This Book
Is an Action

This Book Is an Action

Feminist Print Culture and Activist Aesthetics

Edited by
Jaime Harker and
Cecilia Konchar Farr

University of Illinois Press
Urbana, Chicago, and Springfield

1 2 3 4 5 C P 5 4 3 2 1

♾ This book is printed on acid-free paper.
Library of Congress Cataloging-in-Publication Data
This book is an action: feminist print culture and activist aesthetics / edited by Jaime Harker and Cecilia Konchar Farr.
pages cm
Includes bibliographical references and index.
ISBN 978-0-252-03980-5 (hardback)
ISBN 978-0-252-08134-7 (paper)
ISBN 978-0-252-09790-4 (e-book)
1. American literature—Women authors—History and criticism. 2. Feminism and literature—United States—History—20th century. 3. Women—United States—Intellectual life—20th century. 4. Second-wave feminism—United States. 5. Publishers and publishing—United States—History—20th century. 6. Books and reading—United States—History—20th century.
I. Harker, Jaime, editor. II. Farr, Cecilia Konchar, 1958- editor.
PS228.F45T48 2016
810.9'352042—dc23 2015019098

For our mothers
Donna June Harker and Grace Kurtz Konchar

Contents

Part II

Acknowledgments

As a Master's student at Brigham Young University, Jaime took a class from Cecilia Konchar Farr and learned about academic feminist literary criticism. That meeting started an ongoing conversation that has continued over two decades, through two books, cross-country moves, new jobs, and break-ups (personal and institutional). *This Book Is an Action* is a testament to the power of friendship and feminist sisterhood. Jaime is grateful to have a sustaining mentor and writing partner.

Jaime wants to thank the department of English and the College of Liberal Arts at the University of Mississippi for supporting her travel to the Naiad Press archive at the San Francisco public library and the Sallie Bingham archives at Duke University, as well as to St. Paul, Minnesota, to work on this manuscript in person. She also wants to thank the students in two graduate seminars, "Aesthetics of Protest" and "The Queer South," in which we discussed many of the issues that made it into our introduction. Many thanks for the support of family, friends, and pets. Special thanks and love to Dixie Grimes.

Cecilia is beholden (most beholden) to Jaime for the compelling decades-long conversation that led to this book. Here is to the promise of more conversing, scheming, traveling, and collaborating ahead. Cecilia could not ask for a better colleague and friend. Next time, though, she would like to do Oxford in December and St. Paul in August, instead of the other way around.

Cecilia also acknowledges the gift of time and funding that was the Sr. Mona Riley Endowed Chair in the Humanities at St. Catherine University. For three years, under Sr. Mona's watch, she wrote, read, talked, gadded about, and blissfully enjoyed the life of a scholar. She still thinks of Sr. Mona as her "Guardian Nun"—as are all of the CSJs whose founding vision and years of dedicated service sustain the college still.

And, as always, thanks to Cubs for, among other things, late night grilled cheese sandwiches, and reliably honest editing.

This Book Is an Action

Introduction

Outrageous, Dangerous, and Unassimilable: Writing the Women's Movement

Jaime Harker and Cecilia Konchar Farr

"This book is an action," writes Robin Morgan in her introduction to the iconic second-wave feminist anthology *Sisterhood Is Powerful*. Her claim, that writing can function as activism, just as protests, sit-ins, and marches do, is one of the most interesting legacies of the Women's Liberation Movement of the 1960s and 1970s, and one that has powerful implications for the cultural and literary work that followed. Early feminists wrote in a wide variety of genres—poetry, manifestos, plays and performances, personal and scholarly essays, science fiction and detective novels, avant-garde experimental texts, and coming-of-age novels—and they purposefully explored a range of alternative aesthetics. What united them was a firm belief that books could be revolutionary, that language could remake the world, and that writing mattered in a profound way. This conviction, purposefully linking art and activism, left us an invigorating and diverse feminist canon.

This canon has begun to get more critical attention in recent years; the anniversaries of famous feminist texts (such as Erica Jong's *Fear of Flying*) and the deaths of Women's Liberation activists (including provocateur Jill Johnston and poet Adrienne Rich) have brought feminist literature back into the spotlight. And recent political debates about contraception, abortion, equal pay, voting rights, and marriage equality highlight the continued relevance of early second-wave activism. Yet, much of the long overdue reassessment of the literature of second-wave feminism has been hindered by unsubstantiated claims about its aesthetic inferiority. Current literary scholarship tends to sidestep these constitutive questions of aesthetics, instead arguing for the cultural significance of a wide variety of texts. This has left judgments of literary value to erupt, unquestioned, based on criteria that obscure their cultural investments under cover of ostensibly universal literary merit.

These questions of literary value are particularly apropos of second-wave feminist literature, which, like the literature of other politically inflected literary movements such as the Black Arts Movement, were dismissed by Cold War literary critics as polemical and artistically inferior. Indeed, U.S. literary history has generally reserved its highest aesthetic categories for productions by privileged white men. Meanwhile, a shadow tradition has long existed outside of mainstream U.S. literary culture, where works by nonmale, nonwhite, nonstraight, and nonprivileged writers reside (Farr and Harker 3). Texts relegated to these shadows have been easily dismissed as less significant, less influential, and, emphatically, less beautiful.

To rethink this bias, scholars need to consider aesthetic values within the larger material and cultural conditions that shape them and give them meaning. As Richard Brodhead explains in *Cultures of Letters,* "literary production is bound up with a distinct social audience . . . identified by its readerly interests but by other unifying social interests as well" (5). For him, "writing has no life separate from the particularized mechanisms that bring it to public life" (5), which include "some particular landscape of institutional structures," "some particular group from among the array of contemporary groupings," and "some group-based world of understandings, practices, and values," and a "network of relations that surround it" (8). He concludes, "writing orients itself in or against some understanding of what writing is" (8). Brodhead's insistence that literary texts cannot be separated from the material means of production and the cultural value placed on them remains crucially important when considering aesthetic value. It is a distinctive culture of letters that produces writing, that makes it legible, and that creates standards for its consumption and evaluation. Without that understanding of context, aesthetic assessment is impossible.

This Book Is an Action frames and investigates the distinctive feminist culture of letters that emerged with the reawakened women's movement in the late 1960s and early 1970s. Essays in this collection reflect on the conditions of that culture, its "particularized mechanisms," and on its specific literary artifacts—a sampling of the diverse range of feminist literary production. Together, these essays make a case for the importance of the writings of the women's movement, not just as political and cultural artifacts but also as the texts of an influential and inventive American literary renaissance.

The Literary Roots of Women's Liberation

The Women's Liberation Movement had a literary bent from the beginning. Many of its activists grew up immersed in the distinctive U.S. American tradition of women's writing and reading. Reaching back at least to the seduction novel of the eighteenth century, this tradition was grounded in an expanding print culture, coded feminine, and frequently denounced for its sensationalist or sentimental content and inferior artistry. When most avenues of public expression and political power were denied to women, print culture, particularly novels and periodicals, provided them with a means of self-expression and community.

Feminist critics have recuperated this tradition with a range and nuance to which we cannot possibly do justice to in this introduction. But one depressingly consistent detail of women's literary culture has been the backlash against it. Nathaniel Hawthorne's notorious dismissal of the "damned mob of scribbling women" was a rejection of both women readers and women writers, even as he desired their financial support and envied their success. Women readers have rarely been respected in evaluative discourse, but they have created their own conversations, standards of excellence, and markers of relevance—despite critical disdain for sentimental novels, Oprah's Book Club, and the many manifestations of women's literary culture in between.

In the early twentieth century, this culture became associated with the new term "middlebrow." Joan Shelley Rubin defines middlebrow as an outgrowth of nineteenth-century commitments to the arts and to educational outreach; her studies of key middlebrow institutions—such as the Book-of-the-Month Club and radio shows such as *Information, Please!*—combine an appreciation for their dedication to exposing the masses to "the best that has been thought and said in the world" with a concern about the compromises these middlebrow institutions made (Harker 17). Janice Radway, by contrast, emphasizes the middlebrow's investment in identification and emotion and suggests that it encourages an apolitical personalism, meant to placate the professional-managerial class (17–18). Despite their obvious sympathy toward middlebrow institutions, both Rubin and Radway exhibit reservations about the middlebrow that mirror a larger cultural animus.

Radway was the first to identify *middlebrow* as a gendered term, depicting a feminized popular culture seeking to crush the masculine individual (19). Subsequent scholarship has continued to explore the classification and dismissal of women writers as middlebrow, while also rethinking the values that characterize this category. Middlebrow readers, Radway explains, emphasized emotion and identification and sought out fiction for vicarious experience and practical advice about their own lives (20). The women's book club movement encouraged conversation around books, a communal experience that turned the private experience of reading into a cultural and social experience. Middlebrow reading and writing practices also merged with progressive causes, notably in Harriet Beecher Stowe's *Uncle Tom's Cabin,* in Dorothy Canfield's interwar novels, and in the emergence of the proletarian novel in the early 1930s (Harker). The habits of middlebrow novel readers, in other words, were amenable to political uses and easily linked with later feminist consciousness-raising efforts.

For many feminist writers of the Women's Liberation Movement, fiction became a means for transforming readers' politics. Reading was essential in early conceptions of second-wave feminism, as books became a provocation to conversation about readers' own lives and experiences. Lisa Hogeland argues that consciousness-raising (CR) novels were "the most important form for feminist writers in the 1970s" (8). From popular books such as Marilyn French's *The Women's Room,* Erica Jong's *Fear of Flying,* Marge Piercy's *Small Changes,* and Alix Schulman's *Memoirs of an Ex-Prom Queen,* to smaller feminist press publications such as Audre Lorde's *Zami,* Rita Mae Brown's *Rubyfruit Jungle,* and Isabel Miller's *Patience and Sarah,* CR novels provided millions of women with a vicarious "aha" moment that radical CR groups were producing across the United States. These CR novels were often first-person accounts of individual transformation that discussed once-taboo subjects. Most were explicitly activist and drew overtly on middlebrow reading practices for political aims.

The CR novel is a useful conceptual tool to discuss feminist literary production. It built on a feminine culture of middlebrow reading and capitalized on its proclivities in the claim that literature could "transform consciousness" through identification and emotional experience. But an overdependence on the idea of CR has tended to obscure the broader diversity of literary production of Women's Liberation. As important as they were, *The Women's Room* and *Fear of Flying* do not define all feminist literature. Indeed, though both are often categorized as CR novels, *Fear of Flying* and *The Women's Room* are dramatically different in their language and tone, their style and structure, their literary pretensions, their attitudes toward sex, and their revolutionary resolutions. Among classic CR novels, the differences among them constantly threaten to destabilize CR as a coherent label—and many central second-wave novels cannot be adequately accounted for with that term. Early feminist fiction included science fiction, avant-garde experimentation, historical novels, picaresques, and collective novels. In fact, feminist literary production was not exclusively a middlebrow project. It ranged through genre fiction, women's magazines, and pulps, as well as into the highbrow realms of academic recognition. CR novels are just one strand in the complicated fabric of feminist print culture, which incorporated more radical and experimental patterns that refashioned the mainstream movement. Key to that alternative structure is what came to be known as the Women in Print Movement.

The Explosion of Feminist Print Culture

According to Trysh Travis, the Women in Print Movement was "an attempt by a group of allied practitioners to create an alternative communications circuit—a woman-centered network of readers and writers, editors, printers, publishers, distributors, and retailers through which ideas, objects, and practices flowed in a continuous and dynamic loop" (276). Many of these early feminist bookwomen came of age through 1960s radicalism, and, as Kathryn Adams argues, those "revolutions were built out of books" (184). Second-wave feminism was, again, similarly textual. Activists were eager to create "a communications network free from patriarchal and capitalist control" (Travis 276). That network circulated newsletters and periodicals, which published manifestos, position papers, poetry, news, and book reviews. It included women's presses, which published a wide range of genres and women authors, and women's bookstores, which sold the periodicals and books produced by these alternative genres; it also encompassed women readers, who supported these venues and often joined in as bookstore owners, volunteers, writers, or publishers. Even distributors and operators of the physical presses themselves were a part of the do-it-yourself ethos of Women's Liberation.

The explosion of women's presses across the country, owned by women, publishing women authors, expressly for women readers, introduced a number of writers who had never been published before—many of them writers who could not be published by mainstream presses because of their content. Daughters, Inc., for one, came into being when mainstream publishers rejected June Arnold's second novel, *The Cook and the Carpenter*; she responded by forming one of the most respected presses of the era, the first publisher of Rita Mae Brown, Elena Nachman, and Blanche McCrary Boyd. And when Bertha Harris's third novel, *Lover*, was rejected by Harcourt, Daughters, Inc. stepped in to publish what became one of the most famous experimental novels of the 1970s. Daughters, Inc., taking Virginia Woolf's Hogarth Press as a model, was just one of scores of women's presses that formed over the next two decades. Women's Press Collective, one of the earliest, was based in the Bay Area, and like Diana Press, its collective members owned and operated their own presses—and edited and selected books. Some of their earliest publications, such as Judy Grahn's poetry collections *Edward the Dyke* and *The Common Woman*, were mimeographed and stapled; later editions were produced on presses purchased by the collective (Grahn *A Simple Revolution* 142–143). One of Rita Mae Brown's earliest publications, *Songs to a Handsome Woman*, was a joint production—Brown bought the paper; Diana Press, then based in Baltimore, donated the labor; and they were to split the profits ("Rita Mae Brown"). These presses operated on a shoestring budget, dependent on donated labor and often marked by inexperienced printing and editing, but they produced some of the most remarkable artifacts of Women's Liberation and launched many writers and texts that have become essential to Women's Liberation and to the U.S. women's literary tradition.

Feminist periodicals also emerged across the country. Kathryn Adams notes, "between March, 1968, and August, 1973, over 560 new publications produced by feminists appeared in the United States, each one serving as a mailing address for the movement" (193). These periodicals fostered writers' voices, produced articles such as "I Want a Wife" and "The Myth of the Vaginal Orgasm" that have become standard in second-wave feminist anthologies, constructed local feminist communities, and provided a forum for presses to advertise their books and have them reviewed.

Women's bookstores then provided a new means of distribution. Over time, these bookstores emerged across the country, supporting the nascent feminist presses by connecting them with readers without the expensive advertising that New York firms used. Junko Onosaka called this a "feminist revolution in literacy," and at its height, nearly two hundred bookstores provided a national network for feminist writers and publishers.

The roots of this feminist print culture were formed at the first Women in Print Conference in 1976. June Arnold, after touring women's bookstores with her novel *Sister Gin* in 1975, got the idea of getting publishers, writers, printers, and bookstore owners together to build a collaborative network. More established printers gave advice to younger publishers; new bookstore owners networked with experienced owners; and new networking possibilities were born out of the collaborative conversation. Carol Seajay, an attendee of the conference, went on to cofound San Francisco's Old Wives Tales bookstore and the Feminist Bookstore News, which became essential reading for bookstore owners. All told, the Women in Print Movement created a collaborative publishing and distribution system that, while never a multimillion-dollar operation, was dynamic, solvent, and functional for nearly two decades.

The Women in Print Movement had a symbiotic—sometimes codependent—relationship with the mainstream literary establishment. In the early 1970s, feminism garnered considerable interest from mainstream presses, which published or republished a number of anthologies and feminist novels, including *Fear of Flying*, *Rubyfruit Jungle* (the rights for which were bought from Daughters, Inc. by Bantam paperbacks), and Alice Walker's *The Color Purple* (Loudermilk 20). *Ms.* magazine received major support from New York publishing venues, largely through Gloria Steinem's savvy connections. Many radical feminists remained deeply suspicious of the motives of these mainstream players and publicly trashed feminists for publishing with what June Arnold called the "finishing press" (because their intention was to finish the women's movement [18–26]). But this wide publication of feminist writing, in established presses as well as in left-wing and independent ones, is a key part of the second-wave story.

Though the Women in Print Movement was the cutting edge of textual feminism, it was far from the only significant textual network for feminism, and feminist readers and writers took advantage of all avenues available to them. Feminist print culture is a fascinating subject in its own right, and the essays in the first part of this collection suggest it is a rich field for further exploration. Feminist print culture is also an essential context for understanding the literary artifacts that arose from second-wave feminism.

Activist Aesthetics: Writing Beyond the Boundaries

Feminist print culture, often figured as an exemplary progressive middlebrow form (particularly with reference to CR novels), did not, in fact, prescribe any particular form or style in its heyday. Poetry, for example, was an early focus of feminist presses and in that context developed a distinctive aesthetic of its own, quite different from the allusive, high art, modernist poetry popular in the academy of the time. As Kathryn Flannery points out, poetry was cheaper to print, and feminists perceived it as a democratic form that a variety of women could embrace. Again, as Brodhead argues, what counts as literary is determined in this way—through reading practices and the conventions of material culture in print; aesthetics are not a separate question. An early manifestation of the unique aesthetic of feminist poetry was in San Francisco, in the performances of poets Pat Parker and Judy Grahn.

Parker, an African American poet from Houston, had connections to Black Power and the Black Panthers before joining Grahn, a working-class lesbian from New Mexico, in joint performances at coffee houses across the Bay Area. The Women's Press Collective then published a number of books of their poetry, including Grahn's *Edward the Dyke and Other Poems* and Parker's *Child of Myself* and *Pit Stop*. Both performed on an Olivia Records LP *Where Would I Be Without You—The Poetry of Pat Parker and Judy Grahn*. Performance was key to the aesthetic of feminist communities, extending to poetry readings and an emerging theater scene; in both cases, performances created an immediate kinship between listeners and readers, creating the potential for collective understanding and action. Adrian Oktenberg wrote of Parker's poetry that "she gets down on paper complicated states of feeling, lightning-quick changes of thought, and she deals with complex issues in language and imagery that any bar dyke can understand" (19).

Audre Lorde and Adrienne Rich would later be memorialized as the poet-laureates of the feminist movement, but these early performance pieces by working-class butches—emphasizing accessibility and humor, violence and defiance—were equally important in the development of an activist feminist aesthetic. By the time Lorde wrote, in 1985, that "poetry is not a luxury," feminist poets had long embraced poetry as an egalitarian art form, "a vital necessity of our existence" that "forms the quality of the light within which we predicate our hopes and dreams toward survival and change, first made into language, then into idea, then into more tangible action." If poetry was "the way we help give name to the nameless so it can be thought" (37), it was first given language by black, working-class, and gay poets such as Grahn and Parker.

But Lorde's articulation of a feminist literary aesthetic did the important work of challenging poetry's patriarchal roots and tying feminist poetry to women's diverse experiences. It let feminist thinkers imagine a nonpatriarchal art that does both political and artistic work. She writes simultaneously of survival, change, and tangible action and of revelations, dreams, and giving names to the nameless. And in doing this, she stands on the shoulders of the activist feminist poets before her.

Another important literary legacy of second-wave feminism that pushes the limits of its middlebrow classification was postmodern experimentation, or avant-garde feminism. June Arnold, during the 1970s, was an advocate and exemplar of this version of feminist aesthetics. She and other feminist writers looked to modernist role models such as Virginia Woolf, Gertrude Stein, and Djuna Barnes as they began articulating a theory of language that would later be embraced as *l'écriture feminine*. Based on the notion that mainstream language was fundamentally male, it insisted that the *logos* needed to be broken with a dramatically different approach to language. Monique Wittig's experimental novels, including *Les Guérillères* and *The Lesbian Body*, became touchstones for the feminist avant-garde; Daughters, Inc. later printed her novel *The Opopomax*. In fact, Daughters, Inc. published a number of the most famous experimental novels of the decade, precursors of later feminist postmodernism exemplified by Kathy Acker.

Arnold and Harris not only wrote experimental novels, they also advocated for these novels' aesthetic and political efficacy. Arnold claimed that the novel was, by definition, revolutionary: "Women's art is politics, the means to change women's minds" (28). For her, that transformation was not in the traditional plot of the realist novel but in language and in form. "One of the things we have noticed in reading women's press writings is a change in the language," she wrote. "We've experimented with unpatriarchal spelling and neuter pronouns. I think we've changed our sentence structure, and paragraphs no longer contain one subject," Arnold argued, because women writers aimed for "the inclusiveness of many complex things" (28–29). For Arnold, new language and new form would be the means to a feminist political revolution.

Harris, too, tied lived feminism to aesthetic innovation. She saw lesbian-feminism as a transgressive, resistant identity that would create a revolution in formal structure: "Lesbians, instead, might have been great, as some literature is: unassimilable, awesome, dangerous, outrageous, different: distinguished" (6). Harris's aesthetics here combine a middlebrow focus on emotion with a highbrow emphasis on resistance to identification. Harris and Arnold believed that feminist writing was, by definition, unassimilable and outrageous—in contemporary terminology, innately queer. The queerness of feminist aesthetics contradicts conventional wisdom about the centrality of the middlebrow for second-wave feminism. While one may not agree that women's writing is innately revolutionary or queer, the *belief* in such a concept produced some of the most interesting and overlooked literary productions of second-wave feminism, in their merging of experimentation and activism.

Feminist writers also staged incursions into lowbrow genre fiction, including detective fiction, romance, and science fiction. Rita Mae Brown was the first crossover artist, whose novels for Daughters, Inc. became paperback bestsellers, launching a lucrative popular publishing career that continues today. It quickly became clear that genre fiction was enormously popular with feminist readers, and sales of these books supported both feminist presses and feminist bookstores alike. Naiad Press was a clear leader in this shift in the 1980s; its mysteries and romances turned it into the largest and most commercially successful of all the women's presses.

This appropriation of genre conventions introduced the values of civil rights and gay and Women's Liberation into "language that any bar dyke can understand." Early feminist interventions in aesthetics valued accessibility and immediacy, and this later incursion into popular genres reached audiences that experimental fiction never could. Science fiction allowed for feminist utopian imaginings of a world after the revolution, with possibilities and freedoms unimaginable; mysteries placed women with agency and autonomy in central roles traditionally reserved for hypermasculine characters; romances merged sexual satisfaction and equality and put women's desire at the center. When Catherine Ennis writes a Civil War romance featuring a lesbian couple working for the Underground Railroad, when Jewell Gomez presents an African American lesbian vampire narrative starting in Louisiana in 1850 and ending in 2050, or when Joanna Russ provides four versions of the same woman in alternate realities, the narrative experimentation and formal innovations open speculative possibilities beyond those allowed by other more conventional literary forms.[1]

These forays into genre fiction were about innovation and entertainment, and for many feminist novels and publishers, readers' desires were paramount. Barbara Grier of Naiad Press was happy if feminist reading led to CR and political transformation, but she seemed content with other uses—the construction of identity, a virtual sense of community, even pure pleasure. The goal, Grier insisted, was "to get women to read. Taste will come later" (Beebe). Grier seemed less interested in transforming women than in serving and charming them. For Grier, as for the women she served, reading itself was its own reward. "I suppose if I could," she explained to Houston bookstore owner Pokey Anderson, "I would make better readers, but you can't do that. . . . There is a place in the world for all of it, there's a place for all this reading" (Interview with Brophy). Grier insisted that "all this reading" be considered in feminist aesthetic practices.

That broad view of literature was common in feminist print culture. Literature, with a capital "L," was a cultural category that, for early feminists, had been defined in explicitly patriarchal ways and that had excluded a host of women writers whom many early feminists found exemplary—even the likes of Woolf, Stein, and Barnes, and famously, the lost Zora Neale Hurston. It was second-wave feminist re-visioning that brought this omission to light, and, with uneven success, brought new writers into the mainstream canon.

Feminist re-visioning also led feminist presses to seek out diverse depictions of women's lives. While second-wave feminists have been criticized for failing to account for differences among women, the historical record tells a very different story. From the earliest days of its activist engagements, the Women in Print Movement was obsessed with questions of diversity and cross-cultural work and committed to publishing books that interrogated multiple oppressions, what we now call intersectionality. Questions of race, of class, of sexuality, of region, and of nationality run through the publications of feminist presses, the articles and reviews of periodicals, and the authorship of feminist fiction. Many iconic books by women of color, such as *This Bridge Called My Back* and *All the Women Are White, All the Men Are Black, but Some of Us Are Brave* were published by feminist presses, and feminist print culture included women of color publishing houses, such as Aunt Lute Books and Barbara Smith's Kitchen Table: Women of Color Press. Women's bookstores became the first interracial audience for many women writers of color, leading to the unprecedented popular success and critical recognition of such writers in the 1980s and 1990s. These groundbreaking anthologies and novels such as *The Color Purple* and *Rubyfruit Jungle*, Maxine Hong Kingston's *The Woman Warrior,* and Sandra Cisneros's *The House on Mango Street* have been incorporated into specific canons in area, ethnic, or gender and sexuality studies. Literary history has forgotten their second-wave origins, thus erasing the complex intersectional impulse under what is often derisively, and erroneously, dismissed as "white lady feminism" (Halberstam). The commitment of the Women in Print Movement to encourage identification across lines of race, class, and orientation led to the centrality of texts by women of color in feminist reading and writing communities, and while feminists were not the only audiences for these works, they were an early and important one.

While canon revision was a priority for feminist presses long before it became a principle of academic feminism, maintaining the cultural distinctions that a male literary establishment valued was not. Instead, the central task, as defined by Grahn, was to move beyond stock literary tropes and types "for women's real life stories and for the truth we deserve" (*True to Life* 10). Feminist writers, she argues, "learned their crafts in many different institutions. Not only colleges, but also trade schools, service jobs, office jobs, family, work, and street hustling helped to form their writer's minds. Likewise, their ideas have been gathered from many places: the labor-oriented old Left, the historic lesbian underground, the Black Liberation Movement, the Women's Liberation Movement, and more than anything from life itself" (8). Because of this, Grahn respected the distinctive language of each writer's story, "for the more closely coordinated we allow the content and form of any art to be, the more accurate, useful and whole it is." Grahn's embrace of the multiplicity of feminist literary practices marked the Women's Liberation Movement as a whole, resulting in a number of genres and formal styles. Feminist literary culture—with its emphasis on emotion, identification, and the transformation of consciousness—could be defined as middlebrow, but it produced texts that ranged freely across cultural hierarchies.

Feminist criticism in the 1970s would further develop this expansive understanding of women's writing under the umbrella of "gynocritics," as Elaine Showalter called it. The work of feminist criticism, she writes, "is to construct a female framework for the analysis of women's literature, to develop new models based on the study of female experience, rather than to adapt male models and theories"—again, grounding feminist aesthetics in women's experience and challenging patriarchal paradigms as insufficient. "Gynocritics," she explains, "begins at the point when we free ourselves from the linear absolutes of male literary history, stop trying to fit women between the lines of the male tradition, and focus instead on the newly visible world of female culture" ("Toward a Feminist Poetics" 131). This idea of "women's culture," which implies a separate women's aesthetic, had been circulating in do-it-yourself feminist periodicals long before it entered academic literary criticism where it transformed the study of literature. Annette Kolodny, in her 1980 essay "Dancing through the Minefield," argues that readers have been "unable to assign significance to women's fictions that attend to 'kitchen things'"; instead, they "judge such fictions as trivial and as aesthetically wanting. For her to take useful issue with such a reader, she must make clear that what appears to be a dispute about aesthetic merit is, in reality, a dispute about the *contexts of judgment*" (Kolodny 158, emphasis in the original). Kolodny's claim that the content of women's literature led to its dismissal as "trivial and aesthetically wanting" inspired a widespread call for reevaluation of standards of aesthetic merit. Books by Kate Millett, Elaine Showalter, Nina Baym, Jane Tompkins, Bonnie Zimmerman, Barbara Herrnstein Smith, and Janice Radway built on feminism's earliest critiques of the literary establishment;[2] the issue of who counts as "great" led to a generation of recuperative work.

But even more profoundly, feminist critics made clear that it is not just *who* we read that matters, but *how* we read and, thus, what we value. Feminist literary criticism has insisted that the deepest assumptions of a supposedly disinterested Western aesthetic be called into question. It demands constant reexamination of whose writing is considered "best" and by what standards. VIDA: Women in Literary Arts, founded in 2009 to address "the critical reception of women's creative writing in our current culture," highlights the continued importance of this reassessment (and its unachieved goals) with its annual "VIDA Counts," exposing the ongoing bias in mainstream book reviewing. When only a third of literary novels reviewed in leading literary venues such as the *New York Times Book Review* and the *New Yorker* are by women, it suggests that the sexist bias targeted in these early aesthetic calls to arms continues to flourish (VIDA).

Essays in the Collection

The essays in the first section of this collection examine the structures and systems of feminist print culture. Jennifer Gilley's "Feminist Publishing/Publishing Feminism: Experimentation in Second-Wave Book Publishing" explores two case studies of feminist publishing that illustrate an attempt to infuse feminist politics into the economically driven apparatus of book publishing: *Sisterhood Is Powerful* and *This Bridge Called My Back*. Each book negotiated the mainstream/alternative press divide differently, and their evolution suggests the complexity of feminist publishing during the period. Agatha Beins's "A Revolution in Ephemera: Feminist Newsletters and Newspapers of the 1970s" focuses on periodicals published in New Orleans, Louisiana (*Distaff*), Northampton, Massachusetts (*Valley Women's Center Newsletter*), Cambridge, Massachusetts (*Female Liberation Newsletter*), Iowa City, Iowa (*Ain't I a Woman?*), and Los Angeles, California (*L.A. Women's Liberation Newsletter*, later published as *Sister*). She argues that movement periodicals constituted a vital site of literary experimentation for feminism and complicated the reductive dominant narratives told about Women's Liberation of the 1970s.

Julie Enszer's "'What Made Us Think They'd Pay Us for Making a Revolution?' Women in Distribution (WinD), 1974–1979," analyzes the case study of a feminist book distribution company that animates a central concern of feminists during the 1970s: how to create an economically viable model to continue to support and nurture feminist revolutions. Although Women in Distribution did not survive, it achieved extraordinary success in disseminating books and materials by feminists and lesbian-feminists broadly throughout the United States. Finally, Yung-Hsing Wu's "Closely, Consciously Reading Feminism" considers the fate of close reading in second-wave reading and writing communities, through an analysis of memoirs, literary criticism, and a novel, Marilyn French's *The Women's Room*. She argues that an epistemology of reading that generates closeness among women—irrespective of geography or location—crystallizes a feminist consciousness.

These essays highlight the lively revolutionary spirit that pervaded the material productions of the early Women's Liberation Movement, and, again, their foundational belief in the power of the printed word to incite social change. They also provide archival evidence to ground some of the most persistent debates around feminist cultural production: Did feminism sell out to capitalism? Did it become more interested in culture and personal transformation than in real political change? Did it ignore the experiences of women of color? What these essays reveal is a feminism in the process of becoming—improvisational, experimental, contingent, even tentative. Gilley and Enszer show us the diverse ways feminists tried to negotiate print culture with integrity and creativity and discuss inevitable failures without teleological assumptions about the failure of feminism. Capitalism—making a profit, making a living—was an unavoidable problem that all feminist bookwomen had to accommodate. Beins refuses to allow us to make predetermined assumptions about what feminism valued, how it organized, or who it included, by foregrounding the multiple contexts and unexpected alliances present in mimeographed and collaboratively imagined periodicals. And Wu's careful unpacking of the role of close reading in second-wave feminism shows how essential the trope was from the earliest days and how ambivalent the meaning of close reading would be, before and after "cultural feminism" supposedly sapped the political will of the movement. We see the possibilities in these essays as catalysts, inspiring additional research on the many presses, periodicals, bookstores, and distribution systems of the vital Women in Print Movement that prodded a feminist literary renaissance into being.

The subsequent essays, focused on specific literary texts, build on information about the feminist culture of letters to signal the range of literary production it nurtured and to suggest unmapped possibilities for their critical and aesthetic analysis. We place them here chronologically to evidence the evolution and expansion of feminist literature over time and to attest to the diversity of literary artifacts during particular moments of the Women's Liberation Movement. We begin with Jill E. Anderson's "The Element That Shaped Me, That I Shape by Being In: Alternative Natures in Margaret Atwood's *Surfacing* and *The Edible Woman*," which argues that in Atwood's first two novels, from 1969 and 1971, the two main characters revise common conceptions of nature to instigate their own feminist liberatory politics. Through their embodied experience, they imagine alternatives to the cultural scripts they are offered and find a fluidity and adaptability in nature that provides an early prototype for queer ecocriticism. Lisa Botshon's "The Second-Wave Sandbox: Anne Roiphe's Monstrous Motherhood" examines how Anne Roiphe's 1970 novel *Up the Sandbox!* creates a split narrative for its main character, one of liberation and social change juxtaposed against one of middle-class domestic life, to demonstrate the cultural minefields in place for women who challenge patriarchal norms. Roiphe's ambivalent ending tests traditional notions of the CR novel and points to a nuanced view of white liberal motherhood. Botshon argues that, in her portrayal of the monstrous cleaved self of the mother, Roiphe attempts to wrestle mothering from its patriarchal moorings and set it loose in the playground of feminist politics.

Jay Hood's "Desire and Fantasy in Erica Jong's *Fear of Flying*" reexamines the central voyeuristic fantasy that animates Jong's 1973 novel—the notorious "zipless fuck"—and moves it beyond masochistic theories of female sexuality to propose a productive space, a fantasy heterotopia, where Isadora negotiates the politics of desire and reality for herself. Hood takes on sadomasochism and public sex, elucidated through embodiment and queer theory, to mark this paradigmatic feminist novel as much more complicated and prescient than generations of reviewers enamored of the zipless fuck would have us believe. Jaime Cantrell's "Coming Out and Tutor Text Performance in Jane Chambers's Lesbi-Dramas" traces the phenomenon of feminist drama through three overtly lesbian plays: *A Late Snow* (1974), *Last Summer at Bluefish Cove* (1980), and *My Blue Heaven* (1981). Cantrell demonstrates how the performance of Chambers's plays involved the audience in an experience of lesbian hypervisibility, an opportunity to interact with the political and personal issues that lesbians were confronting at a time when their invisibility was still the American cultural norm. She argues that the appeal Chambers had to mainstream audiences allowed her plays to function as tutor texts, doing political work as they marked the stage as a central place in feminist cultures of letters. Laura Christine Godfrey's "Creating a Nonpatriarchal Lineage in Bertha Harris's *Lover*" identifies the use of the saints in Harris's 1976 novel as a way of creating a feminine and feminist lineage for women seeking to escape the cultural, mythical, and historical confines imposed on their gender. Godfrey demonstrates how Harris offers alternative biological and familial connections both via the saint epigraphs and through the novel's broader context of lesbian separatism. Godfrey's insightful reading introduces a useful interpretive strategy for one of the most lauded and puzzling literary artifacts of Women's Liberation.

Phillip Gordon's "*The Color Purple* and the Wine-Dark Kiss of Death: How a Second-Wave Feminist Wrote the First American AIDS Narrative" proposes a reading of Walker's epistolary novel, published six months after AIDS was first described in medical literature, as an early exploration of how AIDS moved through African and U.S. populations. Indeed, he concludes that Walker's novel is a more accurate depiction of AIDS than other better-known AIDS literature because its timeframe, the 1920s to 1940s, coincides with the initial spread of AIDS throughout areas of Africa—where Nettie and her children live—and predates the arrival of AIDS in the United States, making this version of the story more global in scope and more complete than the versions we now consider our canon of AIDS stories. In addition, Gordon points out, Celie's careful descriptions of the (hetero)sexual economy of her rural Georgia community reveal how women in that community were put at greater risk for sexually transmitted diseases, a taxonomy of sexually transmitted diseases that further elucidates how AIDS spread so devastatingly quickly, and not only in gay communities. Finally, Charlotte Beyer's "'This Really Isn't a Job for a Girl to Take on Alone': Reappraising Feminism and Genre Fiction in Sara Paretsky's Crime Novel *Indemnity Only*" makes a case for the powerful influence the female detective had in translating the advances of second-wave feminism into the cultural mainstream. As Paretsky deployed feminist positions and strategies in the influential 1982 novel *Indemnity Only,* female detectives such as V. I. Warshawski broke ground in genre fiction—questioning patriarchal authority, embracing independence, and willfully taking care of themselves. This essay reappraises the significance of genre fiction, and crime fiction in particular, to second-wave feminism—and of second-wave feminism to the genre novel.

These essays suggest future recuperative work for Women's Liberation literature by placing it in conversation with a broad range of aesthetic concerns. The texts examined here represent just a sampling of a large feminist canon, but they encompass a variety of literary styles, from middlebrow genre fiction (Paretsky), to realistic novels of feminist awakening (French, Jong, Roiphe), to the experimental and surreal (Atwood, Harris). Some authors emphasize performance (Chambers and Harris); others call on intertextual readings (French, Jong). The diversity of these feminist literary texts—including those lumped together as CR novels—suggests how much remains to be done in examining the significance of our second-wave feminist canon.

The themes and topics of this literature also demonstrate what a rich cultural tradition Women's Liberation produced. The texts explored here address various women's issues—motherhood in *Up the Sandbox!, Surfacing,* and *The Color Purple*; eating disorders in *The Edible Woman*; women's sexual desire in *Fear of Flying* and *Lover*; women's autonomy and agency in *The Women's Room, Indemnity Only, The Color Purple,* and *Up the Sandbox!*; lesbian identity in *Lover* and *A Late Snow*; incest in *The Color Purple* and *Lover*; and violence in *Indemnity Only.* But these women's issues are hardly uniform; as Agatha Beins reminds us in her study of feminist periodicals, early feminism was without prescriptive approaches to single issues or broader programmatic dicta. That diversity is apparent in the fictional treatments of these signature feminist issues, just as it is in the intersectional identities of the movement's feminist authors, including a range of regions, races, ethnicities, and sexualities.

But it is just as telling how many of the critical approaches included in this collection do not take feminist themes as their key focus, instead analyzing the texts through book history, popular culture, or genre contexts, and reader response, postmodernist, ecocritical, and queer theories. In this, the critical essays are following the lead of the Women's Liberation itself, a collaborative, cross-disciplinary movement. Second-wave feminism has contributed to or inspired a number of other critical discourses that continue to resonate in the academy, including ecocriticism, queer theory, critical race studies, postcolonialism, and popular culture studies. Not all theorists remember, for example, that Judith Butler's "compulsory heterosexuality" in *Gender Trouble* stems from Adrienne Rich's "Compulsory Heterosexuality and Lesbian Existence," that the manifesto of the Combahee River Collective introduced intersectional analysis, or that Eve Sedgwick's articulation of homosociality and homosexuality parallels Rich's "lesbian continuum." When we read the literature of second-wave feminism only for its depiction of "women's issues," we artificially limit its narrative reach and miss its many other critical and cultural engagements—something this collection of essays aimed to avoid. Instead, these essays delve into the material conditions of publishing (both mainstream and alternative), frame issues within unexpected historical and cultural contexts, explore the intersection of social movements and capitalism, interrogate women's queer desires, and perform superb close readings of formally distinctive literary artifacts.

Insinuating itself onto the reading lists of everyday American women, engaging middlebrow reading practices, making incursions into the avant-garde and genre fictions, the literature of second-wave feminism crossed categories, with forms and language that distinguish this literary moment. The boundaries between these "brow levels" were always more fluid than manifesto writers would have us believe. Daughters, Inc. published novels by both popular novelist Rita Mae Brown and science fiction writer Joanna Russ; Naiad Press, denounced as the pulpiest feminist press of them all, reprinted highbrow writers such as Renée Vivien and Jane Rule. Some of the most interesting experimental writers, such as Bertha Harris and Joanna Russ, incorporated elements from lesbian pulp or wrote genre fiction on the side. And the idea that feminist middlebrow novels are transparent and not formally significant is belied by nearly forty years of feminist analysis of these novels. The truth is that feminist aesthetics do not respect the traditional boundaries that structure much of literary study. We need to keep developing the critical and cultural tools necessary to appreciate the literature of second-wave feminism—middlebrow, highbrow, lowbrow. It is our hope that *This Book Is an Action* will contribute to this development, as we participate in the recuperation and revaluation of second-wave feminism's significant literary legacies. Because, in the end, this book is an action, too.

Notes

1. Catherine Ennis, *South of the Line* (Kansas City: Naiad Press, 1989); Jewell Gomez, *The Gilda Stories* (Ithaca, NY: Firebrand Books, 1991). Joanna Russ, *The Female Man* (Boston: Beacon Press, 1975).

2. Kate Millett, *Sexual Politics* (Urbana: U of Illinois P, 2000); Elaine Showalter, *New Feminist Criticism*; Nina Baym, "Melodramas of Beset Manhood" (Showalter, *New Feminist Criticism*); Jane Tompkins, *Sensational Designs: The Cultural Work of American Fiction 1790–1860* (Oxford: Oxford UP, 1986); Bonnie Zimmerman, *The Safe Sea of Women: Lesbian Fiction 1969–1989* (Boston: Beacon P, 1991); Barbara Herrnstein Smith, *Contingencies*

of Value: Alternate Perspectives for Critical Theory (Cambridge: Harvard UP, 1991); and Janice Radway, *Reading the Romance: Women, Patriarchy, and Popular Literature* (Chapel Hill: U of North Carolina P, 1991).

Works Cited

Adams, Kathryn. "Paper Lesbians: Alternative Publishing and the Politics of Lesbian Representation in the United States, 1950–1990." Diss. U of Texas at Austin. 1994.

Arnold, June. "Feminist Presses and Feminist Politics." *Quest* 3 (Summer 1976): 18–26.

Beebe, Bonnie Ruth, "Happy Birthday, Naiad!" *Lambda Book Report* 6.7 (1998).

Brodhead, Richard. *Cultures of Letters: Scenes of Reading and Writing in Nineteenth-Century America.* Chicago: U of Chicago P, 1995.

Enszer, Julie. *The Whole Naked Truth of Our Lives: Lesbian-Feminist Print Culture from 1969 through 1989.* Diss. U of Maryland. 2013.

Farr, Cecilia Konchar, and Jaime Harker. Eds. *The Oprah Affect: Critical Essays on Oprah's Book Club. Albany:* SUNY UP, 2008.

Flannery, Kathryn Thoms. *Feminist Literacies, 1968–1975.* Urbana: U of Illinois P, 2005.

Grahn, Judy. *A Simple Revolution.* San Francisco: Aunt Lute Books, 2012.

———. Ed. *True to Life Adventure Stories Volume II.* Trumansburg, NY: Cross Press and Diana Press, 1984.

Grier, Barbara. Interview with Mary Brophy. 8 June 1988. Barbara Grier Archive, San Francisco Public Library.

Halberstam, Jack. "Triggering Me, Triggering You: Making Up Is Hard to Do." *Bully Bloggers.* 15 July 2014. http://bullybloggers.wordpress.com/2014/07/15/triggering-me-triggering-you- making-up-is-hard-to-do/. Accessed September 26, 2014.

Harker, Jaime. *America the Middlebrow: Women's Novels, Progressivism, and Middlebrow Authorship between the Wars.* Amherst: U of Massachusetts P, 2007.

Harris, Bertha. "What We Mean To Say: Notes toward Defining the Nature of Lesbian Literature." *Heresies* 1.3 (Fall 1977): 5–8.

Hogeland, Lisa. *Feminism and Its Fictions: The Consciousness-Raising Novel and the Women's Liberation Movement* (Conduct and Communication Series). Philadelphia: U of Pennsylvania P, 1998.

Kolodny, Annette. "Dancing through the Minefield: Some Observations on the Theory, Practice and Politics of a Feminist Literary Criticism." *The New Feminist Criticism: Essays on Women, Literature and Theory.* Ed. Elaine Showalter. New York: Pantheon, 1985. 144–167.

Lorde, Audre. "Poetry Is Not a Luxury." *Sister/Outsider.* Freedom, CA: The Crossing Press, 1984. 36–39.

Loudermilk, Kim. *Fictional Feminism: How American Bestsellers Affect the Movement for Women's Equality.* New York: Routledge, 2004.

Oktenberg, Adrian. Rev. of *Jonestown and Other Madness* by Pat Parker. *Women's Review of Books* April (1986): 17–19.

Radway, Janice. *A Feeling for Books: The Book-of-the-Month Club, Literary Taste, and Middle-Class Desire.* Chapel Hill: U of North Carolina P, 1999.

"Rita Mae Brown." *Ms. Blog.* 4 April 2012. http://msmagazine.com/blog/2012/04/30/national-poetry-month-rita-mae-brown/. Accessed November 6, 2014.

Showalter, Elaine. Ed. *New Feminist Criticism.* New York: Pantheon, 1985.

———. "Toward a Feminist Poetics." *Women Writing and Writing about Women.* Ed. Mary Jacobus. Totowa, NJ: Barnes and Noble Books, 1979. 25–36.

Travis, Trysh. "The Women in Print Movement: History and Implications." *Book History* 11 (2008): 275–300.

VIDA. "VIDA Count 2012: MIC Check Redux." *VIDA: Women in the Literary Arts.* 4 March 2013. http://www.vidaweb.org/vida-count. Accessed September 17, 2014.

Part I

Chapter 1

Feminist Publishing/Publishing Feminism

Experimentation in Second-Wave Book Publishing

Jennifer Gilley

In her book *Feminism and Pop Culture,* Andi Zeisler characterizes the proliferation of second-wave feminist writing as belonging to two categories: the publishing of feminism, referring to books written by feminists but published by corporate presses; and feminist publishing, referring to pamphlets, newsletters, and books both written and published by feminists themselves (64). These two strains of publishing, rather than being distinct, actually fed off each other and, taken together, reveal a nuanced and experimental relationship between second-wave feminism and publishing. Yet historians of this period have not examined the phenomenon of either. Kathryn Flannery, in her book *Feminist Literacies 1968–75,* argues that "publishing is left out of historical studies of feminism because practices of literacy, particularly book publishing, are tainted by their relationship to the power structure" (2). Yet studying the publication histories of second-wave feminist literature actually reveals an array of feminist interventions into traditional modes of publishing, not just by creating alternative feminist presses but by experimenting with different royalty structures and contracts with corporate presses.

In this essay, I will explore two case studies that each illustrate an attempt to infuse feminist politics into the economically driven apparatus of book publishing: *Sisterhood Is Powerful* and *This Bridge Called My Back.* Zeisler cites Robin

Morgan as an example of a "movement participant" who published with a "storied establishment house" (64), but the book to which Zeisler is referring, Morgan's anthology *Sisterhood Is Powerful* published by Random House in 1970, actually belies any such easy categorization. As an anthology meant to capture the cutting edge ideas of the movement, the book contained many pieces that had already circulated via the feminist underground, so it could be seen as having feminist publishing roots. Furthermore, Morgan insisted on incorporating as many feminist principles as possible into the traditional publication process by demanding that only women within Random House work on it and by turning the book into an economic engine for the Women's Liberation Movement, pouring all of her royalties as editor back into the movement through the Sisterhood Is Powerful Fund. Exploring the publication history of *Sisterhood Is Powerful* provides a landmark case study of feminist experimentation in publishing that was inevitably fraught with controversy due to the ideological struggles of the time over economic and political "purity."

For my second case study, I will turn to the feminist press movement for the fascinating publication history of *This Bridge Called My Back: Writings by Radical Women of Color,* which was published first by Persephone Press in 1981, then by Kitchen Table: Women of Color Press when Persephone went out of business. With both presses, the anthology was published under an unusual type of contract in which contributors, rather than receiving a one-time payment at the beginning, would continue to receive payments for every ten thousand copies sold. While laudable for its feminist valuing of the authors' work, this strategy proved to be quite difficult in practice for the presses, but it exemplifies the type of experimentation that the feminist press movement was committed to in the 1970s and early 1980s. Overall, these studies show the variety of ways in which feminists tried to get around the "taint" of publishing's relationship to the power structure in order to enact a feminist sensibility not just in the content of their writing but also in its production and dissemination.

Publishing in Second-Wave Feminism: Some Ideological Context

The politics of publishing were long fraught in Women's Liberation, but they erupted in 1976. June Arnold's article "Feminist Presses and Feminist Politics," published in the summer 1976 issue of *Quest,* stands as the clearest and most-oft quoted articulation of the us versus them political stance on publishing in feminism. Arnold declares that Madison Avenue publishers are "what we can call the finishing press, because it is our movement they intend to finish. They will publish some of us—the least threatening, the most saleable, the most easily controlled or a few who cannot be ignored—until they cease publishing us because to be a woman is no longer in style" (19). Arnold is characterizing Zeisler's "publishing feminism" category as a deliberate co-optation of feminism on the part of corporate publishers for the purpose of deradicalization and then extinction. Arnold would have put Morgan into the "few who cannot be ignored" category (for reasons I will explain later) without any recognition of her attempt to co-opt the corporate publishers for her own ends. Arnold's observation that being a woman was currently "in style" for publishers was a salient one: a *New York Times* article from August 17, 1970, had declared that "the women's liberation movement is about to have its season in book publishing" (32). (It lasted a lot longer than many imagined.) In addition to this overt hostility to feminism on the part of corporate publishing, Arnold also points out that publishing with "the finishing press" supports companies whose "profits go to oppressing women in South America [such as] Gulf and Western, owner of Simon and Schuster" (24). It was also widely known that Random House was owned by RCA, who had military contracts and was therefore considered to be part of the Vietnam-era war machine.

Harriet Ellenberger and Catherine Nicholson, founders of the lesbian feminist journal *Sinister Wisdom*, supported Arnold's view and, in their first issue (October 1976), wrote that "Corporate America controls establishment publishing because control of communications ensures control of politics and industry . . . [corporate presses] exist primarily to kill revolution" (Ellenberger and Nicholson 126–129). The alternative to this was the feminist press, of which both they and Arnold were a part. Ellenberger and Nicholson assert that "the lesbian presses exist primarily to make revolution" both through the ideological content of what they publish and through the material structures that must be put in place to publish this content (126). Ellenberger and Nicholson argue that "by keeping this issue in feminist hands from mindflash to bookstore, we gain all these things: we solidify our ties with each other; we learn the whole time we're doing; we recycle our money; we reach more lesbians with a journal written just for them; we strengthen the chain that will make this possible in the future; and most importantly, we create breakthroughs in the content, in the vision BECAUSE we are so clear about this: we are not justifying our lives before the world, we are talking to women" (129). Although both of these pieces were written in 1976, they reflect political impulses that were certainly in play from the beginning of the second wave (despite the early lack of alternative feminist presses) and are therefore good illustrations of one type of publishing ideal that Robin Morgan and other feminist writers would have had to wrestle with as they made decisions about their work. Overall the feminist print movement, whether for-profit or nonprofit in intent, was considered to be crucial to the publication of feminism for a host of political and material reasons.

Foremost among these reasons was the idea that feminist presses were necessary to publish new work that corporate presses would not touch for ideological or economic reasons, at least until the material was proven to be saleable. Carol Seajay, editor of the influential *Feminist Bookstore News,* wrote that "whatever is newest, groundbreaking and close to the cutting edge of feminist thinking is published by feminist publishers. . . . Often they break new ground with a book, or several books, on a topic and commercial publishers follow this up with several more books on the same subject" (30). Charlotte Bunch, also a veteran member of the feminist print movement seconded this dynamic: "First, I believe that the existence and visibility of feminist (and esp. lesbian-feminist) writing that we have today is largely a result of the existence of feminist presses, periodicals, journals, and books over the past 10 years. (Even that printed by male presses would not have happened if we had not created and demonstrated the market.)" (25). According to Seajay and Bunch, feminist publishing directly feeds into publishing feminism. They would describe this relationship as a parasitic one rather than a symbiotic one, with the life-giving force coming mainly from the new voices surfacing through the feminist press. Bunch draws attention in particular to lesbian-feminist writing because lesbians were a marginalized group even within feminism and considered too marginal and controversial to ever get picked up by commercial presses, at least until Rita Mae Brown's *Rubyfruit Jungle* proved how much money there was to be made in this market. Lesbians, therefore, had to start their own presses to be heard, and women of color were at a similar disadvantage. Barbara Smith, publisher of Kitchen Table: Women of Color Press, explained that "as feminist and lesbian of color writers, we knew that we had no options for getting published, except at the mercy or whim of others, whether in the context of alternative or commercial publishing, since both are white-dominated" (202–207). This lack of access to publication outlets led to the popularity of the slogan "the freedom of the press belongs to those who own the press" in the feminist print movement, and the urgency of getting marginalized voices in print was the primary raison d'être for feminist publishing.

In addition to being the ones most likely to publish cutting-edge material, there was also an ethos surrounding the feminist presses that suggested they would be more committed to supporting the work and its author according to feminist principles rather than purely economic ones. One central tenet of this commitment was to keep books in print. Corporate presses were frequently accused of letting their feminist books go out of print if the first print run did not sell out immediately, while "women's presses keep the book in print until it finds its audience" (Arnold 19). Indeed, a major goal of feminist presses is to keep all of their books in print and the Feminist Press got its start reprinting works of women's literature that had long since gone out of print. Feminist publishers were also expected to have a higher standard in regard to financially compensating authors and contributors. Traditional publishing contracts dedicate a very low percentage of sales to author royalties (10 percent for hardback, 6 to 7 percent for paperback) and never pay any royalties to contributors to anthologies. Contributors generally get a small one-time payment up front that comes out of the editor's royalties. Under the collective ideals of feminism, the anthology is the most politically appropriate vehicle for nonfiction because it contains a wider diversity of voices than a single-author book does, and from an egalitarian point of view, each of those contributors deserves an equal share in the royalties. One feminist writer, Melanie Kaye, even felt that only the contributors to anthologies should get paid, not the editors, because "editors should not make money off other people's work" (Clausen "Politics" 106). Persephone Press, a lesbian feminist press that published extremely influential books from 1976 to 1983, experimented with enacting these types of egalitarian principles in their contracts, but the realities of the publishing business for a small undercapitalized press meant that there was rarely enough cash to pay royalties at all and these experiments failed. I will explore this issue in more depth for my second case study, *This Bridge Called My Back*, which was first published by Persephone Press and then by Kitchen Table under a similar contract.

Another commonly cited benefit of feminist presses is that they targeted a particular audience: lesbians, women of color, or just women in the movement who were presumed to be sympathetic, rather than reaching a mass audience. Arnold writes that "If I publish with a women's press, I reach the women who need and can use what I say" (22). A prominent example of this thinking was the belief of Rosemary Curb, coeditor of the Naiad Press book *Lesbian Nuns: Breaking the Silence*, that the preferred audience for her book would be the same "women's studies audience" that greeted other small feminist press books, not the mass audience the book achieved once stories from it were sold to Penthouse *Forum* and paperback rights were sold to Warner books (Curb 4). (Clearly she and Barbara Grier, publisher at Naiad Press, had different ideas about audience and the desirability of limiting or expanding it beyond narrow political boundaries, as the controversy over *Lesbian Nuns* attests.)

The desire for a limited and politically exclusive audience would have resonated in the lesbian separatist movement but was simultaneously anathema to many other writers who wished their writing to reach a mass audience. Jan Clausen was one such feminist writer, and even publisher (Long Haul Press), who did not embrace the cultural separatism believed by some to be a benefit of feminist publishing: "I sometimes find myself thinking of life in the feminist literary community—even in bustling New York—as 'life in the provinces.' This is my private, rueful phrase for a feminist literary existence which, both for reasons of our choosing and ones not of our choosing, tends to be extremely isolated from other literary communities" (Clausen *A Movement of Poets* 36). When she talks about "reasons of our choosing," she is talking about the us versus them separatist tendencies that I have outlined so far as a major strain of the debate about feminist publishing that came to a head in 1976, but her own article "The Politics of Publishing" acts as a counterargument to these points and shows a much more diverse field of thought, at least among the writers themselves (as opposed to the publishers), with regard to the politics of publishing feminism.

In "The Politics of Publishing," Clausen reports on the results of a survey she sent to "over 35 lesbian writers, editors, and publishers" in June 1976. This survey was occasioned by three controversial events that had brought the debate over feminist publishing versus publishing feminism to the fore. First, the small press magazine *Margins* had requested that Beth Hodges do a sequel to the lesbian publishing special issue she had edited for them, but some women protested that this material should be placed in a feminist magazine instead. Second, an attempt to have a second edition of *The Lesbian Reader* (Amazon Press) brought out by Harper and Row fell through over conflicts about copyright, contributors' fees, and "What kind of compensation we are entitled to expect from the commercial press" (97). The third event was a May 1976 panel discussion on lesbian publishing at the New York City Lesbian Conference. The panel was lead by June Arnold and Parke Bowman of Daughters, Inc., Elly Bulkin and Joan Larkin of Out and Out Books, Fran Winant of Violet Press, and Bertha Harris, and "what many in the audience hoped would be a discussion of practical aspects of publishing and self-publishing quickly turned into an acrimonious debate over the validity of publishing with 'the man'" (97). Amid this maelstrom of community debate, Clausen sent out her survey to get a wide variety of opinions on the political choices faced when publishing. In contrast to the vehement opinions held forth at the panel, "no one categorically ruled out options outside the women's press" (99). In fact, respondents laid out several justifications for choosing commercial presses.

Primarily, authors may choose commercial presses when they have that option in order to reach a wider audience, as these presses have much broader marketing and distribution channels. Irene Yarrow exemplifies this point of view: "My first preference, though it is not without conflict, is to publish with a major commercial press. . . . Reason: to me I write primarily to communicate, to as many women as possible, straight and gay, feminist and nonfeminist, and the major presses vastly surpass the others in reaching power" (Clausen "Politics" 100). Beth Hodges agreed that for certain books, reaching a wider audience overrides all other considerations: "At this stage in the Women's Movement there are some books which all women should have access to. In 1975 it would have been terribly wrong, I think, not to have taken advantage of Knopf's distribution to get *The New Woman's Survival Sourcebook* places any woman could see it" (ibid. 101). In addition to reaching more readers, authors with commercial presses could make more money, allowing them to potentially support themselves as writers. Susan Griffin articulated the feminist ramifications of this economic concern. "I believe that in fact those who are critical of feminist writers publishing with trade houses must face the consequences of their criticism: that the only women who can write without support are the wealthy and those who are not responsible for the care of children" (ibid. 99). Finally, the desire for higher status as a writer, to launch feminist writers into the upper echelons of the literary community as a whole rather than staying in Clausen's imagined "provinces," provided motivation to go commercial. Fran Winant of Violet Press sums up this desire. "The power to grant validation and status is, I believe, the greatest power that the establishment has over writers. They make you a 'real' writer, not just self-published or a 'small press person'" (ibid. 100). The respondents to Clausen's survey overall tended toward a flexible view of feminist publishing and publishing feminism as an interrelated system to be deployed as necessary to get feminist writing out. Adrienne Rich concluded, "at present, we need all the options possible" (ibid. 103).

The reality that feminist publishing and publishing feminism are not diametrically opposed but part of an interrelated whole is most clearly illustrated by books such as Rita Mae Brown's *Rubyfruit Jungle,* which started as a feminist press book but was such a big seller for Daughters, Inc. that the commercial presses came calling and Bantam bought the reprint rights for $250,000 (*Feminist Bookstores Newsletter,* 1.5 8). This sale has to be one of the greatest ironies in feminist publishing history; it occurred in the spring of 1977, less than a year after June Arnold of Daughters, Inc. had written: "There also seems to be a temptation for a women's press to feel flattered when a finishing press offers to buy one of their books—usually one that has been selling well. In this case I think the finishing press sees a chance to make money without doing any work (the women already have put together the book and proved its audience) but I want to repeat that the finishing press is the hard-cover of corporate America and absolutely does not want the independent women's presses to survive. Each time he takes a feminist book from us he weakens us all" (25). As evidenced by her about-face on the issue, however, the sale of reprint rights to corporate presses was quite a boon to feminist presses because the windfall of cash could stabilize their always-rocky finances, keeping them afloat. The corporate presses ultimately made the larger profit, but the books also reached a mass audience. Still, in the culture of the feminist print movement at the time, such a sale of reprint rights to a commercial house was looked upon with suspicion, with implications of "selling out." Many members of the feminist print movement scorned both the corporate profits that were being made off feminist writing and the potential deradicalization of the content.

Arnold's fiery rhetoric in "Feminist Presses and Feminist Politics" clearly stands as the apotheosis of the separatist viewpoint for feminist publishing. She concludes, "It is time to stop giving *any* favorable attention to the books or journals put out by the finishing press. It is time to recycle our money and refuse to let any male corporation make profit—off of us. It is time to understand what male status really means and withdraw support from any woman who is still trying to make her name by selling out our movement" (26). Arnold could afford to have this viewpoint as the owner of a feminist press backed by her own great personal wealth, but it was never the majority viewpoint of the second-wave feminist movement as a whole. By the early 1980s, Seajay noted that the "debate seems to have settled into the practical reality that everyone should publish as often and wherever possible" (30). Beth Hodges, in her response to the Clausen survey, articulated an argument for a holistic view. "I wonder too whether the lesbian presses *should* publish everything . . . If they are busy publishing what others would be willing to publish . . . there's lesbian work that is *not* being published" (Clausen "Politics" 101).

Ultimately, second-wave feminist writers and publishers had to be creative and flexible in attempting to integrate their politics into their overarching goal of making feminist thought and writing available via the inescapably materialist mechanism of publishing. In the very first issue of the *Feminist Bookstores Newsletter*, Andre wrote, "We want to find ways of dealing with the inherent contradiction between being revolutionaries and being in a capitalist business system" (*Feminist Bookstores Newsletter* 1.1 1). Rita Mae Brown also posed this challenge to her contemporaries: "Polarization is the sign of a weak mind. Once you think establishment presses vs. feminist presses you already blew it. The point is to be imaginative" (Clausen "Politics" 110).

In the following case studies, the authors/editors took up this challenge to be imaginative. In the first case, Morgan turned the resources of traditional publishing into tools for feminist empowerment via creative strategies. In the second case, feminist presses experimented even further with challenging the typical financial structure of publishing in an effort to put politics before business. While the two books I am studying are well known, their publication histories are not, largely because their attempts at reconciliation between feminist principle and capitalist profit could be seen as failures. Nonetheless, these innovative interventions are critical to study for what they reveal about how feminist ideas and aesthetics are disseminated and how the materialist process of publication undergirds and influences the feminist movement itself (Gilley 1–9).

Sisterhood Is Powerful

Robin Morgan's 1970 anthology *Sisterhood Is Powerful (SIP)* was a landmark work of the second-wave feminist movement and a major popularizer of radical feminism outside the limited scope of urban-based Women's Liberation groups. As Morgan notes in her memoir, it became "the 'click,' the first feminist epiphany for hundreds of thousands of women, and the staple of mushrooming women's studies courses around the world" (*Saturday's Child* 296). Indeed, the New York Public Library picked *SIP* as one of its Books of the Century, one of eleven books listed under the heading "Women Rise." As an anthology of radical feminist essays, some of which had already been published as pamphlets or by the movement press, *SIP*'s purpose was to collect in one place the diverse voices of Women's Liberation to enable distribution, and thus radicalization, on a massive scale. Morgan achieved this purpose by publishing her collection with Random House, who had the marketing and distribution reach to get copies into every supermarket in America, but radical feminism and Random House made strange bedfellows to say the least. Why would Random House, the very figurehead of what June Arnold would later call "the finishing press" and Carol Seajay would dub LICE (the Literary Industrial Corporate Establishment), be interested in being the ones responsible for mass distribution of essays such as "Notes of a Radical Lesbian," "The Politics of Orgasm," or "The SCUM Manifesto"? How did such a radical book end up being published by "the Man"?

The story begins in 1968, as Robin Morgan first came to national prominence as one of the organizers of and participants in the protest against the Miss America Pageant in Atlantic City, an event that would thereafter be termed by the media as "the birth of the feminist movement" (Saturday's Child 263). Following this event as well as her participation in the WITCH (Women's International Terrorist Conspiracy from Hell) protest of the Bridal Show at Madison Square Garden, Morgan began popping up in the pages of the *New York Times* frequently, culminating in the February 9, 1969, article "Meet the

Women of the Revolution." The *New York Times* love affair with Morgan probably stemmed from the fact that she had been a child star, playing Dagmar on the TV show *Mama*, and was therefore already a celebrity as well as being adept at handling media attention. The February 9th piece features a glamour photo headshot with the caption "Says Robin Morgan, former child actress: 'We will have a revolution in this society'" (Babcox 34). This article launched Morgan as a media darling two months before her Random House contract was signed.

In addition to being known in the New York press and having legitimate movement bona fides as a prominent member of several Women's Liberation groups, Morgan worked in publishing herself at Grove Press (before being fired for trying to organize a union) and had a contact she could call at Random House: John Simon, who became the chief editor of *SIP*. Morgan's proposal for an anthology of writings from the Women's Liberation Movement must have felt like the right opportunity at the right time for Random House: Morgan was both famous and a Women's Liberation insider, and in 1969, "women's lib" was trendy enough to make even such a radical book profitable. Random House said yes, but Simon warned Morgan "to get the material in fast because six months down the line there might not be any interest" (Brownmiller 69). Taking this news back to her feminist group, where she anticipated working on the project as a collective, Morgan was surprised to run into stiff opposition from group members based on issues of money, editorial control, and the feeling that Morgan was on a "personal star trip" (ibid.). She then determined to edit the collection by herself, but she was profoundly aware of the political objections to her undertaking. These objections are best summarized by Ann ForFreedom's article in *Everywoman* after the publication of *SIP*, asking, "How can an institution based on competitive individualism promote cooperative collectivism? If *Sisterhood* is a collective action, why is only one name on it, that of Robin Morgan?" (10). Ideals of collectivity are anathema to traditional publishing processes, but Morgan did her best to meet this challenge with an experiment that was unique in second-wave publishing history.

First, Morgan declares in the opening line of her introduction that "This book is an action. It was conceived, written, edited, copy-edited, proofread, designed, and illustrated by women" ("Introduction" xv). Both for the purpose of protecting the political integrity of the message and for the purpose of promoting the position of women within Random House, Morgan had insisted on working only with women. This part of the experiment did not run as smoothly as hoped, as it quickly became clear that the two female editors Morgan was working with had no "real power in the male-dominated hierarchy of the house, and so were forced into a position of 'interceding' with those who could enforce the decision—men" (xviii). The second part of *SIP*'s "action" was Morgan's negotiation that the book be released simultaneously in paperback so that more women could afford it. This move is very rare in publishing because the publisher wants to make maximum profits off the hardback and wait until interest dies down before releasing the cheaper paperback. Instead, *SIP* was released simultaneously as a hardback for $8.95 and a Vintage paperback for $2.45 in September 1970. Ultimately, though, Morgan's most innovative and radical intervention into the traditional capitalist publishing machine lay in her decision to use the royalties for the book to set up a Sisterhood is Powerful Fund that would pump money directly back into the movement. She was passionately committed to the collectivist roots and purpose of the anthology and wrote in a letter to contributors: "I consider the book as *belonging to* the Movement" (Unpublished letter to contributors 21 Dec. 1971).

In consultation with some of the contributors, Morgan decided on a process for the disbursement of funds that was, as she called it, "ultra-egalitarian" ("The Destruction of Sisterhood Is Powerful" 3). Each royalty check would be divided into seventy portions, one for each contributor, and each portion would be distributed to the "group or institution of the Women's Movement" of the contributor's choice. There were two ground rules: that money was to be distributed to groups, not individuals, in the collectivist spirit of the project, and "the groups had to be *women's* groups concentrating on issues that were of concern *to* women (no caucuses in male organizations)" ("Destruction"). All contributors had received one-time fees for their writings up front, as is usual, but their input and involvement with royalties on the back end was highly unusual and, in fact, proved untenable. After the first royalty check was distributed in this way, the process was dropped due to unreachable contributors, contributors who could not or would not pick a group, and contributors who chose male-left groups instead of women's groups. Beginning with the second round of royalties, Morgan began distributing money to any group that wrote in (and met the ground rules) on a first-come, first-served basis. This allowed for a nonhierarchical but easier-to-administer process. This entire process was carried out through strict business channels via a corporation Morgan and her lawyer Emily Goodman set up called Sisterhood is Powerful, Inc. Morgan was insistent that Random House send royalty checks directly to SIP Inc. and that records relating to the fund's disbursement be made public, all so that she would not appear to be personally giving "her" money away, which, she wrote, "smacks of charity" (Unpublished letter to fund seekers 10 June 1973). In a letter to potential fund-seekers dated June 10, 1973, she argued, "This should NOT be charity; these monies belong, in fact, to the Feminist Movement." The fact that this viewpoint was somewhat unique among other feminist authors/editors did not go unremarked. Morgan also pointed out in that letter "that only a few [other feminist] authors (Shulman, Chesler) have contributed *any* portion of their monetary gains to the Movement, and even that was not done in a regulated way that anyone could check on." Furthermore, Morgan had sarcastically commented in an earlier letter after the lengthy frustration of getting SIP Inc. legally set up, that "It certainly would have been easier to abscond with the funds and build a mansion in Jamaica, like Germaine Greer is doing" (Unpublished letter to contributors).

Thanks to all the hard work and dedication, however, the Sisterhood is Powerful Fund had disbursed $23,000 in direct grants to Women's Liberation groups by 1974 ("SIP Fund"). In this way, Morgan's declaration that "this book is an action" took on its deepest and most provocative meaning (Gilley 1–9). Although Morgan's creation of the SIP Fund with her royalties did not alter the traditional publishing contract in any way, and therefore did not effect any kind of political change at Random House, it did pioneer a way in which the resources of a corporate press could be harnessed to benefit feminism, not just as a distributor of ideas, but as an economic engine. Digging more deeply into the workings of SIP Inc. reveals that its underlying ideological project was at heart one of repurposing "publishing feminism" for the direct benefit of feminist publishing. While popularly known as the SIP Fund, SIP Inc. actually had to be set up as a business corporation because the money was "openly going to political destinations" and therefore could not be a foundation or nonprofit (Unpublished letter to contributors). Morgan decided to set it up as a publishing business that would pay "consultation fees" to groups for information and feedback that they could use to create successive editions of *SIP*. Seen this way, SIP Inc. was essentially supporting feminism so that there would still be a movement underway to report on in the next edition. In more practical terms, fully one-third of the groups receiving money from SIP Inc. were feminist publishers (Morgan "Destruction" 5–6). In her memoir, Morgan realizes the impact of this specific aspect of the whole *SIP* project. She notes that the fund gave "seed money grants to what [would] become a massive alternative feminist media: newspapers, magazines, publishers" (*Saturday's Child* 307–308). *SIP* as an anthology not only reached the mass audience that only a corporate press could provide, but it also generated monies that were funneled directly to feminist presses, who would be free to publish things Random House would not.

This awkward but idealistic phenomenon survived from the fall of 1971, when the first royalties came in, to the fall of 1973, when Lucinda Cisler, one of the book's contributors, filed a federal suit against Random House and Robin

Morgan for allegedly plagiarizing her pamphlet "Women: A Bibliography" in *SIP*'s bibliography (Morgan "Destruction"). Morgan claims that Cisler had called her and, in need of money, asked for some of the *SIP* royalties. Morgan turned her down due to the policy of not granting funds to individuals, and a month later, Cisler launched her suit. She also details the process by which the *SIP* editorial team came up with their own bibliography and notes that Cisler had never, in the three years since the book was published, said a word to Morgan about the bibliography being plagiarized. A feminist media frenzy ensued as *Off Our Backs* covered the lawsuit in their October and December 1974 issues, publishing letters from both Cisler and Morgan, and including letters from various prominent feminists who wrote in defense of one or the other. The outcome of the case was that Random House, against Morgan's wishes, settled with Cisler out of court for $10,000 and immediately froze the royalties for both *SIP* and Morgan's book of poetry *Monster*, until this amount, plus the legal fees in the amount of $13,356.92 could be recouped (Morgan "Destruction"). The entire cost of the lawsuit came out of the royalties, not out of Random House's profits, as stipulated in the original contract. With no royalties coming in for at least three years (this was the same amount of money that SIP Inc. had distributed in its first three years), Morgan was forced to shut down SIP Inc. because it would not be able to pay its yearly taxes, and thus, the grand historical experiment was ended. Because *SIP* stayed in print for at least thirty years, royalties must have been resumed at some point, but Morgan never brought the SIP Fund back to life.

This Bridge Called My Back: Writings by Radical Women of Color

Just as the publication history of *Sisterhood Is Powerful* reveals both the limits and possibilities of publishing feminism with corporate presses, the story of *This Bridge Called My Back: Writings by Radical Women of Color* offers an equally compelling excavation of the intersection between economics and politics in feminist publishing. *This Bridge* and its second publisher Kitchen Table: Women of Color Press are accorded nearly mythical status within feminist and women's studies circles due to the crucial work they did breaking the silence about racism in the second wave and paving the way for theory and activism that would refuse to prioritize gender over race, sexuality, disability, etc., in a hierarchy of oppression. Yet, despite its deep and abiding influence within the movement, the book is unknown outside feminist circles and went out of print with three separate publishers before being revived for a fourth edition by SUNY Press. This path could be attributed to the book's radical politics; an anthology of bilingual writings by third-world lesbians would undoubtedly never be a commercial bestseller in the way that *SIP* was. But I would argue that the publication choices made by the book's editors, Cherríe Moraga and Gloria Anzaldúa, are also largely responsible both for the book's political authenticity and its long periods of unavailability.

Moraga and Anzaldúa met in 1977 at a Feminist Writers Guild meeting in San Francisco and bonded quickly as the only women of color in the group. Two years later, Anzaldúa went to a workshop offered by Merlin Stone, where Merlin encouraged Anzaldúa to create the anthology she had realized was needed back when she taught classes on Chicana women at University of Texas–Austin. Galvanized, Anzaldúa convinced Moraga to coedit the anthology with her and sent solicitations for materials to *Conditions* and the *Feminist Writers Guild Newsletter* (Anzaldúa "Turning Points" 58–59). Just like Robin Morgan before her, Anzaldúa's vision for the work was a populist one. On a copy of the draft call for submissions for *This Bridge* in 1979, Anzaldúa wrote a note to Cherríe and Merlin saying, "I think we should try to get a mainstream press to publish us—we need to reach a broad audience, not just a feminist one" (Unpublished letter soliciting manuscripts 19 April 1979). While I cannot find evidence of any mainstream presses expressing interest in this first edition, on August 24th of that year, Barbara Beltrand of South End Press wrote to Anzaldúa expressing great interest (Beltrand). South End is neither a mainstream press nor a strictly feminist one, but a well-capitalized nonprofit, collectively run publisher dedicated to radical social politics that would have reached beyond the feminist audience. Meanwhile, however, Moraga had made connections with Persephone Press, a white lesbian radical feminist press in Watertown, Massachusetts. Sally Gearhart, who had been Moraga's advisor in graduate school, had published *Wanderground* with Persephone in 1978 and brought *This Bridge* to their attention. Additionally, Adrienne Rich had read Moraga's essay "La Guera" and recommended it for inclusion in Persephone's anthology *The Coming Out Stories* as well as recommending *This Bridge* (Moraga *Xicana* 219). As a small lesbian press, Persephone did not have a lot of capital, but they did offer the chance to convert feminist theory into action by supporting a lesbian business and altering traditional economic paradigms. Persephone publishers Pat McGloin and Gloria Greenfield were committed to experimenting with breaking down hierarchies of remuneration and control within the publishing relationship. Moraga and Anzaldúa decided to publish with Persephone and the first edition of *This Bridge* came out on June 1, 1981.

The Persephone contract for *This Bridge* is a model of feminist philosophy. Persephone was known for offering royalties that were twice that offered by commercial presses, and indeed they contracted to pay 12 percent in royalties, when 6 percent was usual for paperbacks. They also pledged not to sell mass market rights to "non-feminist publishing enterprises" and to sell translation rights only to "non-sexist, non-racist, and non-conglomerate publishing enterprises." These clauses imply a separatist inclination in the great feminist publishing/publishing feminism debate discussed earlier in this chapter, and, indeed, the contract also evoked the question of intended audience that was common to that debate. Clause 25 of the publishing contract states: "It is the understanding of the Publishers and the Editors that the priority market for distribution of the said Work is women of color, and the Publishers respectively agree to promote and market the said Work accordingly. Priority market will be determined by the Publishers allocating fifty per cent (50%) of all marketing dollar expenditures, marketing research time, and resources of said Work to women of color" (Publishing contract between Persephone Press and Cherrie Moraga). Finally, and perhaps most radically, Persephone agreed to experiment with continuing to compensate contributors throughout the publishing history of the book, although this was an informal agreement and not written into the legal contract. According to a July 1981 letter to contributors from Moraga and Anzaldúa, each contributor would receive a fee for their work to be deducted from the editor's royalties and reflecting payment for the first ten thousand copies sold, but for every subsequent ten thousand copies sold, contributors would receive another payment in the same amount to be paid half by Persephone and half from the editor's royalties (Unpublished letter to contributors 22 July 1981). This attempt to compensate contributors beyond an upfront fee is unheard of in publishing and reflected the feminist belief that those whose intellectual contributions created the book should be the beneficiaries of the economic wealth generated, rather than those who merely performed the materialist labor of publishing.

The problem with this feminist ideal of reallocating the economic wealth from the publishers to the editors and contributors is that for a small undercapitalized press run by women without deep pockets, there is no economic wealth. Because bookstores do not pay publishers for books until long after they are sold and they are also free to return unsold copies, there is no income for a long time after publication. Generally, all of the money that does finally come in is needed to finance the next print run of copies if the book is selling well. In this way, a successful book can leave a small publisher without any actual income to pay royalties out of (or a salary for the publisher herself) for a very long time. Greenfield called this "death by too much success" (Unpublished letter from Gloria Greenfield). This constant lack of liquid capital plagued most feminist publishers and while Persephone was able to get bank loans for years to tide them over until funds came in, eventually a credit crunch and a huge bill to the Internal Revenue Service for back taxes put Persephone out of business at the height of its success (Greenfield and McGloin). Although the royalty rate and continuing compensation for contributors probably did not cause the business to collapse per se (as they were never fully paid), McGloin and Greenfield complained bitterly to the *Gay Community News* that "they felt constantly conflicted about whether to operate Persephone in accordance with [publishing] industry standards and be financially healthy, or to do what they thought they as lesbian feminists should do, even when it seemed to be financially unwise" (Clark 1). In a special report released on April 13, 1983, Persephone documented their struggle to stay in business and reported that they had tried to sell the press to a larger publishing house who would assume the liabilities. "All four publishing houses rejected the purchase proposal for the same reason: our contracted royalties were ridiculous" (McGloin and Greenfield). Ultimately, Beacon Press did purchase Persephone, but around this same time, Moraga had cofounded Kitchen Table: Women of Color Press with Barbara Smith and Audre Lorde and she wanted to publish *This Bridge* with Kitchen Table (Enszer chapter 2).

The frontispiece of the Kitchen Table edition of *This Bridge* paints the transition from Persephone Press to Kitchen Table as one fraught with racial tension: "When Persephone Press, Inc., a white women's press of Watertown, Massachusetts and the original publishers of *Bridge*, ceased operation in the Spring of 1983, this book had already gone out of print. After many months of negotiations, the co-editors were finally able to retrieve control of their book, whereupon Kitchen Table: Women of Color Press of New York agreed to republish it. The following, then, is the second edition of *This Bridge Called My Back*, conceived of and produced entirely by women of color." Indeed, there had been a mediated discussion among Pat McGloin, Gloria Greenfield, Gloria Anzaldúa, Elly Bulkin, Audre Lorde, Cherríe Moraga, and Barbara Smith on January 30, 1982, about issues of anti-Semitism, race, and the control publishers have over authors, but the archival record presents a more nuanced picture than the one suggested by this frontispiece (Enszer chapter 2). McGloin and Greenfield were very committed to publishing the work of women of color at Persephone and the accusation that *This Bridge* had gone out of print is a debatable one. Anzaldúa wrote, in a letter to Moraga dated May 2, 1983, "I am not *sure* that *Bridge* is out of print, they may have squirreled away a few boxes. I told you

I had ordered and received 10 copies around Mar. 12. I also told you that when I wrote to them in March telling them that I had some corrections and requested that they tell me when Bridge would go into next printing, they wrote back to you and me (letter dated March 28) stating that the reprint 'was not immediate' and that I should send the corrections soon. Chorizo, we cannot use this letter as 'evidence' because it does *not* state that *Bridge* is out of print" (Unpublished letter from Anzaldúa to Moraga2 May 1983). *This Bridge* was effectively out of print because Persephone could not afford to print more copies, but they had not deliberately abandoned the work. Additionally, Moraga herself reported in a September 15, 1983, letter to Anzaldúa, "Went up to Boston last week, got back *Bridge* sin problemas, only their bad attitudes." Persephone's intent toward *This Bridge* was not as villainous as the second edition frontispiece suggests, but nonetheless, issues of distrust over power and control in publishing clearly lead to Moraga's desire to take the reins herself via Kitchen Table.

Correspondence between Moraga and Anzaldúa from this period when Moraga was working to retrieve rights to *This Bridge* and organizing a second edition to be published by Kitchen Table shows that the continuance of *This Bridge* as a feminist press publication was contested, rather than a foregone conclusion, at least by Anzaldúa. On May 2, 1983, Anzaldúa writes in a letter to Moraga, "As I told you on the phone, it might be a good thing at this time for Bridge to be published by a press such as Beacon where non-feminist Third World people (and others) would have excess [*sic*] to the book as I think most of the feminist community has been exposed to it" (Unpublished letter Anzaldua to Moraga). Anzaldúa's desire for a wider audience was just as strong as it had been four years earlier when she originally wrote that note on the call for submissions, but she voiced this desire only in private. In a 1982 interview with Linda Smuckler, she was asked directly who she wanted to publish *This Bridge* with next and she said, "I'd like to publish with Kitchen Table Press, the third-world women's press" (Anzaldúa "Turning Points" 61). Smuckler pursued the question: "Do you think about trying to publish in larger presses, in presses that can publish more copies, that do greater publicity? Do you ever think of reaching a greater audience through that medium, rather than through Kitchen Table or Persephone?" Anzaldúa replied, "No, I think it's a myth that larger presses always publish more copies and reach a wider audience. Bridge has sold about eighteen thousand copies, but if a major press handled it, it wouldn't have gotten out, and we wouldn't have gotten as much of the royalties. The big publishers sit on a book for two years; then they remainder it or it rots—after it's out, it rots in the warehouses. Very few of the books they print get out. Most of the books are tax write-offs. It's a big business, often a swindle." ("Turning

Points" 62). At the end of this speech she urges Smuckler to "talk to Cherríe and other people who know more about it," which, given her private beliefs, suggests that this line of thinking about corporate presses represents Moraga's viewpoint more than her own. In that same year, Moraga had presented this viewpoint in a letter cowritten with Barbara Smith articulating her displeasure with Persephone Press for rejecting a poetry collection by Hattie Gossett that ended up going to South End Press. Smith and Moraga felt it would get "so much less than the visibility it deserves" at South End (Enszer 34–35). Clearly, Moraga felt that publishing with a small lesbian press, or subsequently a small women of color lesbian press, was the only way to respect the political integrity of the work, market it to its proper audience, and reap financial benefits for its editors and contributors. Anzaldúa publicly agreed with her in the Smuckler interview claiming, "I've never wanted to publish with a mainstream publisher" ("Turning Points" 63), but the fact that this directly contradicts her private correspondence indicates either a desire to present a solid front of support for feminist publishers or a deep-seated ambivalence over whether a mainstream press or a feminist press would be better suited to achieving her vision. Unsurprisingly, as Moraga had been involved with Barbara Smith and Kitchen Table Press since 1981, the second edition of *This Bridge* was published by Kitchen Table in late 1983.

The relationship between *This Bridge* and its new publisher started out as idealistic and principled as it did at Persephone. Moraga reported in a September 1983 letter to contributors that "Gloria and I have negotiated a contract with Kitchen Table where each contributor will once again receive her original contributors' fee payment after the first 10,000 copies have been sold and for every subsequent 10,000 copies sold thereafter" (Unpublished letter from Moraga to contributors 1 Sept. 1983). Five years later, this contract point, along with the usual cash flow problems that made paying royalties difficult and unpredictable, had created great animosity between Barbara Smith, now the sole publisher at Kitchen Table, and Moraga, despite their previous relationship as lovers and cofounders of the press. An October 13, 1988, letter from Smith to Moraga is frank: "Our decision to take on the payment commitments to contributors that had originally been offered by Persephone was a major error (and this policy was undoubtedly one of the factors that contributed to them declaring bankruptcy). Given the tiny margin of earnings available from independent book publishing, there is hardly sufficient money to pay for the production of new books, reprintings of previous titles, royalties, rent, telephone, supplies, and office staff let alone being obligated to pay contributors again and again" (Unpublished letter Smith to Moraga 13 Oct. 1988). The fact that Moraga persisted in trying to get her royalties from Kitchen Table despite their always precarious existence is evidenced by a 1990 letter from Smith to Anzaldúa: "They [Kitchen Table employees at the National Women's Studies Association conference] also said that Cherríe had informed you that she was receiving monthly installment payments on the royalties due to her. This was an arrangement that we were pressured to make with Cherríe and it is in fact a hardship to pay her in this manner. Up until the time that this arrangement was initiated, *all* authors, including myself, were paid royalties on the same schedule" (Unpublished letter from Smith to Moraga 29 Aug. 1990). This antagonism between Smith and Moraga left Moraga considering the option to reclaim the rights to *This Bridge* and dispiritedly concluding "possibly *Bridge* has seen its day" (Unpublished letter from Moraga to Anzaldúa 24 Oct. 1988).

This Bridge is still a vital work today and most definitely had not "seen its day" in 1988, but its publication road continued to be bumpy. Going out of print when Kitchen Table went under in 1995, *This Bridge* was reissued in a third edition in 2002 by Norma Alarcón's Third Woman Press. Once again, this choice of publisher was contested by Anzaldúa, even more forcefully than the first two times. On April 29, 2000, Anzaldúa wrote to Moraga, "You think Third Woman will be easiest and less work for us, I don't agree. I do agree that it would be more politically correct. At this point I'm in favor of a bigger press like Routledge because it has better circulation, worldwide outreach, more publicity, and better money" (E-mail Anzaldúa to Moraga). For Anzaldúa, the experiment in feminist publishing had to a large extent failed. While feminist presses had gotten *This Bridge* into print and offered the ideal of melding feminist politics with economics, the book was now out of print, had never been able to sustain its editors financially, and had not reached beyond feminist circles with its message of bridging. A year earlier, in 1999, South End Press had come calling again, offering to reissue *This Bridge* as part of its classics series, but Anzaldúa felt that even South End was too small at this point and that the 11 percent royalties they offered were not enough (Unpublished letter from Hayes to Anzaldúa). Once again, she lost the argument and *This Bridge* soon went out of print with Third Woman.

Anzaldúa's foreword to the Third Woman Press third edition explains her bridging philosophy in a way that poses the underlying question at the heart of the feminist publishing/publishing feminism debate: "Bridge has multicultural roots and . . . is not 'owned' solely by mujeres de color, or even by women. Like knowledge, Bridge cannot be possessed by a single person or group. It's public; it's communal. To exclude is to close the bridge, invite separatism and hostilities. Instead we (Third World feminists) must invite other groups to join us and together bring about social change" ("Foreword" xxxvi). How can a text that originates in a place of radical marginality reach a mainstream audience and invite others in while remaining true to its feminist, noncapitalist roots? In her 2011 book, *A Xicana Codex of Changing Consciousness: Writings, 2000–2010*, Moraga's essay "The Salt That Cures: Remembering Gloria Anzaldúa" elucidates the political differences that had evolved between herself and Anzaldúa that underlay their differences in publishing philosophy. Anzaldúa's vision of the bridge, as has already been noted, was not exclusive but meant to include those in privileged positions. Her follow-up to *This Bridge*, created without Moraga and entitled *This Bridge We Call Home*, included writings by men and white women. Moraga disagreed with this move because of her belief that U.S. women of color feminism still has a strategic need to develop an autonomous identity. "From my perspective, to be 'inclusive' of (even) queer men and white women, at this stage of a U.S. feminism of color, would be to suggest that our movement had developed beyond the need for autonomous dialogue entrenos" (*Xicana* 123). This philosophy of empowerment through separatism guided *This Bridge* through its three editions, and the book had an enormous ideological impact on the movement, but it also painfully illustrated the limits of feminist publishing.

Anzaldúa published *This Bridge We Call Home* with Routledge, finally reaching the wider distribution network she had always longed for, but also contending with compromise. She writes in the preface, "The anthology we originally conceived was even more inclusionary than the book you hold. The challenge AnaLouise and I faced was to be as inclusive as possible within the page and word limitations set by our publisher. Due to the current economics in the book publishing industry and the subsequent conviction that teachers would not include a big and pricey book in their syllabi, we had to reduce our original 1,300 page manuscript to 850 pages, the original 108 pieces to 80, and the 113 contributors to 87" (Anzaldúa "Preface: (Un)Natural Bridges" 4). Moraga published *Xicana Codex* with Duke University Press, but thanks her agent in the foreword "for his tenacity and uncompromising loyalty to my vision, even when it doesn't 'please the market'" (xx). Interestingly, Moraga's switch to an academic publisher may have signaled a philosophical change of heart: *This Bridge Called My Back* is now slated to be published in a fourth edition by SUNY Press in 2015. This will be the first time it has been published by a nonfeminist press.

Conclusion: Is Reconciliation Possible?

Julia Penelope, in her article "The Perils of Publishing," laments that "no reconciliation seems possible between political conscience and economic survival"

(3). Yet many feminist authors, editors, and publishers have devoted their lives, resources, and energy to attempting just such a reconciliation. Because many of these experiments either failed economically or were suspect politically, histories of the feminist movement generally ignore them, glossing over the means by which feminist text is made available and distributed. Issues of class and race are central. In the case studies presented here, Robin Morgan could afford to dedicate her royalties to the movement because of her middle-class status. No one involved in the creation or publication of *This Bridge*, on the other hand, had access to any kind of privilege or resources. Exploring the history of experimentation in feminist publishing/publishing feminism, therefore, is crucial to our understanding of how the economic apparatus of publishing affects the ideological direction of feminism and allows us to make informed choices about the path forward.

Works Cited

Anzaldúa, Gloria. E-mail to Cherríe Moraga. 29 April 2000.

———. Foreword, 2001. *This Bridge Called My Back: Writings by Radical Women of Color*. Ed. Cherríe L. Moraga and Gloria E. Anzaldúa. Berkeley, CA: Third Woman Press, 2002. xxxiv–xxxix.

———. "Turning Points: An Interview with Linda Smuckler (1982)." *Gloria Anzaldúa: Interviews/Entrevistas*. New York: Routledge, 2000. 58–59.

———. "(Un)natural Bridges, (Un)safe Spaces." Preface. *This Bridge We Call Home: Radical Visions for Transformation*. Ed. Gloria E. Anzaldúa and AnaLouise Keating. New York: Routledge, 2002. 1–5.

———. Unpublished Letter Soliciting Manuscripts for the New Anthology. 19 April 1979. Gloria Evangelina Anzaldúa Papers.

———. Unpublished Letter to Cherríe Moraga. 2 May 1983. Gloria Evangelina Anzaldúa Papers.

Arnold, June. "Feminist Presses and Feminist Politics." *Quest* 3.1 (Summer 1976): 18–26.

Babcox, Peter. "Meet the Women of the Revolution." *New York Times Magazine* 9 Feb. 1969: 34.

Beltrand, Barbara. Unpublished Letter to Gloria Anzaldúa. 24 Aug. 1979. Gloria Evangelina Anzaldúa Papers.

Brownmiller, Susan. *In Our Time: Memoir of a Revolution*. New York: Random House, 1999.

Bunch, Charlotte. "Feminist Publishing: An Antiquated Form?" *Heresies* 3 (1977): 24–26.

Clark, Jill. "Persephone Press Folds, Some Titles Purchased." *Gay Community News* (Boston) 5 Aug. 1983: 1.

Clausen, Jan. *A Movement of Poets: Thoughts on Poetry and Feminism*. New York: Long Haul Press, 1982. 36.

———. "The Politics of Publishing." *Sinister Wisdom* 2 (Fall 1976): 94–115.

Curb, Rosemary. Press Release to *Off Our Backs, Gay Community News, Womanews, Plexus,* and Other Alternative Women's Publications Concerned. P. 4. 12 June 1985. Barbara Grier-Naiad Press Collections, 1956–1999. San Francisco History Center, San Francisco Public Library.

Ellenberger, Harriet, and Catherine Nicholson. "Dear Beth." *Sinister Wisdom* 1 (Fall 1976): 126–129.

Enszer, Julie. "The Whole Naked Truth of Our Lives: Lesbian Feminist Print Culture from 1969 through 1989." Diss. U of Maryland. 2013.

Feminist Bookstore News 1.1 (Oct. 1976): 1.

Feminist Bookstore News 1.5 (April 1977): 8.

Flannery, Kathryn. *Feminist Literacies 1968–75*. Urbana: U of Illinois Press, 2005.

ForFreedom, Ann. "Review of Sisterhood is Powerful." *Everywoman* 2.1.12 (Jan. 1971): 10.

Gilley, Jennifer. "This Book Is an Action: A Case for the Study of Feminist Publishing." *International Journal of the Book* 9.1 (2012): 1–9.

Gloria Evangelina Anzaldúa Papers. Benson Latin American Collection, University of Texas Libraries, the University of Texas at Austin.

Greenfield, Gloria. Unpublished Letter to Persephone Authors. 19 May 1982. Gloria Evangelina Anzaldúa Papers.

Greenfield, Gloria Z., and Pat McGloin. Persephone Press Special Report: Letter to Persephone Authors. 13 April 1983. Gloria Evangelina Anzaldúa Papers.

Hayes, Loie. Unpublished Letter from Loie Hayes at South End Press to Gloria Anzaldúa. 13 July 1999. Gloria Evangelina Anzaldúa Papers.

Lichtenstein, Grace. "Women's Lib Wooed by Publishers." *New York Times* 17 Aug. 1970: 32.

Moraga, Cherríe. *A Xicana Codex of Changing Consciousness: Writings, 2000–2010*. Durham, NC: Duke UP, 2011.

———. Unpublished Letter to Contributors. 1 Sept. 1983. Gloria Evangelina Anzaldúa Papers.

———. Unpublished Letter to Gloria Anzaldúa. 24 Oct. 1988. Gloria Evangelina Anzaldúa Papers.

Moraga, Cherríe, and Gloria Anzaldúa. Unpublished Letter to Contributors. 22 July 1981. Gloria Evangelina Anzaldúa Papers.

Morgan, Robin. "The Destruction of Sisterhood Is Powerful, Inc.: A Report to the Women's Movement." Unpublished MS. August 1974. Robin Morgan Papers.

———. "Introduction." *Sisterhood Is Powerful: An Anthology of Writings from the Women's Liberation Movement*. Ed. Robin Morgan. New York: Random House, 1970. xv.

———. *Saturday's Child: A Memoir*. New York: W. W. Norton, 2001.

———. "SIP Fund, 1970–1974. Rough Statement." Unpublished MS. Robin Morgan Papers.

———. Unpublished Letter to Contributors. 21 Dec. 1971. Robin Morgan Papers.

———. Unpublished Letter to Fund-seekers. 10 June 1973. Robin Morgan Papers.

Penelope, Julia. "The Perils of Publishing." *Women's Review of Books* 2.12 (Sept. 1985): 3–6.

Publishing Contract between Persephone Press and Cherríe Moraga and Gloria Anzaldúa. Aug. 1980. Gloria Evangelina Anzaldúa Papers.

Robin Morgan Papers. David M. Rubenstein Rare Book and Manuscript Library, Duke University. Durham, NC.

Seajay, Carol. "Feminist Publishing in the U.S." N.d. Essay. *Feminist Bookstore News* Records. Gay and Lesbian Center, San Francisco Public Library.

Smith, Barbara. "A Press of Our Own: Kitchen Table: Women of Color Press." In *Communications at the Crossroads: The Gender Gap Connection*. Ed. Ramona R. Rush and Donna Allen. Norwood, NJ: Ablex Publishing Corporation, 1989. 202–207.

———. Unpublished Letter to Cherríe Moraga. 13 Oct. 1988. Gloria Evangelina Anzaldúa Papers.

———. Unpublished Letter to Gloria Anzaldúa. 29 Aug. 1990. Gloria Evangelina Anzaldúa Papers.

Zeisler, Andi. *Feminism and Pop Culture*. Berkeley, CA: Seal Press, 2008.

Chapter 2

A Revolution in Ephemera

Feminist Newsletters and Newspapers of the 1970s

Agatha Beins

The April 1974 issue of *Sister*, a Los Angeles feminist newspaper, calls to readers for their assistance:

> Sisters! Please contribute to the June *Sports* issue. Send your favorite newspaper, magazine or personal black & white photographs of all women in all sports. Articles, poetry, essays stories are needed. I would also like your lists of women athletic greats of the past & present. Also you can help by monitering TV reporting of women in sports. For each newscast you watch, tally the number of sports items about men and the number of items about women. Indicate the city, station, network affiliation if any, and what time of day the broadcast was. Even if you just do one broadcasts—send it in to: SISTER—Sports Issue Westside Women's Center.[1] ("Women in Sports" 14)

This announcement gives insight into the dynamic and multifaceted place of periodicals in the U.S. Women's Liberation Movement in the 1970s. In addition to covering events nationally and internationally, feminist periodicals paid particular attention to the quotidian happenings where they were published and many also contained calendars that announced meetings, demonstrations, actions, and celebrations to come. Thus they serve as important chronicles of contemporary life. *Sister*'s interest in newspaper, magazine, and personal photographs points to the multifaceted nature of feminism: in addition to intervening in the public, legal, and political spheres, feminists viewed all aspects of public and private realms as potential sites for transformation. Not only did periodicals provide information, but readers also often participated in this record of feminism, which suggests that being a part of the newsletter is a form of participating in the Women's Liberation Movement. Lastly, the end of the announcement gives women and feminism a place in time. By recognizing "women athletic greats of the past & present," the announcement creates a legacy of resistance to gender norms that has been going on for a decades, if not centuries.

Feminist periodicals played such a wide variety of roles in the 1970s in part because of the lack of formal, institutionalized systems through which feminists could circulate information and in part because of the textual qualities of periodicals as a genre. As an inexpensive and effective way to record and communicate news, periodicals were one of the few reliable ways for women to learn about feminist happenings in their city and throughout the world.[2] The resource- and money-intensive process of getting a book into readers' hands meant that only a select few women could find their written work in monographs or anthologies, whereas access to cheap offset printing and mimeograph machines created multiple and repeated chances for a wide range of women to produce feminism in print through periodicals. Additionally, as we can see from the *Sister* announcement, the editors were looking for a variety of different kinds of contributions, reflecting the multitextual qualities of periodicals. These publications contain a variety of genres of writing and art, including articles, reports on events, position statements, narrative essays, editorials, announcements, letters, reprints from other publications, poetry, fiction, photographs, drawings, cartoons, how-to pieces, and advertisements. Periodicals thus juxtapose more objective, factual, or unequivocal pieces with creative and fanciful pieces, putting many different voices in conversation within a particular issue and across multiple issues. A method of analysis that builds on this spatial and temporal intertextuality illuminates the rich, contradictory, and dynamic elaboration of feminist theory and practice.

In this essay I use feminist periodicals to demonstrate the significance of the local, quotidian, and daily scale at which Women's Liberation occurred in the 1970s. Offering local interpretations of grander ideals, shifts in ideas and ideals through time, a variety of different texts and voices, and local specificity, periodicals temper and texture the political images that characterized feminism on a national scale. In their content and in their intertextuality, periodicals highlight how feminist ideals were manifested in different communities and how communities developed distinct practices to reach these ideals. To illustrate the complexity and provisionality of feminism during this time, I focus on four different facets of periodicals: spatial intertexuality, temporal intertextuality, the significance of location, and the way periodicals make feminism visible at a local, quotidian scale.

I read feminist periodicals as emerging conversations rather than as fully formed manifestations of already crystallized feminist ideals. The voices in these periodicals collectively struggle to articulate an imagined future and unearth a hidden past, and this struggle appears not only within the pages of a single issue but also diachronically. Presenting feminism in a particular community over a period of time, each periodical pieces together a narrative of the way feminism as a collective identity formed and re-formed in that site. The multiple voices weighing in on an idea and the re-presentation of an idea through different issues of a periodical show that feminists did not simply arrive at an unwavering consensus in their political programs (Hesford 122). Thus, borrowing from Caitlin DeSilvey's formulation of anticipatory history, I argue that periodicals "unsettle the narrative foundations that stabilize" feminism as transparent and fully knowable (DeSilvey 35). This disruption is an effect both of the textual variety in periodicals and also of the ways in which different pieces interact intertextually. Images, for instance, can clarify meaning in an article or make it more ambiguous, and the metaphorical qualities of poetry can complicate seemingly straightforward political interventions to address sexism. In other words, if we look at an article in isolation from its broader textual context, meaning may appear to be transparent and fixed, but when we can see the full page or full issue, a different narrative may emerge.

As a chronicle of feminist activism, periodicals constitute a performative archive. At the time of their publication they not only provided concrete evidence of feminism's presence but also enacted what they recorded (see Johnston 15–16). Periodicals are performative also in the sense that they prescribe the world. Kathryn Thoms Flannery explains that "more than just 'reflecting,' the newsletters, newspapers, and journals helped shape those ideologies and issues of the growing movement" (29; see also Myerson et al.; Felski 78). That is, the textual and visual utterances in periodicals describe the world and "the world is also made to fit the words" (Hall 185).

My essay draws from a primary source archive that includes a set of feminist newsletters and newspapers published in five different communities: Iowa City, Iowa; Los Angeles, California; New Orleans, Louisiana; Northampton, Massachusetts; and Cambridge, Massachusetts. These sites represent geographic breadth and highlight places not often included in the national histories of the Women's Liberation Movement. I have chosen also to focus on multi-issue feminist periodicals, or periodicals whose purpose is not to address a specific aspect of Women's Liberation—such as art, women's health, or lesbian feminism—because they reflect and construct feminism as a social movement more broadly.

Spatial Intertextuality

Alternative and underground newsletters and newspapers in the 1960s and 1970s were radical collages, juxtaposing typed and handwritten text, photographs and hand-drawn graphics, signed and unsigned articles, and layout that appears professionally done alongside typos, misnumbered pages, and crooked lines of text. At times this aesthetic is the result of an active commitment to antiprofessionalism (Flannery 53), at times it is part of a fierce commitment to include as many women as possible in the publication process, and at times, editorial collectives simply did not have enough time or woman power to thoroughly edit the issue. Regardless of the cause, the effect, as Flannery describes, is "a riot of variations rather than a consistency of positionings, [and a] mix of ideas and forms" (41).

Feminist periodicals are thus particularly apt for an intertextual analysis. In this section, I look at intertextuality in a spatial sense, conducting close readings of the different pieces placed on a single page to argue that an individual piece (an article, poem, essay, etc.) gains meaning in relation to the other items on the page. Therefore, if we shift scale and, instead of looking only at a single article or essay, take the page or multiple issues of a periodical as a unit of analysis, we can nuance the meanings of the claims and ideas presented. In this and the following sections, I focus particularly on how a method that uses spatial and temporal intertextuality produces Women's Liberation in the 1970s as an unfinished, continually unfolding set of ideals and practices.

The first issue of *Distaff*, a New Orleans newspaper published between 1973 and 1982, offers a conversation between different genres of writing and visions of feminism.[3] On page 5 there is an article by Clay Latimer titled "The Legal Identity of the Married Woman," which explains some of the ways that women are legally and contractually bound to their husbands upon marriage (5). Advertised as "the first article of a series on this subject" with a title placed prominently in bold font, it takes up almost the entire page, likely to draw a reader's attention, which marks this topic as important to the editors and the local community. The article is primarily informative and practical. Latimer discusses court decisions and recent legislation and goes into detail about the Civil Code of Louisiana, which provides a basis for state laws. Paying particular attention to sexism embedded in language, Latimer explains that according to the code husbands have "rights" while wives have "duties," and that "the wife is *bound* to live with her husband and to follow him wherever he chooses to reside; the husband is *obliged* to receive her and to furnish her with whatever is required for the convenience of life, in proportion to his means and condition" (emphasis in the original). Although Latimer does not prescribe a particular course of action, the article implies that reform of existing governmental structures will bring us closer to social justice, since she concludes with the hopeful comment that there are currently more options "by which [married women] may, with extended effort and some legal implementation, establish their own individual identities."

The content of this piece largely reflects what José E. Muñoz would describe as pragmatic politics, or an approach to social justice that relies on "ontological certitude" (11) that fixes identity categories and political practices. Working within the confines of juridico-legal discourses, Latimer presumes that "woman," and thus "wife," are transparent and coherent identities that gain meaning and validity through existing laws and social norms. We also see an understanding of political activism that directly and linearly connects the future to the present: if women work within the legal system now, then, at some point in the future, they may become autonomous individuals in the eyes of the law. Muñoz critiques this political framework because it prevents us from imagining a future that does not emerge directly from a present that emerged directly from the past (see also Weigman 118). It becomes more difficult—if not impossible—to imagine a different future and to imagine the future differently.

Nestled in the lower right-hand corner of the page dominated by Latimer's article and only eight lines long is a poem by Sheila Hope Jurnak, "Movement Two." It is unobtrusive and could be overlooked fairly easily. However, its brevity is forceful:

> Without meaning to
> I turned 35
> three marriages six children
> too busy to look where I'm going.
> Today I want
> rainbows
> cheeseberries
> purple onion cookies. (5)

Latimer's ideas perhaps echo in the poem, inflecting Jurnak's wife/mother character with ontological certitude characterized by marital burdens of duty and obligation. Yet, in this poem Jurnak moves away from the predictable and the knowable. The last four lines imagine a future that breaks from the demands of pragmatic politics. The poem does not call for changes to the Civil Code of Louisiana to make the legal contract of marriage less sexist or for an oppositional politics that simply rejects marriage, family, men, or motherhood. It does not engage a rhetoric of equality or reform. Rather, Jurnak moves us to a fanciful, hopeful place, one that bears no normatively logical relation to the conditions of being a mother/wife depicted in the first four lines of the poem and in Latimer's article. Rainbows, cheeseberries, and purple onion cookies offer no clear antidote to the political and identitarian norms of motherhood and marriage and instead create space for a future in which heretofore unimaginable feelings can be named and desires can be satisfied. We start with a rainbow, which is something familiar, but nonetheless exists as an object purely for pleasure. The rainbow in the sky has no utilitarian function but merely allows us to enjoy it without having to give anything in return. Purple onion cookies suggest a kind of gastronomic rule breaking: the pleasure and sweetness of a cookie in contrast to the astringent, tear-inducing qualities of an onion. At the same time, cheeseberries push us into ontological uncertainty: are they berries made of cheese, are they an imagined kind of berry, are they cheese mixed with berries, or are they something else completely? Muñoz claims that "queerness in its utopian connotations promises a human that is not yet here" (26), and, importantly, this promise is not just about offering a path toward a different epistemology; it also involves relating to the world in an affectively different way. Jurnak's cheeseberries and purple onion cookies, in particular, symbolize this yearning for a world that bears a resemblance to the present one obliquely, if at all.

Such a chimerical list of desires can work to complicate the self-determination for women that Latimer's article demands. The juxtaposition of Latimer's article and Jurnak's poem shows the importance of polyvocality in feminist periodicals. Giving idealistic visions for change and concrete guides for getting us closer to these visions, Latimer and Jurnak manifest feminism as a social movement that was neither hopelessly utopian nor rigidly pragmatic. Refusing a simple definition or representation of feminism and a single path for realizing feminist objectives, periodicals invite a methodology based on intertextuality that recognizes that any single piece in a periodical likely gains meaning in relation to the other text and imagery in that issue.

Intertextual readings can enrich our analyses of periodicals as primary source artifacts. Sometimes different pieces are clearly connected, such as editorial introductions to articles or editors' responses to letters they publish. Other times, though, these dialogues formed unpredictably, based on readers' idiosyncratic interpretations and editors' decisions about layout that were based more on efficient use of space than on content of different pieces. The creative writing, in particular, opens up feminism's plasticity since poetry and personal essays often lend themselves to multiple interpretations. The inclusion of multiple forms of writing on a single page reflects one kind of intertextuality, and, as I discuss in the next section, we can also think of intertextuality in a temporal sense. Reading multiple issues of a periodical shows how feminism forms and re-forms through time, which both complicates and disrupts the coherence of the dominant concepts associated with feminism.

Temporal Intertextuality

The editors of the Iowa City feminist newspaper *Ain't I a Woman?* did not shy away from making overt, strident, and unequivocal demands, from the first issue published in June 1970 until the paper folded in May 1974. Half of the front page of the second issue is filled with a manifesto titled "to meet the needs of women." After a brief introduction, a series of eleven demands addresses topics such as child care, health care, education, labor, and media. It concludes with a demand for an all-encompassing program for liberation: "WE DEMAND THE RIGHT OF SELF-DETERMINATION FOR ALL PEOPLE. There must be an immediate end to the exploitation of women, blacks, third world peoples. All forms of oppression and exploitation must be ended. We demand our freedom as women but not at the expense of the freedom of other people. Being rich by making others poor, being free by enslaving others, is not worth fighting for. We demand that all people be liberated. Power to all the people or none." The Iowa City feminists demonstrate the expansiveness of their vision for a feminist future in these demands. Though grounding the different demands in the inequalities sexism produces, they also explicitly include men, children, and people of color in their vision of liberation. Moreover, the mixture of spheres—family, media, education, medicine, sexuality, and day care—represent the wide range of feminist concerns. Virtually no aspect of society can be left as it is; liberation must occur everywhere, for everyone, and in the smallest niches of our private lives.

Muñoz cites the manifesto-like piece "What We Want, What We Believe," published in 1971 in the activist periodical *Gay Flames,* as an example of a performative utopian text.[4] It lists sixteen demands addressing a variety of topics and echoing the tone and content of *Ain't I a Woman?* in its bold conclusion:

"We want a new society—a revolutionary socialist society. We want liberation of humanity, free food, free shelter, free clothing, free health care, free transportation, free education, free art for all. We want a society where the needs of the people come first" (quoted in Muñoz 19). Similar to *Ain't I a Woman?*, *Gay Flames* demands not inclusion in existing structures and institutions but a set of human relations that does not yet exist. Both manifestoes reject a pragmatic, assimilationist political agenda, creating the potential for new identities, ways of thinking, modes of belonging, and relationalities.

At the same time, the tone of *Ain't I a Woman?*'s manifesto appears conclusive, which, according to Muñoz, would be a form of anti-utopianism since it produces the world as knowable and known and often prescribes forms of action to reach a purported ideal. However, the polyvocal nature of periodicals and their seriality mean that even definitive statements are necessarily provisional. Subsequent issues elaborate, albeit indirectly, on the ideas in a previous issue, expanding statements that might otherwise seem unequivocal. And even if a demand itself may not change, the complexity of the paths carved to realize it become apparent. For example, different issues of *Ain't I a Woman?* address "the sexism which permeates our cultural media" (the sixth demand). In addition to the shortcomings of popular culture, readers learn about biases within Women's Liberation media related to geography (more attention is paid to large urban areas in the northeast), lesbianism (it is often overlooked), and class (there is a lack of socioeconomic class consciousness), which together demonstrate that we cannot end sexism only in mainstream and alternative media ("Big City, Little City"; Brown; "So Far Our Analysis Labels"). Feminist media also reproduce inequalities that need to be eradicated to achieve self-determination for all.

Reading the full run of *Ain't I a Woman?* (thirty-two issues in all) as an extended conversation suggests that not all of the demands for self-determination were equally important to the editorial collective. Although the range of topics addressed remains broad, the editors' priorities surface through different issues. The third issue covers health care, day care, and lesbianism, and includes three full pages of writing about the state of Women's Liberation and the path to revolution more generally (*Ain't I a Woman?* July 24, 1970). Day care, health care, and the state of the Women's Liberation Movement reappear in the fourth issue in addition to pieces about consumerism; race, class, and gender oppression in a local factory; and North and South Korea (*Ain't I a Woman?* August 21, 1970). As the newspaper continues, certain topics and certain views about those topics gain prominence. Six months after the first issue (December 1970), the editors began identifying as "a collective of 10 women functioning either as a front for a world wide conspiracy of Radical Lesbians or the house cornfield of the Women's Movement" (*Ain't I a Woman?* December 11, 1970, 10). And one third of the twelve pages in issue 12 (February 1971) is devoted to reflections on and analyses of lesbianism: there is a reprint of the widely circulating piece "The Woman Identified Woman" by the New York City–based Radicalesbians, and three pages of poetry and prose responding to it. The cell continued to publish one- to two-page-long pieces, usually personal narratives or analytical essays, about sexuality.[5] Even as the significance of lesbianism grew, the paper continued to emphasize child care, the state of Women's Liberation as revolutionary or reformist, socioeconomic class, and collectivity as a revolutionary practice. Nonetheless, this focus on women and sexuality produces the tenth demand, "an end to discrimination against our lesbian sisters," as more important than others.

Complicating feminism through temporal intertextuality, feminist periodicals disrupt the perspectives and prescriptions offered in definitive statements like manifestoes and position papers as well as in feminist slogans that circulated nationally such as "sisterhood is powerful" and "the personal is political." This kind of intertextuality, importantly, occurs because after an issue's publication, the editors, writers, and readers move on to the next one, which alters—reinforcing, disrupting, and/or revising—the ideas presented in the previous issue. As a result, the grammatically simple demand "self-determination for all people" fractures and reassembles as subsequent issues of the periodical present differing versions of self-determination and different modes of reaching it. In addition to showing that feminist ideals are not necessarily self-evident and that achieving them is a complex and dynamic process, periodicals also show that both are site-dependent. Not only are some concerns more salient than others, the particularities of these concerns vary based on locale.

Place Matters

The Equal Rights Amendment (ERA) permeated U.S. feminist activism in the 1970s. Supported by groups such as the National Organization for Women, the League of Women Voters, the Women's Equity Action League, and the American Federation of Labor and Congress of Industrial Organizations, as well as by hundreds of small groups throughout the country, this amendment received widespread attention. Its focus on eradicating discrimination based on sex fits squarely within one of the dominant narratives about feminism, namely that it is a movement singularly for and about women. Thus the assumption that feminism is focused solely on gender, allows for certain efforts—such as the Equal Rights Amendment or the fight to legalize abortion—to stand in for feminist politics more generally. Periodicals, while affirming the significance of gender and sexism, display the complexity of activism within Women's Liberation in the 1970s. As the previous sections have shown, the aesthetic, rhetorical, and textual qualities of periodicals present information and ideas as a pastiche, which can disrupt ideological and teleological certainty and coherence. This section brings in an additional factor, namely location, to analyze how place interacts with the ideas presented in periodicals. The fact that most feminist periodicals did not circulate far from where they were created and included contributions primarily from local women meant that local issues and concerns had a significant impact on the content.[6]

Mimeographed on 8 1/2 by 11 inch paper, the *Valley Women's Center Newsletter* was published from 1971 to 1977 in Northampton, Massachusetts, by the Valley Women's Center.[7] The ERA itself—a national issue, an icon of Women's Liberation—did not receive much coverage in the newsletter. There are a few announcements that give readers brief updates, and in one issue readers are encouraged to contact their senators to support its passage, but the fact that the ERA was a national campaign did not seem to make it more important or worthy of readers' attention.

For example, in the November 1971 issue, the newsletter tells readers, "WOMEN UNITED, a Washington-based group lobbying for women's rights, urges that women write or call their senators to urge passage early next year of Equal Rights Amendment" (Announcement: *Valley Women's Center Newsletter,* 3). Presented as part of a list with announcements about other local, national, and international news, all in the same font size and type, these various items appear to have equivalent importance. Some names and phrases are capitalized: "A small group of women in New Haven are starting a WOMEN'S RESEARCH PROJECT, beginning with the relation of women to corporation," and "A telegram sent by some women at VWC to WOMEN ELECTED IN SEPTEMBER 20 NORWEGIAN ELECTIONS (women captured 48 of 85 seats in Oslo's city council, 46 or 85 in Trondheim, 27 of 47 in Asker) has reached women in Norway." Capitalization draws the reader's attention to certain phrases within the list but does not mark particular announcements as more important. Based on this layout, information about the ERA is equivalent to information about a regional research project or an international political victory.

When national issues get taken up in communities, periodicals also show how the particularities of those communities shaped the way an issue was presented to and created a feminist public (Marshall 470). The Los Angeles periodical—published as the mimeographed *L.A. Women's Liberation Newsletter* from 1970 to 1972 and then as the newspaper *Sister* until 1979—featured reproductive rights in many of its issues. In the summer of 1970, the third issue of the newsletter names the "three major demands of women's liberation": "1) equal employment 2) abortion and 3) child care" ("August 26th Strike" 1). The women's center in Los Angeles specifically offered abortion referrals ("Definition of the Women's Center" 3), and the newsletter mentioned struggles for abortion rights locally and throughout the world.[8] It is no surprise to see abortion highlighted here. Yet, despite the early emphasis on abortion in the newsletter, it became only one part of the self-help health activism in Los Angeles. Feminist self-help health activism, though focused on reproductive health, was more broadly about demystifying the body, giving women the skills and confidence to take responsibility for their own health and to stand up to the conventional medical establishment.

The Los Angeles–based Feminist Women's Health Clinic (FWHC) played a significant role in making self-help health into a nationally known movement. The clinic primarily focused on gynecological aspects of women's health, but Carol Downer, one of the center's founders, expressed a broader ideological premise on which her view of self-help health was based: "Yes, we dare to want POWER. We want to take over women's medicine—nothing less" (quoted in Morgen 25; see also Murphy 48). When two of the women involved in the clinic, Downer and Colleen Wilson, were arrested for practicing medicine without a license in September 1972, *Sister* published extensive coverage of their trials. In January 1973, it published a two-page timeline along with a retelling of the events in the form of a comic that spanned four pages, an article by Downer about the future of the FWHC, and an article by a woman summarizing the trial ("Historical Feminist Trial...... Chronology"; Clement; Downer; Gutzoff). In all, almost half of the issue was devoted to the FWHC. And just six months later, the editors published the July issue with a self-help health theme that included a piece from a medical student at UCLA, a two-page essay by Downer explaining the concept of self-help health, an article about a Philadelphia clinic that offered abortion services, a piece about how to use a speculum to see one's cervix, a "Menopause Dialogue" based on a conversation among ten different women who met at the FWHC, and an article about Downer's trial.[9]

The FWHC also stimulated more abstract articles. For example, the May 1974 issue contains a letter that occupies almost half the page and a full-page article, both of which are analyzing and critiquing the structure and politics of the FWHC (Tafoya et al.; Macker). These pieces, while not directly addressing women's health, offer a more complex picture of what it meant for a woman to gain greater control over her own body and the practices necessary to achieve this objective. Reproductive health collectives and organizations also have their own political perspectives and modes of organizing, both of which affect the services offered. The attention to Downer and Wilson's plight moreover demonstrates that the politics of women's health is more complex than granting someone access to an abortion or to contraception. It is about access to information, demystifying one's body, being able to trust the medical establishment, making informed decisions about medical care, and, importantly, developing structures and organizations that support reproductive justice efforts. And, as I have discussed in this section, the complexity of the Women's Liberation Movement derives from a specific locality. Without the FWHC and Downer's often-controversial personality and praxis, the picture of feminist health activism in Los Angeles would likely have been painted quite differently.

Feminism in Practice

Because of mainstream media coverage, certain events became emblematic of feminism. The Miss America Pageant protests, the sit-in at the *Ladies Home Journal* office, the national and international conferences, and the Women's Strike for Equality were critical to raising feminism's visibility across the nation and catalyzing participation.[10] However, as T. V. Reed notes in his analysis of civil rights movement activism, the "large-scale, dramatic events that captured media attention did not arise spontaneously [but] were made possible by countless hours, months, and years of work by local activists from all classes and segments of the black community" (4). Reed draws our attention to the often unnoticed but necessary tasks required to support and sustain social movements. In other words, moving toward utopian visions requires concrete resources in the present, hours of labor, mundane repetitive tasks, and constant struggles to secure resources.

Feminist periodicals—because of their ephemerality, their seriality, and their attention to these material facets of the movement's present—chronicled the concrete and practical efforts that constituted feminism. They show us on a micro scale the daily labors, the networks and relationships, and the struggles and conflicts within which women worked out their feminist praxis. Attention to feminism at this scale disrupts not only the hegemonic narratives of grand protests but also the fixity of meaning associated with concepts such as the personal is political, issues like reproductive rights, and assumptions about who is a feminist.

Periodicals themselves were one of those endeavors that required a consistent and constant input of time, labor, skills, and money. *Female Liberation* demonstrates this need through their appeals to readers for support. In the summer of 1971, the editors, for example, described *Female Liberation* as in "very grave financial shape" (in part because of the costs of printing the newsletter, which was "over $75 per week") and ask readers to give whatever money they can (Announcement, *Female Liberation Newsletter,* 4). This request was followed in the next issue by an editorial titled "HELP WANTED!!!!!" in which readers are reminded that "Every Friday we need people to collate, fold, staple, stamp, and address the Newsletter" (3). In an early September issue, there are two brief announcements requesting readers' assistance for the newsletter. And just one week later, the editors state: "Volunteers needed to help put out the Newsletter. 10am–5pm" (Calendar item 4). Four consecutive newsletter issues remind readers five different times about the labors that go into making sure that the next issue will arrive in their mailboxes. Some of these tasks may involve unskilled, tedious labor, but they are nonetheless necessary, as yet another editorial in *Female Liberation Newsletters* tells readers: "If you're looking for ways to help out the women's movement, and keep Female Liberation going with its vital work, we have two suggestions: help us with the Newsletter and with our Orientation work. We still need people to put together the Newsletter (editing, gathering material and TYPING) also with collating, folding and stapling. Newsletter meetings are Tuesday night at 5:30 p.m., and the production work for the Newsletter is done all day Thursday, mostly in the morning" ("Taking Care of Business" 6). This pattern continued almost ceaselessly, and, in fact, the initial printing schedule became unsustainable. In February 1972, the editors announce that instead of publishing weekly, the newsletter would now come out every other week (Announcement, *Female Liberation Newsletter* 6). These calls to reader show that sustaining a periodical was not a trivial or insignificant endeavor. Serial publications voraciously demanded women's time and energy, and the fact that so many appeared during the early 1970s indicated the political and social significance to their makers and readers. Thus, this labor that was critical *to* feminism and *as* feminism, like the quotidian work Reed describes in the civil rights movement. In this sense, periodicals are valuable both as a chronicle of the myriad daily activities constituting feminism and also as primary sources that embody some of these daily activities.

Ain't I a Woman? invites readers to participate in the feminist revolution as well, although in a way that does not reflect conventional modes of feminist activism. On a page and a half titled "Sisters Smash Sexism, Technocracy & Planned Obsolescence," a collage of hand-drawn diagrams, handwritten notes, and typed text instructs the reader to troubleshoot and then fix problems with her stereo ("Sisters Smash Sexism"). Although fixing a stereo is not a revolutionary act in and of itself, this piece gives such a repair a political context: making these repairs, particularly if you are a woman, defies the sexist and capitalist status quo. The editors of *Ain't I a Woman?* presume a reader's capability and, specifically, presume a female reader's capability. At a time when a woman could not apply for a credit card without her husband's signature and before affirmative action created a space—albeit small—for women to enter manual labor fields (Antolovich, Eisenberg), for women to attempt such a repair is significant and noteworthy.

The multitextuality of periodicals highlights the process through which "Sisters Smash Sexism, Technology, & Planned Obsolescence" invites readers to participate. Looking at this piece as a kind of collage, we see it comprises a mixture of typed text, handwritten text, and hand-drawn images. The typed sections are more formally instructive: "Check wires in speaker and into amplifier; you may have to have them soldered if they're broken off, but tape could do. Tighten parts with pliers" (10). With clear and basic language, it could be easily understood by a layperson, and the neutral, informed, and knowledgeable tone gives the writer authority. Various hand-drawn diagrams with different parts labeled accompany the instructions. One presents the stereo (intact) from a bird's-eye view (10) and another depicts four different washer rings in the order in which they need to be reassembled (11). Although adding to the credibility of the instructions, the hand-drawn images are less precise than the typed language. Corners are not 90-degree angles. Where someone's hand wavered, the lines are not straight. And some of the drawings almost obscure part of the typed text. Giving us a glimpse of this piece's creator(s), a handwritten section—subtitled "Good Words"—personalizes the writer with its punctuation and language: "Portable stereos are made to wear out + fuck up + be hard to take apart. I keep remembering how electronics is a very male thing—all those screws + sockets. . . ." The anonymous writer then assures readers, "The repairs listed here are mostly mechanical + you don't have to understand much electronic shit (I don't). You learn it by doing it. . . ." (10; ellipses in the original). Handwriting humanizes the writer as well as the process of fixing a stereo and counters not only the way that electronics is a "male thing" with "all those screws + sockets," or rigid mechanical items. Ellipses carry the weight of these unsaid assumptions about the boundaries of femininity and the expectations of masculinity.[11] This set of dots also suggests that readers will be able to empathize with the parenthetical "I don't [understand much]" and fill in the blank with their own insecurities produced by a capitalist patriarchy. Recognizing that machine innards may be alien to readers, the writer acknowledges the affective obstacles to attempting home repairs and presents her own fallibility in a way that encourages readers to perceive themselves as able. But more than telling readers "you *can* do this," the piece politicizes a small, likely "personal" act, making part of a larger feminist revolution.

As these how-to pieces and the announcements about Women's Liberation schools and women's center classes demonstrate, the idea of a feminist revolution is more complex than inclusion simply based on identity. Periodicals illuminate feminism as a form of belonging based on praxis and not just on being a woman, so the *potential* for inclusion within feminism rather than a priori inclusiveness becomes the default position. Identity, however, is not irrelevant. The titular phrase "sisters smash sexism," in its alliteration, emphasizes that women are being urged to participate in this form of revolutionary activism. Nonetheless, rhetorically and theoretically, periodicals produced the "we" of Women's Liberation as something that could include all women—even all people—but that is also not based on identitarian certitude. It is, instead, grounded in "a human that is not yet here," as Muñoz puts forth (26) because practice and not ontology becomes a mechanism for inclusion.

Conclusion

An editorial from the Baltimore-based *Women: A Journal of Liberation* reads, "An important part of the women's liberation movement has been the many publications that have emerged from the struggle. They have been key in providing an exchanges of ideas and bringing new women into the movement" (Editorial 10). Carol Seajay, a prominent figure in the Women in Print Movement, noted in an interview that "the socialists and the leftists knew that if you want to change something, you start a newspaper and distribute it. You give the ideas to people and they'll take the ideas and run with them" (Onosaka 15). Not only did periodicals maintain communication and spread information (Baxandall 2001), many women, when describing their introduction to the Women's Liberation Movement, state that reading a feminist book or periodical first propelled them to action. Taking these factors into account underlines the importance of looking at feminist periodicals as more than containers of content. The richness and significance of feminist newsletters and newspapers result from their textuality and the contexts of their production. The eclectic mix of different kinds of texts in a periodical opens up possibilities for different ways of reading the content and analyzing the ideals expressed by feminists. In addition to spatial intertextuality, seriality meant that new information was routinely being offered. Articles covered current events and breaking news, and events calendars gave readers repeated snapshots of what was going on in their local community. Reading periodicals diachronically shows how, across time, different content reconsiders, revises, and adds to ideas presented of previous issues.

Unlike the anthologies *Sisterhood Is Powerful* (Morgan) and *Sisterhood Is Global* (Morgan) or widely circulating periodicals like *off our backs* and *Ms.* magazine, most feminist periodicals did not aim to encompass feminism on a national or international scale. Through reprints and excerpts from other publications, contributions from women who were geographically distant, and coverage of events in a wide range of places, it is clear that editorial collectives were concerned with people and issues that reached far beyond their own city's limits. Nevertheless, what the collectives chose to include reflects the social, cultural, historical, economic, and emotional topographies of their experiences and communities. We can thus see how national-scale values such as reproductive rights were negotiated in ways that reflect the particularities of each community.

Also in contrast to publications like mainstream periodicals and books, feminist periodicals opened up a realm of cultural, mechanical, political, and literary practice to women who might never otherwise consider themselves able or skilled. Readers became writers, artists, editors, and publishers, and the variety of textual genres meant that women could be cultural producers through different forms of writing (see also Jordan). Since feminism as a social movement aimed for transformation at a cultural level, this kind of media production was an important form of political engagement (Bunch), and having access to the means of production allowed women to control the way they were represented. Regarding content, periodicals were also "how-to" guides. They gave women instructions for specific tasks such as fixing appliances, changing the oil in one's car, doing a self breast exam, and applying for welfare benefits. They also guided women in how to be feminists more generally: content both described and prescribed what qualified as feminism.

The ways periodicals recorded feminism during the 1970s portray the Women's Liberation Movement as an assemblage of local groups, actions, and publications that is difficult—if not impossible—to circumscribe with one grand narrative. Therefore, feminist periodicals help us unpack and better understand the ways that utopian ideals of feminism in the 1970s were informed and constrained by the very local material, political, economic, and textual conditions within which feminists were working. Through intertextual and intergenre conversations that extended spatially and temporally, periodicals expressed revolutionary hopes for a wildly different, liberated future, but ones that were grounded in particular places and among specific communities. They reveal feminism as an identity, culture, and politics that complicates the reductive dominant narratives told about Women's Liberation of the 1970s.

Notes

1. In order to reflect the content of newsletters and newspapers as it appeared in the original, I do not change the capitalization, punctuation, spelling, wording, and emphases in quotations or use *sic* to indicate errata.

2. On the significance of the media in feminism see Hesford.

3. This issue is labeled a preview issue and was not given a volume or issue number. The next issue, published in February 1973, is officially labeled volume 1, issue 1.

4. On the manifesto as performative, see also Puchner.

5. See, for example, Shelley; Hart[?]; "Punching Out a Woman"; Editorial, *Ain't I a Woman?*; and "Female Culture/Lesbian Nation."

6. There is an important and growing body of literature exploring U.S. feminism in particular communities. See, for example, Beins and Enszer, Pomerleau, Gilmore, Valk, Gilmore and Kaminski, Ezekiel, and Kesselman.

7. Late 1973 to 1975 represents a time of flux for this community, and in early 1974, feminist activists formed the Valley Women's Union. The newsletter became a project of the union in early 1974, and although it did not change in format, it became the *Valley Women's Union Newsletter* in October 1975.

8. On activism in Holland, see "Dolle Mina," *L.A. Women's Liberation Newsletter*, March 1971, 2; on activism in France, see "Letter from a Sister in France," *L.A. Women's Liberation Newsletter*, May 1971, 3; folder 1 Register of the Los Angeles Women's Liberation Movement Collection, 1970–1976, SCL.

9. This issue was published July 1973.

10. The strike for equality was an action held on August 26, 1970, to recognize the fiftieth anniversary of the passage of the Nineteenth Amendment, and which culminated in protests throughout the United States, including one in New York City that included around twenty thousand women.

11. For an analysis of the ellipsis, see Brody (chap. 2).

Works Cited

Announcement. *Female Liberation Newsletter*. 23 Aug. 1971: 4. Sophia Smith Collection, Smith College, Northampton, Massachusetts (hereafter SSC).

Announcement. *Female Liberation Newsletter*. 28 Feb. 1972: 6. SSC.

Announcement. *Valley Women's Center Newsletter*. 10 Nov. 1971: 3. Valley Women's Center Records, 1971–1977, box 4, folder 1. SSC.

Antolovich, Gabrielle. "Electrical Union Looks to Recruit More Women." *Business Journal* 17 Feb. 1997: 27.

"August 26th Strike." *L.A. Women's Liberation Newsletter* Summer 1970: 1. Register of the Los Angeles Women's Liberation Movement Collection, 1970–1976, folder 1. SCL.

Baxandall, Rosalyn. "Re-Visioning the Women's Liberation Movement's Narrative: Early Second Wave American Feminists." *Feminist Studies* 27.1 (2001): 225–45.

Beins, Agatha, and Julie R. Enszer. "'We Couldn't Get Them Printed' So We Learned to Print: *Ain't I a Woman?* and the Iowa City Women's Press." *Frontiers: A Journal of Women's Studies* 34.2 (2013): 186–221.

"Big City, Little City." *Ain't I a Woman?* 24 July 1970: 10. Iowa Women's Archives, University of Iowa, Iowa City (hereafter IWA).

Brody, Jennifer DeVere. *Punctuation: Art, Politics, and Play*. Durham, NC: Duke UP, 2008.

Brown, Rita Mae. "Hanoi to Hoboken, a Round Trip Ticket." *Ain't I a Woman?* 2 April 1971: 10–11. (Reprinted from *off our backs*.)

Bunch, Charlotte. "Reading and Writing for a Feminist Future." *Passionate Politics: Feminist Theory in Action*. New York: St. Martin's, 1987. 217–21.

Calendar item. *Female Liberation Newsletter*. 11 Sept. 1971: 4. SSC.

Clement, Carol. "Cervix Comix." *Sister*. Jan. 1973. Southern California Library, Los Angeles, California (hereafter SCL).

"Definition of the Women's Center." *L.A. Women's Liberation Newsletter* Summer 1970: 3. Register of the Los Angeles Women's Liberation Movement Collection, 1970–77, folder 1. SCL.

DeSilvey, Caitlin. "Making Sense of Transience: An Anticipatory History." *Cultural Geographies* 19.1 (2012): 31–54.

"Dolle Mina." *L.A. Women's Liberation Newsletter*, March 1971, 2. Register of the Los Angeles Women's Liberation Movement Collection, 1970–1976, folder 1. SCL.

Downer, Carol. "F.W.H.C.—Future Plans." *Sister*. Jan. 1973, SCL.

Editorial. *Ain't I a Woman?* 2 April 1971, 10. IWA.

Editorial. *Women: A Journal of Liberation*. 26 Feb. 1971: 10; Women's Liberation Collection, box 7, folder 12. SSC.

Eisenberg, Susan. "Women Hard Hats Speak Out." *The Nation* 18 Sept. 1989: 272–75.

Ezekiel, Judith. *Feminism in the Heartland*. Columbus: Ohio State UP, 2002.

Felski, Rita. *Beyond Feminist Aesthetics: Feminist Literature and Social Change*. Cambridge, MA: Harvard UP, 1989.

"Female Culture/Lesbian Nation." *Ain't I a Woman?* 4 June 1971, 8–9. IWA.

Flannery, Kathryn Thoms. *Feminist Literacies, 1968–75*. Urbana: U of Illinois P, 2005.

Gilmore, Stephanie. *Groundswell: Grassroots Feminist Activism in Postwar America*. New York: Routledge, 2012.

Gilmore, Stephanie, and Elizabeth Kaminski. "A Part and Apart: Lesbian and Straight Feminist Activists Negotiate Identity in a Second-Wave Organization." *Journal of the History of Sexuality* 16.1 (2007): 95–113.

Gutzoff, Gretchen. "Yummy, Yummy Yogurt for Treating Yeasty Beasties." *Sister*. January 1973. SCL.

Hall, Kira. "Performativity." *Journal of Linguistic Anthropology* 9.1 (2000): 184–87.

Hart[?], Lois. "Lesbian Demands: A Woman Speaks." *Ain't I a Woman?* 9 Oct. 1970: 4–5. IWA.

"HELP WANTED!!!!!" *Female Liberation Newsletter.* 30 Aug. 1971: 3. SSC.

Hesford, Victoria. *Feeling Women's Liberation*. Durham, NC: Duke UP, 2013.

"Historical Feminist Trial...... Chronology...... From the Beginning." *Sister* Jan. 1973: 6, 8.

Johnston, Hank. "Protest Cultures: Performance, Artifacts, and Ideations." *Culture, Social Movements, and Protest.* London: Ashgate, 2009. 1–29.

Jordan, Tessa. "*Branching Out*: Second-Wave Feminist Periodicals and the Archive of Canadian Women's Writing." *ESC* 36.2 (2010): 63–90.

Jurnak, Sheila Hope. "Movement Two." *Distaff.* Jan. 1973: 5. Newcomb Archives, and Vorhoff Library Special Collections, Newcomb College Institute, Tulane University, (hereafter NAVL).

Kesselman, Amy. 2001. "Women's Liberation and the Left in New Haven, Connecticut, 1968–1972." *Radical History Review* 51 (Fall):15–33

Latimer, Clay. "The Legal Identity of the Married Woman." *Distaff.* Jan. 1973: 5. NAVL.

"Letter from a Sister in France." *L.A. Women's Liberation Newsletter*, May 1971: 3. Register of the Los Angeles Women's Liberation Movement Collection, 1970–1976, folder 1. SCL.

Macker, Hope. "Healing or Hassles?" Letter to *Sister*. May 1974: 9. SCL.

Marshall, Barbara L. "Communication as Politics: Feminist Print Media in English Canada." *Women's Studies International Forum* 18.4 (1995): 463–474.

Morgan, Robin, ed. *Sisterhood Is Powerful*. New York: Random House, 1970.

———, ed. *Sisterhood Is Global: The International Women's Movement Anthology*. Garden City, NY: Anchor/Doubleday, 1984.

Morgen, Sandra. *Into Our Own Hands: The Women's Health Movement in the United States, 1969–1990*. New Brunswick, NJ: Rutgers UP, 2002.

Muñoz, Jose. *Cruising Utopia: The Then and There of Queer Futurity*. New York: New York UP, 2006.

Murphy, Michelle. *Seizing the Means of Reproduction: Entanglements of Feminism, Health, and Technoscience*. Durham, NC: Duke UP, 2012.

Myerson, Marilyn, Sara L. Crawley, Erica Hesch Anstey, Justine Kessler, and Cara Okopny. "Who's Zoomin' Who? A Feminist, Queer Content Analysis of 'Interdisciplinary' Human Sexuality Textbooks." *Hypatia* 22.1 (2007): 92–113.

Onosaka, Junko. *Feminist Revolution in Literacy: Women's Bookstores in the United States*. New York: Routledge, 2006.

Pomerleau, Clark A. *Califia Women: Feminist Education against Sexism, Classism, and Racism*. Austin: U of Texas P, 2013.

Puchner, Martin. "Manifestos—Poetry of the Revolution." *Poetry of the Revolution: Marx, Manifestos, and the Avant-Gardes*. Princeton, NJ: Princeton UP, 2006. 1–7.

"Punching out a Woman." *Ain't I a Woman?* 20 Nov. 1970, 5. IWA.

Radicalesbians. "The Woman Identified Woman." *Ain't I a Woman?* 19 Feb. 1971: 2. IWA.

Reed, T. V. *The Art of Protest: Culture and Activism from the Civil Rights Movement to the Streets of Seattle*. Minneapolis: U of Minnesota P, 2005.

Shelley, Martha. "Stepinfetchit Woman," *Ain't I a Woman?* 11 Sept. 1970: 10. IWA.

"Sisters Smash Sexism, Technocracy & Planned Obsolescence." *Ain't I a Woman?* 12 March 1971: 10–11. IWA.

"So Far Our Analysis Labels Common to All Women What Is Common Only to Middle-Class Women." *Ain't I a Woman?* 20 July 1971: 8–11. IWA.

Tafoya, Zoe, Terry, Lorey, Sue, Janie, and Karen. "The Feminist Women's Health Center—'The Tyranny of Structurelessness.'" *Sister* May 1974: 8. SCL.

"Taking Care of Business." *Female Liberation Newsletter.* 1 Nov. 1971: 6. SSC.

"to meet the needs of women." *Ain't I a Woman?* 10 July 1970: 1. IWA.

Valk, Anne. *Radical Sisters: Second Wave Feminism and Black Liberation in Washington, D.C.* Champaign: U of Illinois P, 2008.

Wiegman, Robyn. "What Ails Feminist Criticism? A Second Opinion." *differences: A Journal of Feminist Cultural Studies* 11.3 (1999): 107–136.

"Women in Sports: June Issue of *Sister*." *Sister.* April 1974: 14. SCL.

Chapter 3

"What Made Us Think They'd Pay Us for Making a Revolution?"

Women in Distribution (WinD), 1974–1979

Julie R. Enszer

In late 1974, three women, each with experience marketing and distributing lesbian-feminist materials, wondered: Was there a need for a distributor dedicated to feminist and lesbian work? Was an independent feminist distribution company economically viable? Could a small distribution business enact feminist principles in the capitalist marketplace? Helaine Harris, Cynthia Gair, and Lee Schwing asked these questions and seized the opportunity to create a feminist distribution company. Together, they started Women in Distribution (WinD).

Early feminist publishers, such as Diana Press, the Women's Press Collective, and Daughters Publishing Company, Inc., operated as both publishers and distributors. In addition to editing books, typesetting pages, burning plates, running print machines, and binding books, publishers, devoted to putting feminist and lesbian-feminist books into women's hands, distributed the books they created. During the early 1970s, Women's Press Collective, Diana Press, and Daughters marketed their books through advertisements in lesbian and feminist periodicals, flyers, makeshift catalogs, and community readings. Feminist publishers and writers sold their books primarily hand-to-hand and through the mail. While these sales strategies are rewarding, they are also labor-intensive. In direct sales, orders come through the mail or on the telephone; publishers (or individual authors) then pack and ship books directly to the purchaser/

reader. Direct-to-consumer distribution benefits small publishers, connecting them intimately with readers. Publishers know immediately the demand for their books and often receive instant feedback from readers.

Distribution consumes resources; it requires time and money, which for small publishers are always in short supply. For publishers, the labor of distribution rivals the labor of editing, designing, proofreading, and producing a book or journal. Distributing a bound book—getting it into the hands of readers eager to pay for it and read it—is a specialized function. In Robert Darnton's model, distributors are "shippers" and include "agent, smuggler, entrepôt keeper, wagoner, etc" (68). In the contemporary communications circuit, distributors are a link between publishers and retail booksellers. Publishers need good distributors—people and businesses that thrive on marketing and promotion and that have solid relationships with bookstores and other retail outlets.

Gair, Harris, and Schwing wanted to reduce the burden on feminist publishers; they wanted feminist books and journals to reach even more women, inspiring them to join the feminist revolution. During the Women's Liberation Movement (WLM), an eclectic mix of small feminist businesses developed to support the creation and dispersal of creative printed work by women. Eventually, feminist bookstores became the economic engine for selling feminist books, but prior to the explosion of feminist bookstores and the maturation of a feminist bookstore marketplace, feminists developed their own distribution strategies.

The story of WinD mirrors the growth in feminist publishing during the late 1970s and reinforces the power and influence of poetry, in particular, and of feminist writing more generally during the WLM.[1] WinD illuminates how feminist businesses negotiated feminist principles within a capitalist economy and demonstrates how feminist businesses experienced the increasingly neoliberal economy in the United States, naming it a threat to feminism and lesbian-feminism. Ultimately, feminist innovation and invention, embodied in the work of Gair, Harris, and Schwing, extended the economic engine of feminism. Between 1974 and 1979, WinD shaped a revolutionary feminist landscape in Washington, DC, and throughout the United States. In the three and a half decades since it closed, the legacy and afterlife of WinD continues.

The Story of WinD

Origins

In 1970, Helaine Harris left her home in Houston, Texas, at the age of sixteen. Harris spent time in the Oakland-Berkeley area (California) and New Mexico working in the antiwar movement. She eventually landed in Washington, DC. In Washington, she lived in an "antiwar commune" and worked on "the Revolutionary People's Constitutional Convention, which was held in Philadelphia" (Harris interview). Then Rita Mae Brown came to town, and The Furies collective began.

Twelve women between the ages of eighteen and twenty-eight started The Furies. Part communal living cooperative, part consciousness-raising group, part revolutionary cell for radical feminism, The Furies were a vital force in feminism and extraordinarily influential, in part because of the newspaper that they published for eighteen months in 1972 and 1973. *The Furies: lesbian/feminist monthly* hit the streets of Washington, DC, in January 1972. In the front-page manifesto, written by Ginny Berson, The Furies declared, "We are angry because we are oppressed by male supremacy. We have been fucked over all our lives by a system which is based on the domination of men over women, which defines male as good and female as only as good as the man you are with. It is a system in which heterosexuality is rigidly enforced and Lesbianism rigidly suppressed. It is a system which has further divided us by class, race, and nationality" (1). Speaking on behalf of The Furies, Berson expressed a number of iconoclastic views in this opening salvo: lesbianism as a necessary choice for feminists, the failure of the "straight women's movement" and the "male left" to address lesbian issues, and the necessity for lesbians to develop a "common politic" of "Lesbianism as a political issue" (ibid.). The Furies used their own living and working community as a site for experimentation to analyze and understand oppression as well as to develop a vision for broader social change. Anne Valk accurately describes the Furies playing "a pivotal role in bringing attention to lesbians' presence in the women's movement and legitimizing lesbian feminism as a political issue" (152). In addition, The Furies articulated lesbian separatism as a vibrant political theory and feminist practice, an ideology that lesbians would embrace over the next decades for further experimentations.

The Furies were short-lived. By June 1973, the newspaper ceased publishing and the collective disbanded. After The Furies, women from the collective organized a number of influential feminist projects. Collective members "devised new means to spread feminist theory and culture throughout the city (Washington, DC) and into mainstream America. In doing so, they built an infrastructure that supported the feminist movement and substantively broadened both the movement's ideological foundation and the diversity of its adherents" (Valk 153). One of the projects that immediately emerged from The Furies was Olivia Records. Jennifer Woodhul, Lee Schwing, Ginny Berson, and Helaine Harris started Olivia Records. At Olivia, Harris and Schwing worked on distribution.

Shortly after Olivia Records' genesis in Washington, DC, Woodhul and Berson realized that, to be successful, the business needed to be in Los Angeles, the center of the music industry. Woodhul and Berson moved west where Olivia Records grew to be a vibrant and influential women's music company, selling hundreds of thousands of albums and producing concerts at an array of venues including Carnegie Hall.[2] Today, Olivia remains a thriving entertainment and travel company, though the company no longer produces music. Harris and Schwing stayed in Washington. With Cynthia Gair, a feminist activist who came to Washington from Michigan, Harris and Schwing started WinD.

Genesis

WinD began modestly with a capital investment of $1,200; part of the money was a loan from Cynthia Gair's parents (Dear Sisters letter).[3] Harris remembers "the women's movement in that time was kind of a personal movement." Harris, Schwing, and Gair knew the producers of feminist books, magazines, and other print materials that they wanted to distribute. They called them on the telephone or took trips to visit them, securing distribution agreements (Dear Friends letter, Mazer Archives; personal interview with Helaine Harris; Skype interview with Cynthia Gair).

On November 11, 1974, Harris, Gair, and Schwing formally launched WinD as a national distribution company with a letter to feminist colleagues and activists. They cited the "upsurge of woman produced and woman oriented products such as books, calendars, periodicals, records, and posters" as the reason for the company.[4] Recognizing the desires of producers of feminist materials to "get into the hands and influence a great many women, women already in the movement and those not yet a part of it," WinD wanted to aid producers of woman-oriented products with effective distribution (Dear Friends letter from Harris, Gair, and Schwing). By distributing feminist materials, Harris, Gair, and Schwing hoped to catalyze the movement, bringing in new activists and spreading feminist consciousness. Shortly after the letter that launched WinD, Lee Schwing left the trio of WinD founders to pursue other feminist passions relating to spirituality. Together, Harris and Gair continued to build WinD.

In April 1975, WinD mailed its first catalog, a small blue flyer, measuring 8.5 × 7 inches. This catalog featured eleven books and included a statement about WinD. A copy of the catalog in the Atlanta Lesbian-Feminist Alliance archives demonstrates the labor and personal engagements of the business: it is hand-addressed by Gair in red ink to an individual woman at Atlanta Lesbian-Feminist Alliance, perhaps someone she knew personally, and postmarked April 21, 1975 (WinD flyer). In this first catalog, WinD proclaims, "We want to be the liaison between you, the retail outlet, and the small press and independent publisher." The catalog further notes, "The items in this preview catalog represent a wide range of personal/cultural/political viewpoints of women today" (ibid.).

Even though the initial offerings of WinD were small—small enough to fit on a single-sheet flyer—the catalog reflected the range of creative printed work that feminists produced in 1975: periodicals, books, and music. In spite of its modest presentation, the array of materials foreshadowed what was to come for WinD: a broad catalog of interest to women throughout the United States. This first catalog promised the second in September 1975 followed by a spring catalog in March 1976.

In the fall of 1975, Harris and Gair published their second catalog. The September 1975 catalog featured twenty-nine books, records, posters, and postcards. A year later, in September 1976, WinD had 186 titles and over 200 accounts from "women's centers, women's bookstores, universities, libraries, and establishment bookstores across the country" (Dear Sisters letter). WinD not only aggregated the producers of feminist print culture, they built a more extensive market to distribute the materials. To understand the scope of the feminist marketplace, in 1977 in *Feminist Bookstore News* (*FBN*), Carol Seajay listed ninety-four feminist bookstores, the majority in the United States, but a handful in other countries ("Bookstores"). Gair and Harris built a market for creative, feminist printed work that more than doubled the number of feminist bookstores in the United States.

Although feminist collectives and cooperatives proliferated during the WLM, these were only one model of economic engagement. WinD, like Diana Press in Baltimore, Maryland, and Daughters Publishing Company in Plainfield, Vermont, was a business. Harris and Gair wholly owned the business and knew that it would succeed or fail by the dint of their labor. Also like their colleagues at Diana and Daughters, WinD had a revolutionary intention: to facilitate the feminist transformation of the world.

By April 15, 1975, even the *Wall Street Journal* (*WSJ*) recognized that feminists engaged a variety of broad-based strategies to remake the economic lives of women. In a front page article titled, "For Some Feminists Owning a Business Is Real Liberation," Bill Hieronymus reported on Diana Press, "a Baltimore-based publishing and printing concern owned and operated by women." To the *WSJ*, Diana Press cofounder Coletta Reid boasted, "Men don't touch any job that we do" (Hieronymus 1). Hieronymus continued, "Diana Press not only shows male job applicants the door, it refuses to accept male customers. (The owners say they have more business than they can handle from women.)" While feminist separatism may have been provocative to readers of the *WSJ* given Hieronymus's choice to use it as the lead, for feminist businesses, separatism was quite ordinary and, in fact, an important strategy for remaking the economic landscape for women. Hieronymus explained that "a host of new feminist businesses have come into being since the women's liberation movement began to gather steam in the late 1960s." Reid told the *WSJ* that the aim of Diana Press, in addition to making a profit "is to promote the feminist cause and bring more women into business at all levels." This ethos suffused Diana Press, other feminist publishers, and other feminist businesses like WinD. In 1975, feminist businesses were intent on transforming American capitalism; they used separatism as an important strategy to achieve economic and political objectives.

Originally, Harris and Gair operated WinD from the basement in their group house in Washington, DC. When they decided to rent space for the business, they first moved to Alexandria, Virginia, just south of Washington. Unfortunately, that space did not work; previously, the building had been a dry cleaner, and "when they [the dry cleaner] left, they took all of their big machines which had been mounted into the floor; the first time it rained, the whole place flooded" (Harris interview). Water is an anathema to paper-based businesses. WinD then moved to a five thousand square foot warehouse in northeast Washington, DC, off Bladensburg Road. Harris remembers that it was a tiny, cold space without heat. Gair remembers it as a "great space" with high ceilings, light, and dry (Gair Skype interview). From this location, Harris said, "We did everything. All hand-written, there were no computers. Everyone participated in taking orders, selling, and packing orders" (ibid.).

Starting and operating WinD was an employment strategy for both Harris and Gair. In the early 1970s, job opportunities for young women, particularly young women without college educations, were limited. Harris recalled, "I wanted to do something else than be a waitress, frankly." While they were running WinD, Harris completed her GED, but she did not have a college degree; Gair completed three years of college at the University of Michigan, but did not graduate (Harris interview, Gair interview). By creating their own jobs through entrepreneurship, Gair and Harris secured more meaningful and significant work than what was available to young women in the marketplace. They also ensured their engagement in the feminist movement by making a business rooted in feminism.

From the beginning, WinD supported Harris and Gair as two full-time employees. Gair remembers that they each received a salary of $8,000.[5] As the business grew, they added two part-time employees, a bookkeeper, and a woman who "helped us pack." By building WinD as a business, Harris and

Gair joined a group of feminist entrepreneurs who supported themselves with work that furthered their feminist principles and visions. Individually and collectively, these feminist entrepreneurs nurtured a vibrant Women's Liberation Movement.

Growth and Sustenance

Gair and Harris ran WinD as a classic small business: each of the principals wore many hats to fulfill the variety of tasks and functions that the business required—and often each of them learned new skills as they did the work. Everything that WinD did was done by women: picking and packing books, shipping books, acquiring books for distribution, acquiring clients to purchase the books and materials that they stocked, creating catalogs, handling correspondence, and bookkeeping. Harris and Gair split some responsibilities. Gair was responsible for WinD's bookkeeping and accounting. She became "the queen of cash flow" and "that was how WinD survived." Producing the catalogs, which became gorgeous, elaborate productions, was a shared responsibility, though each woman specialized in different components of catalog production. Gair designed and laid out the catalogs. Harris did the typesetting; she had learned typesetting while working on the special lesbian edition of *Motive Magazine*.[6] Harris recalls, "typesetting was really tedious, but it was actually a job, a skill that I used for many years to help support myself" (Harris interview). Graphics for the WinD catalogs came from the Works Progress Administration project files at the Library of Congress. Harris remembers, "You could actually go into the library at that time and go through the files" (ibid.). These freely available images provided visual elements for all of the WinD catalogs.

The summer of 1976 was telltale for the feminist print movement. June Arnold, a firebrand activist and owner of Daughters, hatched the idea for a summer gathering of women involved in printing and publishing. Arnold, Charlotte Bunch of *Quest Magazine*, Coletta Reid of Diana Press, and Nancy Stockwell of *Plexus* planned the 1976 Women in Print (WIP) Conference. The conference ran a full week from August 29 through September 5 at a Campfire Girls' campground in Omaha, Nebraska. The organizers selected Omaha because it is in the middle of the country, equidistant for women on both coasts (and convenient for no one). One hundred thirty-two women attended the conference representing eighty "newspapers, magazines, publishing houses, printing companies, bookstores, and distribution services" (Kelly 2). The eight days of the gathering were intense and enormously generative for different lesbian-feminist projects around the country. The WIP Conference contributed to the growth of WinD. Harris and Gair used the gathering to organize a new kind of support for WinD.

Writing to the attendees of WIP in advance of the gathering, Gair and Harris outlined what they wanted to discuss at the WIP conference. Acknowledging that the profit margins for WinD were small, Gair and Harris revealed that they needed strategies to make their business more economically viable. For Gair and Harris, finding business solutions for WinD was not simply an internal problem; they presented the situation to the WIP community as a challenge. At the WIP Conference, Gair and Harris, together with the community of feminists gathering for the conference, wanted to talk about how their business could work economically and support the work of others in the movement (Dear Sisters letter). The fate of WinD was not only in the hands of Gair and Harris, it was also shared within a broader feminist community.

In their advance letter, Gair and Harris offered a strategy to sustain WinD and framed the adoption of this strategy as political action. One challenge facing WinD was cutting "down the effect of male competition" (ibid.). Although feminists were invested in creating an alternate world that was feminist and female-centered, the daily realities of life at WinD meant that they operated "in direct competition with male distributors (who have access not only to establishment books, but also to many of the very same books that we distribute)" (ibid.). To eliminate this competition, Harris and Gair wanted feminist publishers to cease working with male-owned distributors and instead provide exclusive distribution rights to their books to WinD. They wrote, "If we are truly trying to set up a network through which feminists in print can support each other, and since feminist distribution companies are set up to distribute books by women to women then there is no need to distribute through male distribution organizations" (ibid.). In short, Gair and Harris wanted publishers to sign exclusive distribution agreements with WinD, guaranteeing that WinD was the only sales channel to bookstores and retail outlets for publishers they represented.

To bolster their argument, Gair and Harris argued, "There are now feminist distribution companies which deal effectively with many of the problems of distribution and are working out the other problems" (ibid.). The nature of the "other problems" is unclear, but there are always issues between publishers and distributors. Feminism and shared political commitments may mitigate some of these issues, but they do not eliminate them. Feminist publishers complained about WinD's distribution policies, the quality of shipping, and catalog representation, among other issues. WinD, on the other hand, had to deal with issues arising from missed publication dates, lack of stock, and publishers with unrealistic sales expectations. All of these issues typify the usual tensions between publishers and distributors. In addition, the sheer physical variety of materials published by feminist publishers created distribution challenges, particularly with storage and shipping. Although many of the materials published by feminist presses complied with book standards, some of the best-selling feminist books were unique in size.[7] Grahn's *Edward the Dyke and Other Poems*, for instance, was 8 1/4 × 7 inches, more square than rectangular. Moreover, the volume of staple-bound books without a perfect spine emblazoned with a title creates storage problems; staple-bound books do not sit upright on shelves easily and, without the title on the spine, they are difficult to identify when picking and packing for shipment. One solution to the myriad of challenges is mutual support within the feminist publishing community. Gair and Harris conclude their letter with the plea, "We can only survive only if we are supported by feminist presses" (Dear Sisters letter). In their appeal, Gair and Harris emphasize mutuality as crucial if feminist publishing is to survive and thrive.

Many publishers granted exclusive distribution rights to WinD, but some, including one of their biggest clients, Diana Press, resisted. For the next two years, Gair and Harris tried to convince Diana Press to sign an exclusive agreement. Reid and Czarnik refused (Letter from Cynthia Gair to Diana Press). While there would have been benefits to WinD for such an agreement, primarily increased sales for WinD and new accounts because every bookseller would have had to order from WinD, the benefits to the publishers would have been minimal—and may have even meant a loss in sales. Commercial publishers secure exclusive distribution agreements because of their size and reach. Large distributors have aggressive sales forces, strong fulfillment practices, and good customer service. For small distributors, such as WinD, the tension between securing exclusive distribution rights and having a distribution network large enough to support those rights was a business conundrum. WinD needed to grow to hire more people and expand their distribution, but, undercapitalized, growth was difficult.

How Gair and Harris made this request for exclusive distribution rights—through an open letter to WIP Conference participants—demonstrates a method of thinking about and addressing problems in community contexts. Harris and Gair outlined the issues in a letter to all conference participants and then discussed it at the conference, embodying feminist principles of mutuality and open, transparent communication. Harris and Gair's request demonstrates the interconnections between the burgeoning feminist businesses; women saw themselves not in antagonistic or competitive relationships but in relationships of solidarity and mutuality.

This example also highlights the currency of separatist practices in feminism. Separatism is a political practice embraced by feminists in the 1970s. Even though separatism is often described as lesbian separatism and assumed to involve only lesbians, separatism was not, and is not, exclusive to lesbians. For WinD, proposing a separatist business practice had political, theoretical, and economic value.

WinD experienced enormous growth during its four years of operation. In 1979, Harris and Gair wrote, "Each year between 1975 and 1978 our sales doubled. Our list of titles increased from 30 in 1975 to 600 in 1979. The number of bookstores and libraries that regularly order from us rose steadily from 25 in 1975 to 600 in 1979" (Dear Friends letter July 1979). The sales data from Diana Press demonstrates the economic impact of WinD on small publishers. In 1975, WinD sold 1,711 books from Diana Press and paid Diana Press $1,748. In 1976, the number only increased modestly, in part because Diana Press published fewer new books; WinD sold 2,204 books from Diana Press and paid Diana $1,971.74. In 1977, the numbers increased nearly four-fold. In 1977, WinD sold 8,089 books from Diana Press and paid them $13,926. In 1978, the number slipped slightly with 6,619 books sold with a payment of $12,950, still a strong performance. In 1977 and 1978, these are significant sales numbers—and significant revenue—for Diana Press. Strong numbers continued in the early part of 1979 (reports are available through March 1979) with WinD selling 2,575 books from Diana Press and paying them $5,416 (multiple source documents compiled from "WinD" folder, Diana Press Papers). Neither Gair nor Harris recall the gross revenue for WinD, but both agree that Diana Press represented between 10 and 20 percent of total receipts. Thus, the gross revenue for WinD in 1978 (the most productive year) may have been between $64,000 and $130,000 (Harris interview, Gair interview).

Between 1977 and 1979, WinD's distribution network increased substantially as well. In 1979, the mailing list for WinD was "100+ pages long and contain[ed] 2,500 names and addresses." Within the list were 700 bookstores, approximately 900–1200 libraries, 200–400 women's studies departments, and a variety of publishers and individuals (Dear Publisher-who-until-recently-distributed-with-WIND). There was an eager audience of readers for feminist creative work. WinD was an important part of an increasingly sophisticated network of businesses selling feminist products.

Dissolution

In spite of the growth in sales both for individual publishers and to an ever-broadening group of retailers, WinD continued to lose money each year it operated. By the spring of 1979, Gair and Harris anticipated more losses as the business continued to grow. Together, they realized their business was not viable. Harris recalls, "It was just difficult work," then continues, "We were able to pay ourselves for the period that we were in business, four people. That was not horrible. And then we just saw, we just couldn't do it" (Harris interview).

Harris and Gair realized that they could no longer operate the business after an accountant analyzed their books and explained to Gair that there was "no way to make money in the business" (Gair interview). Distributing books requires high volume and a quick turn; that is, distributors must sell a lot of individual books quickly in order to break even or yield a profit. Gair and Harris explain, "The challenge for all distributors is that distribution works as a way to earn money only through high volume" (Dear Friends letter July 1979). In addition, in distribution, like publishing, the margins are small. WinD purchased books on consignment at 50 percent of retail price. WinD sold the book at 60 percent of retail to bookstores and other retail outlets. The 10 percent difference between purchase and sale price was the revenue retained by WinD. Gair and Harris explained, "If we sell $1,000 worth of books in a week we make a 'profit' of $100. Over half of that $100 will be spent on packing costs and most of the remainder will go for publicity—for catalogs, flyers, promotions, etc. That leaves little or no money for salaries, rent, and overhead" (ibid.). Reflecting on the business, Harris noted, "we probably should have started at a higher percentage" for a distribution fee, but "we didn't have enough business knowhow. We had the will, we were quick learners, but not quick enough" (Harris interview). With retrospect and her business savvy today, she observed, "the margin was way, way, way too slim. And we didn't have enough start up capital. And I think our turn[around?] would have had to have been a lot quicker" (ibid.).

During a tense few months in 1979, Harris and Gair proceeded to wind down the company in an orderly fashion—returning books to small, feminist publishers to ensure that they would not be held during the bankruptcy proceedings, informing their two employees so that these women could make other plans, and paying as many bills as possible to feminist small businesses and suppliers, ensuring that their losses in the bankruptcy were not severe (Gair interview, Harris interview).

In a July 1979 letter, Harris and Gair informed other feminist publishers and suppliers that "we have decided that Women in Distribution must be dissolved" (Dear Friends letter July 1979). They said, "Three main factors have influenced our decision: . . . the financial position of WinD; the activities of the small and women's presses; and the activities of the major publishers" (ibid.). The financial position of WinD was unsustainable. Even if WinD raised its distribution fee from 10 percent to 15 percent of retail sales, there was not enough revenue to support the business. Moreover, the volume of books being sold was not large enough, even if they expanded the company's mission and distributed books from other, nonfeminist small presses. Finally, the addition of feminist books to major, commercial publishers' catalogs concerned Gair and Harris; they believed it challenged, potentially fatally, the existence of small feminist presses. The collapse of WinD into bankruptcy in August 1979 represented a significant financial, practical, and symbolic loss to feminist publishers.

Legacies from WinD

The demise of WinD shocked and saddened the feminist community. Carol Seajay published an emergency issue of *FBN* when she learned that WinD closed. In addition to paying tribute to the work of Harris and Gair, Seajay published mailing addresses for publishers, urging bookstores subscribers to *FBN* to order directly from feminist presses. In this emergency issue, Seajay's practicality providing advice and assistance to bookstores shines. In her usual chatty, familiar voice, Seajay confides,

> Remember as you order that some of these publishers have never done distribution before and that some of them have had the bulk of their distribution done by WIND. For the first group it means never having dealt with packing, shipping, invoicing, filling orders, creating minimums that work for them and us. For the second group it means a whole shift in workload. Which all adds up to this: that as bookstores we can expect (or should I be more positive and say "we should not be surprised to see") a whole raft of problems. I hope that all the bookstores will be able to take the hassles in stride and take the time to write to the publishers with suggestions and solutions to the problems. Probably if a publisher gets 18 letters in a month saying that a minimum order of 28 copies of her only book is to high a requirement for a 40% discount suggesting that she cut it to 3 or 5, she/they will probably change their discount schedule. Or 15 letters saying "If you pack your books in used newspapers, the print rubs off on the books and they look dirty" will probably solve the problem fast. So lets all take the moment to write such notes as the problems come up. (Steal the time from resenting the same thing when it happens next time.) Pass on your insight/need/experience/understandings. We have to teach each other. If we all spend the next few months writing notes we'll solve a lot of problems before the Christmas Madness (I mean "Season"!) descends on us. (*Feminist Bookstore News* 2)

Seajay dispenses her signature practical advice and simultaneously highlights the labor of operating WinD. This spirit of information sharing and camaraderie infused *FBN,* in particular, and the broader feminist publishing community, in general.

While Seajay reflected on the immediate practical challenges that faced booksellers and readers, other feminist print activists considered the economic and theoretical implications of the demise of WinD. Sherry Thomas, one of the owners of the Old Wives' Tales, a feminist bookseller in San Francisco, learned about the WinD bankruptcy while visiting Harriet Desmoines and Catherine Nicholson, editors and publishers of the lesbian-feminist journal *Sinister Wisdom.* The three recognized "that we may be entering a new period of difficulty, a time to reaffirm our commitment to keeping feminist theory, art, culture alive in the world" (ibid.). This insight proves prescient. The end of the 1970s and the beginning of Ronald Reagan's presidency in 1981 mark a different world for feminists. The new decade brings fewer direct and indirect public resources to support the creation and distribution of cultural projects. Thomas also intuitively recognized, "Somehow, in whatever form, we will always go on. It's our lives we're talking about, creating the possibility of our survival" (ibid.).

"Creating the possibility of our survival," particularly creating the possibility of economic survival, is one of two important legacies of WinD. Upon hearing about the end of WinD, Harriet Desmoines quipped, "What made us think they'd *pay* us for making a revolution?" Yet, being paid, finding economically sustainable activities that contributed to building a feminist revolution, was a key issue for feminists in the late 1970s. The story of WinD illuminates how feminists negotiated feminism and capitalism, using multiple, creative strategies during the 1970s. One of the legacies of WinD is how WinD illuminates feminists' multiple engagements with economics. The other legacy is how the story of WinD demonstrates the complex negotiations of feminists among multiple feminist theories during the 1970s.

Feminist Economies

In 2012 Charlotte Bunch reflected, "Our radical feminist projects were financially unsustainable. . . . People tithed and gave money and had a tremendous work ethic but we didn't have a sustainable model. . . . We didn't have an economic plan. We thought we could do it because we worked hard" (Interview with Charlotte Bunch). During the heady, early days of the WLM, women believed that revolutionary transformation was just around the corner, but by the mid-to-late 1970s, it became clear that the feminist revolution was not imminently at hand. Feminists grappled with how to make a living and build a life while still expressing feminist commitments.

These ostensibly contradictory impulses—the need to earn a living and the need to express feminist commitments—provided a generative environment for feminists. Building feminist businesses was one strategy that women identified to nurture the revolution while refusing to engage in patriarchal workplaces. Building feminist businesses, however, was not without its own internal contradictions and tensions. For some feminists with an anticapitalist framework, feminist entrepreneurs such as Gair and Harris embraced the capitalist marketplace, while for other feminists, with another, equally important, framework of transformative social change, feminist entrepreneurs refused to engage patriarchal workplaces and instead created feminist workplaces to support themselves. Thus, feminist businesses are not only an active negotiation between feminism and capitalism, but also an active *refusal* of capitalism in favor of working only with other feminists.

One response, therefore, to Desmoines's quip, "What made us think they'd *pay* us for making a revolution?" is: feminists! Feminists like Gair and Harris grappled with the question of how women could support themselves economically and still contribute to the feminist revolution. Through their work they asserted that feminists could get paid for making a revolution. In the over thirty years since WinD closed, economic viability both for individual women and for the feminist movement remains a crucial feminist issue.

The story of WinD also affirms the significance of capitalism as a field of engagement for feminists. Gair and Harris both wanted WinD to be a for-profit company—when they created it and when they closed it. When it became clear that WinD was not sustainable as a for-profit venture, some friends and colleagues encouraged Gair and Harris to convert it to a nonprofit. During the late 1970s, in addition to a flowering of feminist publishing, there was a vibrant small press movement of publishers and distributors.[8] Many of these small presses, originally for-profits, became nonprofits, with funding from the National Endowment for the Arts (Harris interview). Gair and Harris chose not to incorporate as a nonprofit. They wanted to build a for-profit business; they wanted to support themselves through their work; they wanted to engage capitalism as feminists.

The ideas and philosophies enacted by feminist businesses such as WinD during the 1970s foreshadow social enterprise and socially responsible entrepreneurship, a movement that coalesced during the late 1980s and 1990s.[9] Gair and Harris's commitment to building for-profit businesses and their belief that businesses offered important opportunities for feminists and lesbian-feminists portend the movement of socially responsible businesses. Gair and Harris, along with other feminist entrepreneurs from companies such as Olivia Records, articulate these values and ideas before the language of social enterprise distills.

WinD also demonstrates how broad economic environments shape economic realities for women and for feminism. In 1979, the United States was inching to a major recession with unemployment at 6 percent in August 1979 and the gross domestic product showing only modest growth in 1979.[10] WinD experienced early the effects of the slowing U.S. economy. In the letter announcing the end of WinD, Gair and Harris wrote, "We have been experiencing extreme difficulties collecting from many of our bookstore accounts in the last six months. Bookstores that have been reliable in the past are now paying 90 to 120 days late. Some are not paying at all" (Dear Friends letter July 1979). Late payments of accounts receivable, an early sign of a slowing economy, had a negative effect on WinD. In addition, Gair and Harris wrote, "Several stores have gone out of business, leaving large due amounts unpaid" (ibid.). The loss of small feminist bookstore accounts not only created the problem of bad debt for WinD but also reduced their overall future sales. Gair and Harris continued, "In the last three months, we have seen sales go down twice their usual summer rate of decrease. More bookstores are making returns, rather than pay for shipments" (ibid.). The slowing and sluggish U.S. economy combined with the lack of access to capital to weather difficult periods and leverage growth, which women widely understood as a challenge for feminist businesses, was the death knell for WinD. Ultimately, the cultural capital of shared feminist commitments, central to WinD's business model, was unable to compensate for the slowing U.S. economy.

Recognizing the imbrication of feminist activities and the U.S. economy brings into focus the effects of capitalism on feminism and provides alternative explanations of different feminist formations and various strategies for feminist engagements. U.S. and global capitalism shape daily experiences in women's lives in significant and mundane ways. Increases and decreases in personal income, employment and unemployment, and expanding and constraining economic opportunities affect individuals, including feminists, concretely. For example, while industry-level issues of volume and margin played a key role in Harris and Gair's closing WinD, the macroeconomic issues—increased unemployment and slowing gross domestic product growth—facing the United States contributed to the urgency of closing WinD. The story of WinD highlights how macroeconomic issues shape the daily experiences of women's lives and the trajectory of social change movements. Attending to macroeconomics in analyses of feminist history changes narratives about the WLM. Macroeconomics illuminate successes and failures within the context of the economic and political realms of women's lives, relocating causes of successes and failures from the personal and interpersonal to the structural and institutional.

Feminist Theories

Just as the story of WinD offers opportunities to grapple with complex economic negotiations among individuals, small businesses, and macroeconomic systems, the story of WinD also illuminates complex negotiations among multiple feminist theories during the 1970s. Multiple descriptions of feminism coexisted in the daily practices of feminists, countering a schema that emerges in later scholarship and persists today.[11] In the first WinD catalog, Harris and Gair describe the material for distribution as "personal/cultural/political." The combination of these three words demonstrates the currency of all three words to capture the burgeoning material production of feminism. The slashes in the descriptor reflect the multiplicity of feminist visions for material production and the inability of (patriarchal) language to neatly describe or categorize these visions.

Similarly, in the 1976 letter to colleagues prior to attending the WIP Conference, Gair and Harris described their feminist commitments: "From working in Olivia Records we knew how to create a basic business structure and recognized the contradictions and problems involved in setting up a corporate structure with matriarchal/socialist goals" (WIP letter). Gair and Harris unite the terms *matriarchal* and *socialist* to describe their political orientation. As in the initial WinD catalog, the slash indicates how feminists yoked multiple ideologies together, expressing the excitement of the WLM at the time, the emergency of different feminist ideologies, and the ability of feminists to embrace multiple theories. *Matriarchal* and *socialist* overlap and diverge in the meanings they suggest; yet both commitments were important to Gair and Harris. *Matriarchal* expresses a world controlled by women, deriving its values through mothers, matriarchs, rather than through fathers, patriarchs. *Matriarchal* also suggests a systemic alternative to patriarchy. Lesbian-feminists envisioned matriarchy as, not simply, a flip of patriarchy in which women, not men, controlled resources but rather as a different system, egalitarian and not oppressive. Gair and Harris explain, "In WinD we have been trying to develop a feminist business which is non-hierarchical, does not exploit workers, is actually worker-controlled and does not exploit the consumer" (ibid.). They wanted to create a business that was not exploitive to workers and consumers, echoed the values of socialism, and embraced feminist principles with an absence of hierarchy and self-determination.

Ultimately, WinD enacted a variety of different types of feminisms and articulated new understandings of feminism. The story of WinD counters the schematic narrative of Echols in *Daring To Be Bad* which emphasizes a fleeing from radical feminism to cultural feminism and offers more complexity to Hogeland's discussion of the feminist literary sphere (Echols 3–6, Hogeland 1–18). During its five years of operation, WinD achieved extraordinary success in disseminating books and materials by feminists and lesbian-feminists broadly throughout the United States. The legacies of WinD, however, extend beyond the books and materials that they distributed.

WinD's legacies are in the belief that women can build businesses to support themselves and simultaneously do good work. WinD's legacies are in contemporary movements for socially responsible entrepreneurs. WinD's legacies are in vibrant, emergent feminist ideologies that center economic justice and that do not police labels and boundaries but instead negotiate complex realities of women's lives with a vision of making them better. WinD's legacies are in actions to do things by, for, and with women—and only women. Knowing the story of WinD enables us to see the legacies of WinD more clearly. WinD's legacies surround us; the legacies of WinD are in our continued search for an economic analysis and transformative economic strategies that embrace feminism and lesbianism.

Afterlives

In the last issue of *The Furies* (May–June 1973), Lee Schwing and Helaine Harris wrote an article titled "Building Feminist Institutions." In this article, they argue that a crucial next step for feminism and lesbian-feminism is dealing with "money and survival" in "an extensive, concrete way." Schwing and Harris argue that building lesbian-feminist institutions would "meet our economic and survival needs." The article is a call for lesbian-feminist owned businesses. Schwing and Harris analyze the many benefits of these imagined institutions: freeing women's time, giving women control of their bodies and their lives, "providing economic security for women," and opportunities to learn new skills. They conclude, "These institutions will kindle our energies and give us space to research talk and have insights into developing our ideology and strategy. This should help create another step towards a feminist society" (2). WinD was one important step that Harris, Schwing, and Gair took toward creating a feminist society.

Now, more than thirty years since WinD's bankruptcy, Harris and Gair have taken other steps to create a feminist society. Since the early 1980s, Harris has pursued her feminist visions through another business: Daedalus Books. Daedalus is a bookseller specializing in overstock (remainder) books. Daedalus buys overstock (excess) inventory from publishers and sells them direct to consumers at a steep discount. Daedalus is a vibrant part of the U.S. publishing landscape.

Harris describes Daedalus as an "ethical" company that treats "employees really well, pays well, and helps people grow" (Harris interview). While not explicitly a lesbian-feminist company, Daedalus Books expresses the principles of lesbian-feminism as Harris and Schwing articulated them in *The Furies*.

Like Harris, Gair also continues to express feminist values in her professional life. After WinD closed, Gair finished her bachelor's degree at the University of Maryland; then, she enrolled in the business school and studied finance, initially planning to become an accountant. Gair took her MBA from George Washington University and spent the next twenty-five years working in business, including with a venture capital firm, always focusing on her values of social responsibility and economic justice.

The final afterlife of WinD is the reminder that feminist and lesbian print culture is a stake for freedom. In the letter announcing WinD's bankruptcy, Gair and Harris ring a bell for freedom of speech and expression. Gair and Harris note that increasingly trade and large corporate publishers publish titles of interest to feminists and lesbians: "We feel this phenomenon is disastrous . . . for the growth of WIND and other alternative distributors and publishers" (Dear Friends letter July 1979). The adoption of feminist titles by commercial, trade publishers was—and continues to be—a Janus-face phenomenon. For authors, trade publishers helped their work reach a larger public through robust distribution and presence in a wide range of nonspecialist bookstores. For feminist publishers and bookstores, the adoption of feminist titles by trade publishers means fewer manuscripts available to feminist publishers, smaller sales margins, and increased competition for books. Feminists discuss and debate the tense relationship between small presses and commercial presses throughout the 1970s and 1980s. Feminists such as Gair and Harris wanted to preserve and defend the diverse and vibrant intellectual culture created through the feminist communications circuit; they believed that commercial publishers usurped lesbian-feminist ideas and exploited them for capitalist profit, benefiting patriarchy and not contributing to the feminist revolution. They also feared the cooptation of the lesbian-feminist subculture, representing an erosion of freedom of speech and expression. In short, Gair and Harris felt that the phenomenon of feminists and lesbians publishing with trade publishers was disastrous "for freedom of speech and expression" (ibid.).

While publishing and distribution are business and economic activities, to publish and distribute books by feminists and lesbians is also a political activity—an activity that makes a stake for free speech and uncensored expression. Feminist print culture contributes to a diverse intellectual, social, and political climate for women. If the political elements of lesbian and feminist publishing are lost, as Gair and Harris note, it is at our own peril. Gair and Harris envisioned defending freedom of speech and expression as a vital afterlife of WinD. This afterlife is one that we are all called to defend continuously.

Acknowledgments

I am grateful to Helaine Harris and Cynthia Gair for doing the work of WinD and for their willingness to discuss it with me nearly thirty years later. As always, Agatha Beins provided insightful comments and early enthusiasm for this essay. Jaime Harker's editorial comments made the essay stronger and clearer. Deep appreciation for the multiple sources of support for my research and writing, including the Catherine Prelinger Award from the Coordinating Council for Women in History, a Woodrow Wilson Dissertation Fellowship in Women's Studies (special designation as Ostriker Fellow in honor of Alicia Ostriker), a dissertation research grant from Schlesinger Library at Harvard University, a Mary Lily Research Grant from the Sallie Bingham Center for Women's History and Culture at Duke University, and a Phil Zwickler Memorial Research Grant from Cornell University Library. Gratitude to my colleagues in the Women's Studies department at the University of Maryland, particularly Deborah Silverton Rosenfelt and Katie King, and as always, appreciation to my ideal reader, Martha Nell Smith.

Notes

1. For a discussion of the significance of poetry in the WLM, see Honor Moore's introduction in *Poems from the Women's Movement* (New York: Library of America, 2009); Kim Whitehead's *The Feminist Poetry Movement* (Jackson: UP of Mississippi, 1996); Jan Clausen's *A Movement of Poets* (Brooklyn: Long Haul Press, 1982); and Linda Garber's *Identity Poetics: Race, Class, and the Lesbian-Feminist Roots of Queer Theory* (New York: Columbia UP, 2001). For a discussion of the significance of writing and publishing during the WLM more generally, see Lisa Maria Hogeland, *Feminism and Its Fictions;* Kate Adams, "Built Out of Books—Lesbian Energy and Feminist Ideology in Alternative Publishing," *Journal of Homosexuality* 34.3 (1998): 113–141; Trysh Travis, "The Women in Print Movement: History and Implications," *Book History* 11 (2008): 275–300; Jan Whitt, "A 'Labor from the Heart': Lesbian Magazines from 1947–1994," *Journal of Lesbian Studies* 5.1/2 (2001): 229–251; and Kathryn Thoms Flannery, *Feminist Literacies 1968–75* (Urbana: U of Illinois P, 2006).

2. A history of Olivia Records is absent from the current feminist historiography of the WLM. Perhaps the best narrative of the history of Olivia Records is a 2006 interview with Judy Dlugacz, one of the founders: Patrick Lettelier, "Judy Dlugacz: Olivia President and Founder Talks about Women's Music, Lesbian Travel, Retirement Resorts and the Job of a Lifetime. (Cover Story)." *Lesbian News* 31.6 (2006): 22–23.

3. In 2014 dollars, $1,200 is the equivalent of $5,682.61. Source: http://www.westegg.com/inflation/, accessed 1 April 2015.

4. Kathryn Flannery notes that "ordinary women engaged in literate production on a remarkable scale" as a part of the women's movement in *Feminist Literacies 1968–75*, 23.

5. A salary of $8,000 in 1978 is equivalent to a salary of $28,640.74 in 2014. Source: http://www.westegg.com/inflation/, accessed 1 April 2015.

6. *Motive* was a publication of the United Methodist Church; the final two issues of the journal were thematic, a *Lesbian-Feminist* issue and a *Gay Men's Liberation* issue. The women who edited the Lesbian-Feminist issue, Joan E. Biren, Rita Mae Brown, Charlotte Bunch, and Coletta Reid, founded The Furies right as they published the Lesbian-Feminist issue of *Motive*.

7. Standard book sizes for hardcover books, paperback books, mass market paperback books, and children's books maximize the efficiencies in distribution for storage and shipping.

8. For more on the small press movement, see Abe Peck's *Uncovering the Sixties: The Life and Times of the Underground Press* (New York: Pantheon, 1985); John McMillian's *Smoking Typewriters: The Sixties Underground Press and the Rise of Alternative Media in America* (New York: Oxford UP, 2011); Peter Richardson's *A Bomb in Every Issue: How the Short, Unruly Life of Ramparts Magazine Changed America* (New York: The New Press, 2009); and Donna Lloyd Ellis "The Underground Press in America: 1955–1970" *Journal of Popular Culture* 1 (1971): 102–124.

9. The prominence of Anita Roddick and The Body Shop is an early indication of this movement; Roddick published a memoir explaining her business philosophy in 1995, *Body and Soul: Profits with Principles—The Amazing Success Story of Anita Roddick & The Body Shop* (New York: Three Rivers Press). Bill Shore's *Revolution of the Heart* (New York: Riverhead Books, 1995) is another marker of the popularity of this philosophy.

10. Source: http://www.sjsu.edu/faculty/watkins/rec1980.htm (accessed 2 Feb. 2012.) Of course, the economic recession of 1979–1980 seems mild compared with the recession of 2008–2009.

11. The most prominent discussion of feminist classification is Chela Sandoval's response in *Methodology of the Oppressed* (Minneapolis: U of Minnesota P, 2000) to the schema of Alison Jaggar and Paula S. Rothenberg in *Feminist Frameworks: Alternative Theoretical Accounts of the Relations between Women and Men* (New York: McGraw-Hill, 1978). Recently, Claire Hemmings reexamined this tension in *Why Stories Matter: The Political Grammar of Feminist Theory* (Durham, NC: Duke UP, 2011).

Works Cited

Berson, Ginny. "The Story of the Furies." *The Furies: Lesbian/Feminist Monthly* 1.1 (January 1972): 1.

Bunch, Charlotte. Personal Interview. 19 July 2012.

Catherine Nicholson Papers. Rare Book, Manuscript, and Special Collections Library, Duke University, Durham, NC.

Darnton, Robert. "What Is the History of Books?" *Daedalus* 111.3 (1982): 65–83.

Dear Friends Letter. July 1979, Catherine Nicholson Papers, box 13, folder "Women in Distribution," 1977–1981.

Diana Press Papers. File drawer 2, folder "WinD." Mazer Archives, Los Angeles.

Echols, Alice. *Daring To Be Bad: Radical Feminism in America 1967–1975*. Minneapolis: U of Minnesota P, 1989.

Gair, Cynthia. Skype Interview. 20 June 2013.

———. Letter to Diana Press. 7 Oct. 1977. Diana Press Papers.

Gair, Cynthia, and Helaine Harris. Dear Sisters Letter. 10 Aug. 1976. Diana Press Papers.

Harris, Helaine. Personal Interview. 14 May 2013.

Harris, Helaine, Cynthia Gair, and Lee Schwing. Dear Friends Letter. 11 Nov. 1974. Diana Press Papers.

Hieronymus, Bill. "For Some Feminists Owning a Business Is Real Liberation." *Wall Street Journal* 15 April 1975.

Hogeland, Lisa. *Feminism and Its Fictions: The Consciousness-Raising Novel and the Women's Liberation Movement*. Philadelphia: U of Pennsylvania P, 1998.

Kelly, Janis. "Conference of Women in Print." *off our backs* 6.8 (Nov. 1976): 2.

Schwing, Lee, and Helaine Harris. "Building Feminist Institution." *The Furies* final issue (May-June 1973): 2–3.

Seajay, Carol. *"Bookstores." Feminist Bookstores Newsletter* 2.2 (1977): 3–5.

———. Dear Publisher-Who-until-Recently-Distributed-with-WIND. 7 Oct. 1979. Catherine Nicholson Papers, folder "Sinister Wisdom Bookstore Copies of Possible Interest, 1976–1980."

———. *Emergency FBN. Feminist Bookstore News* 3.3 (Sept. 1979): 2.

Valk, Anne M. *Radical Sisters: Second-Wave Feminism and Black Liberation in Washington, D.C.* Urbana: U of Illinois P, 2008.

WinD Flyer. N.d. Atlanta Lesbian Feminist Archive ca. 1972–1994, box 11, folder "Women Publishers and Presses." Rare Book, Manuscript, and Special Collections Library, Duke University, Durham, NC.

WIP Letter. N.d. Catherine Nicholson Papers, box 13, folder "Women in Distribution, 1977–1981."

Chapter 4

Closely, Consciously Reading Feminism

Yung-Hsing Wu

Common wisdom has it that close reading and the political sensibilities of contemporary criticism could not be more different. Their antithesis derives from the view that close reading, bound to the primacy of the text, turns a blind eye to the historical, institutional, and social dynamics that shape and are shaped by literature and those readers in its orbit. Just as familiar is the underlying belief that close reading is politically suspect; its appreciation of the textual object is an expression of the privilege of its practitioners. Critical of close reading, both perspectives are also retrospective, and familiar from accounts in which literary studies, shedding the New Critical yoke in the decades following the end of the Cold War, emerges with the fervor of political commitment.[1] Put at the extreme, close reading is doubly alienated from the intellectual practices—of feminism, ethnic studies, gay and lesbian studies, queer theory—that eventually displaced it.

While feminism is one protagonist in this narrative of opposition, I argue that it also undoes it, thanks to a history in which the interrelation of closeness and reading emerges quite differently. Less visible than the feminist critique of "disciplined" close reading, this history articulates a feminist belief in the *closeness* of reading, locating it in the theory and politics of consciousness-raising (CR) that defined the print culture of second-wave feminism and in the disputes over reading that popular novels of that moment produced. From within the movement to those depicted in literature, these scenes of reading demonstrate that for feminism, reading has signified the feeling of closeness associated with identification. Thus if second-wave feminism seized small print ventures—newsletters, pamphlets, magazines, and journals—for collaboration and outreach, that was due in part to the view that reading, because it involved identification, would crystallize a consciousness women had not possessed before, or had not felt so intensely, so intimately. The line from reading to identification through closeness was understood to be as sure as it was direct. Popular feminist fiction, meanwhile, made this line a matter of dispute. Certain that the power of *Diary of a Mad Housewife* (1970), *Memoirs of an Ex-Prom Queen* (1972), *Fear of Flying* (1973), and *The Women's Room* (1977) lay with the readerly identifications they produced, industry commentators and activists remained skeptical that fiction could possess any political relevance. Asking whether Mira Ward was a sufficient model for readerly politicization, or whether *The Women's Room* offered an accurate portrait of the circumstances "real" women faced, such queries articulated anxieties about the mediations of the fictive. And even as readers flocked to these novels, feminist fiction itself expressed uncertainty about the political efficacy of reading—an ambivalence echoed, for instance, in *The Women's Room*, which originates Mira's feminism in reading only to leave it behind.

Taken together, these snapshots suggest one explanation for the coalescence of early feminist literary criticism. If this discourse came of age when it began to argue for the distinctiveness of female authorship and writing, I argue that a closeness associated with reading has been present all along, particularly as an implicit logic about textuality. Just as feminist CR believed that reading could generate closeness among women, and just as feminist fiction of the 1970s was regularly cited (and decried) for an intimacy of identification it was said to create for women readers, early feminist literary criticism was marked by an investment in the political promise of closeness. For feminist literary critics of that first academic generation, many of them steeped in New Criticism, this sensibility marked a shift from closeness described as a familiar stance toward textuality to one with distinctive affective and political valences. In other words, this sensibility yoked the question of women reading to consciousness: to its nascence, whether sudden or gradual, and to its qualities of strangeness, pain, even joy. While their assumptions led them to find reading in very different places, their critical desires stemmed from the shared view that reading, wherever it is found, can be a place for politics.

The Closeness of Print

The mimeograph machine was "the first large purchase" the Women's Liberation D.C. office made in 1968. The machine, Charlotte Bunch recalls, embodied the belief that "getting more copies into more women's hands would ensure that change would happen" ("Reading and Writing" 219). In making this assertion, Bunch articulated a view shared by feminists across the country, who in the next ten years would turn to a variety of outlets to put feminism on the page. Less splashy than events staged to capture mainstream and media attention, print provided a ready instrument for access and exposure, and activists in New York, Boston, Chicago, as well as Austin, Seattle, Los Angeles, and San Francisco were quick to seize the opportunities it afforded, establishing two hundred periodicals and presses nationwide by the early 1980s (ibid. 220, Lauret 72). The contribution print made to feminism resided both in its ability to get the message out and in shaping the coherence of the movement behind the message.

The coherence of the feminist vision depended as much on its being received, and if the staff of *off our backs* or Daughters, Inc. counted on print's greater range, they did so believing that reading would promote CR. In what follows, I argue that an affinity between politicization and reading drove second-wave feminism, and that CR and reading could dovetail precisely because the emphasis on intimacy and attention in the former echoed a similar conviction about readerly identification. A political logic of closeness, one that regarded shared emotion as the catalyst for consciousness, turned in part on thinking that the feelings evoked by reading could yield a similar awakening. For, as Daughters, Inc. cofounder June Arnold put it, "the reader could see her own or her sister's experience portrayed" (qtd. in Loudermilk 16) in such a way that prompted her identification. According to this view, novel-reading occasioned an intimacy no less powerful than the sort that developed in person. The imaginative leap demanded by fiction was reason to argue for its particular importance to feminist politics.

Consider first that the movement's desire for connection constituted a political logic of closeness. In 1969, the authors of the "Redstockings Manifesto" claimed that the oppression of women itself marked a form of closeness: "we have lived so intimately with our oppressors, in isolation from one each other [that] we have been kept from seeing our personal suffering as a personal condition." The task of feminism would be to sever these bonds and replace them, as a New York Radical Feminists leaflet asserted, with "a place for women to be friends, exchange personal griefs, and give their sisters moral support" (Morgan xxviii). Thus when Sarachild called on women to be "with" feeling, she urged them to "share our feelings and pool them" and predicted that this intimacy of affect would "lead us to ideas and then to actions." Her 1968 outline in "A Program for Feminist Consciousness-Raising" would go further and specify, as other similar statements did, that trust would actually produce the capacity to detach—to analyze and abstract. This is Pamela Allen's point about the "free space" that she and the members of the Sudsofloppen group sought:

"after *sharing*," she writes, "we know that women suffer at the hands of a male supremacist society" (emphasis mine). Far from assuming that feeling and thinking are irreconcilable, Allen posits that knowledge follows feeling when the latter is "free" to surface. And even if this freedom troubled Jo Freeman, who worried that the looseness of CR could mean "political impotency," it also remained, she acknowledged, the creative strength of the feminist movement. Or, as Robin Morgan writes in the introduction to the landmark *Sisterhood Is Powerful*, "the theory comes out of human feeling . . . *that's* truly revolutionary, as anyone knows who has listened to abstract political speeches" (xviii, original emphasis). The crux of feminist thinking resided in displacing theory's usual origins from the head to the heart.

There is no more vivid proof that the political promise of shared emotion was understood in terms of closeness than the example of the feminist press. Morgan is emphatic when she writes that working on "this book [*Sisterhood Is Powerful*] seems to have been the most responsible" for her feminism and remembers that she had insisted "on working with women at Random House" during its production (xv–xvi).[2] This was certainly the spirit of the first Women in Print conference, which in August 1976 brought together women to "discuss what we had learned [about publishing] and how we could cooperate more" (Bunch, "Women's Publishing" 223). The conference vision, mirroring the CR belief in personal correspondence, sought to make print a CR occasion. It is significant that Bunch in her own account notes that "there wasn't any one result to point to": if things felt nebulous, that was a function of the atmosphere, which emphasized agendas and schedules less and "what is now called 'networking' and developing resources for improving cooperation" more. She points twice to the way in which the conference benefited attendees through the relationships it made possible; these relationships, and the information and know-how they fostered, defined the vision of the feminist press through the identifications the participants felt. When Bunch says the conference helped people remember "that our problems were not ours alone," when she recalls "a magnificent feeling in that early women's liberation sense of finding each other," she is describing the conference in the language of CR that has identification at its core.

The Women in Print Conference embodied a self-reflexivity characteristic of feminist print efforts. Unlike the *Ladies Home Journal* sit-in that aimed to expose the sexism rampant in mainstream women's magazines, Women in Print was more concerned to develop a print infrastructure out of feminist closeness.[3] A similar impulse was visible as early as 1968, when the New York Radical Women released *Notes from the First Year*, the group's first collection of writing

(Brownmiller 26). Featuring essays and speeches, the collection also included transcripts of CR sessions in order, Shulamith Firestone notes, to "give the reader some sense of what a typical discussion is like at the weekly Thursday night meetings." Analysis and advice was one thing—from the beginning both Redstockings and the Radical Feminists had distributed mimeographed flyers with tips for organizing CR groups, and in its first issue, *Ms.* included a piece offering suggestions for newly formed groups—but the reproduction of actual CR talk emphasized the belief that spontaneity fostered productive thinking (Brownmiller 79).[4] In the transcript of "When Women Rap about Sex," *Notes from the First Year* shows participants moving from one topic to another, from casual sex to halitosis to masturbation, and thus reveals that their model of talk eschews structure for emergence (Firestone).[5] Meanwhile other magazines and journals took to heart the movement's principle that "dividing work and responsibility and sharing power" was a mark of feminist difference (Bunch, "Building" 234). Marilyn Webb recalls, for instance, the "informal hierarchy" attempted at *off our backs* (Brownmiller 74). And at the D.C. journal *Quest*, writers regularly developed essays out of in-house conversation, their own CR defining the work of the journal (Bunch, "Building" 234). Bunch recalls that *Quest* tried to sustain this mutual dynamism through loose leadership and a rotating development committee that introduced nonstaff writers. These invigorated the *Quest* office, she writes, with "fresh experiences, perspectives, and enthusiasm," intensifying it as a hub of CR closeness (235).[6] While it detached the journal's identity from full-time staff, it strengthened the identifications among them that in turn propelled the work forward.

The closeness of print had, however, another side to it. If print brought feminists close in a variety of endeavors, it did so because of a parallel assumption that reading could also compel intimacy. To the extent that second-wave feminists convened on print as their political medium of choice, they did so because they believed that women, through reading, would reach a similar closeness after having identified themselves as and with one another as women—and that that creation of awareness would be generative. Even as individual groups differed in their views regarding the purpose of CR—to what extent was it a means to an end? To what extent was it its own end?—most proceeded from the opinion that something would come out of it.[7] And that thinking was brought to bear, almost seamlessly, to reading. Robin Morgan at the end of her introductory comments to *Sisterhood Is Powerful* thus writes herself into a scene of reading: "*You, sister, reading this*: I have no earthly way of knowing if you are already involved in women's liberation, and if so, how deeply; perhaps you have never yet been to one women's meeting, but only read and heard things about the movement in magazines and TV; perhaps you find you have picked up the book out of anger, or defiance, or on a dare, or from genuine curiosity, or cynical amusement" (xxxv, original emphasis). Up until this direct hail, Morgan has drawn parallels between *Sisterhood Is Powerful* and the movement, suggesting that the difficulties the anthology faced during its production—economic, intellectual, social, cultural, and political—are emblematic of the obstacles feminism has faced. Her turn to address her reader, to imagine an identity and set of circumstances for her, departs from that broader sensibility, but it involves no less a leap than the critical empathy Sarachild urges in her description of CR. Even as she admits that she does not know the reader or her politics, Morgan claims her as a sister precisely by speculating that they as women have in common their experiences of and responses to feminism. Perhaps more to the point, Morgan renders that speculation in terms of her reader's response to *Sisterhood Is Powerful*. Reading, she implies, performs closeness in an echo of the feminist principle that shared expression would carry the movement onward.

While Morgan includes in her address her uncertainty about her reader, the address itself seeks to close that distance. The device proceeds with the hope that reading will produce in Morgan's "sister" a sense of identification. Meanwhile the gesture to posit a literary origin for feminist awareness emphasizes the extent to which identification [in that context] was understood as a political ground. Gloria Steinem, writing about exchanges she has had with audiences throughout her career about female community, recalls Louisa May Alcott's *Little Women* and asks, "Where else . . . could we have read about an all-female group who discussed work, art, and all the Great Questions—or found girls who wanted to be women and not vice versa?" (85). And in *The Female Eunuch*, Germaine Greer offers an explicit statement somewhat rare for the popular treatises of the 1970s, writing that "half the point of reading novels and seeing plays and films is to exercise the faculty of sympathy with our own kind, so often obliterated in the multifarious controls and compulsions of actual social existence" (162). The comment occurs in her discussion of love, at a moment when Greer, imagining love unfettered by ideology, turns to novel-reading for inspiration. In this way her thinking about a "faculty of sympathy" anticipates June Arnold's reasoning that in novels "reader and author could communicate on an intimate personal level," that "the reader could see her own or her sister's experience portrayed" (qtd. in Loudermilk 16).[8] The convergence brings Greer's political analysis of culture directly in contact with Arnold's assessment of print politics. Here novel-reading vitalizes the project of CR, amplifying it in both scope and force. Self-awareness finds one impetus in the specific intersubjectivity of novel-reading—a dynamic that involves the relations of women readers to authors, to characters, and to one another.

Reading in *The Women's Room*?

And yet because novels were peopled by fictional characters, their significance to CR troubled those both within the movement and outside it. Especially vivid is the case of *The Women's Room*, published fifteen years after *The Feminine Mystique* and seven years after *Sexual Politics*. Trouble resulted from the view that when CR appears in narrative form, it has designs on the reader's outright identification. Whether or not the novel's contemporary readers actually identified with the account of Mira Ward's feminist development, most accounts—the popular and the scholarly—stated a version of this claim: that because the narrative is so insistent in its construction of a female readership it compels, almost irresistibly, readers to identify with Mira.[9] This claim is borne out usually in citations to the novel's quick ascent to best-sellerdom (to the top of the *New York Times* list in two months), where the fact of purchase is understood as confirmation of readerly identification, and in equally frequent references to the novel in feminist remembrances, which point to *The Women's Room* as inspiration for women who had yet to feel the touch of politicization. "[*The Women's Room*] came at a time when the mass consciousness was changing," recalls Charlotte Sheedy, the agent who picked up French's novel. "It wasn't for those of us who had been in the movement, it was for them, the ones who were just beginning to understand about consciousness raising and the politics of housework. People started debating it in their living rooms" (Brownmiller 256). Like other explanations of the novel's phenomenal appeal, Sheedy's begins by asserting its specific purpose for a specific audience. *The Women's Room* "was for them": it represented the spread of CR to the domestic realm of living rooms and housework, and in Mira Ward's progress toward feminism, it posits readers who in following her narrative will also follow her example.

This view that the novel would all but guarantee a new politicization of its readers unified reviewers of varying, and at times, opposed political and theoretical dispositions. To be more specific, two views that defined the early reception of *The Women's Room* while simultaneously finding the novel wanting contrasted sharply, as Lisa Hogeland, Kim Loudermilk, Marie Lauret, and Anna Wilson have noted, with the novel's mainstream success. These two strands of rather more ambivalent reception articulate the stance, on the one hand, of highbrow literary culture, which equated its popularity with poor readerly taste, and on the other hand, the view of the feminist movement, which early on viewed the novel, its politics, and French with suspicion. What is more, while publishers and reviewers from the mainstream and feminist press alike were convinced that French's *The Women's Room* was irresistible in compelling readers' identification, they also found fault with its representation of Mira, arguing that she was not a proper model of feminist awakening. Fiction apparently made identification a sure thing, but it came with a risk. For in the reading of fiction, the suspension of belief demands a suspension of self as well, and, as a result, how women readers might respond to characters became a central question. Millions of women may have devoured the story of Mira Ward's gradual feminist awakening, but these two discourses—of expert aesthetic judgment on the one hand and social transformation on the other—rendered the novel and its readers' responses to it as insufficient. Meanwhile the novel's critical reception in the twenty years after its publication has been no more certain, as feminist scholarly regard for the novel has shifted along with its own disciplinary and institutional anxieties.

All this ambivalence about reading intensifies in *The Women's Room*, which does not ascribe to reading the force that its readers are said to have discovered in it. While the novel identifies Mira as a reader, it is uncertain about the political work reading can do, turning instead to shared community and intimacy among women as the catalyst for new awareness. *The Women's Room* is in this way a "novelization of consciousness raising," but that novelization deploys the act of reading against itself, figuring it as an early source of identification for Mira that ultimately cannot provide what she needs (Hogeland 42). Indeed if the arc of *The Women's Room* follows Mira from her youth, married years, and time in graduate school post divorce, and overlays those moments with a developing articulation of her own feminist consciousness, then it is worth noting that the novel associates Mira's reading with her prefeminist self, practically dropping her private readerly self as her politics emerge. In other words, in the arc of *The Women's Room*, solitary reading gives way to a feminism defined by the closeness of the communal. Mira begins her feminist journey in books, but the novel turns (her) away from that origin to define feminist awareness through her relations with women.

Her girlhood features voracious reading—the narrator observes that Mira had finished "all the books they would allow her to take from the library" by the age of fourteen (11)—and characterizes her high school years in terms of the literature in which she hoped she "could find herself and her problems" represented (16). Hardly a social creature in these moments, Mira opts to read to discover what she finds troubling about the world in which she lives. That her problems are about gender is no less surprising than the fact that what she reads fails her. Reading widely, from "every thin, saccharine 'girl's book' she could find" to "trashy novels," from "Jane Austen and Fanny Burney and George Eliot and Gothic novels of all sorts" to "Daphne du Maurier and Somerset Maugham and Frank Yerby and John O'Hara, along with hundreds of nameless mystery tales, love stories, and adventures" (16), Mira seeks an account of herself she can recognize. But casting so wide a net, one that does not distinguish among the canonical, the middlebrow, and genre fiction, yields no answers to her questions about the asymmetries that structure gender. Her belief in literary quality—learned in school—makes the impact of these asymmetries all the more clear. Bored by school reading, Mira still absorbs the constructions of female purity that such reading compels, believing that "women were always pure and true and clean, like Cordelia and Marina and Jane Eyre" (17).

From the outset, Mira's reading possesses a feminist impulse, and the novel, situating that impulse in her isolation, associates lack with what she reads. Reading fuels more reading, but in a strictly negative fashion; the narrator compares Mira to "the person who gets fat because they eat unnourishing foods and so is always hungry and so is always eating," and describes her "drowned in words that could not teach her to swim" (16). Reading is not productive but the sense remains that it could be, if only Mira had access to texts that satisfied her. This dynamic is all but reversed early in her marriage, when during her husband's stint in medical school, she finds that "she could not concentrate even though it [the TV] was off. She suspected the problem was not just tiredness; when she picked up a serious book, one that made her think, she thought. And that was unbearable, because to think involves thinking about one's life. She read at night, read voluminously. It was like the beginning of her adolescence. She read junk: mystery novels, light social satirists like O'Hara and Marquand and Maugham. She could not handle anything more" (37). While Mira continues to hold to a notion of literary seriousness, the difference lies in her feeling that such thinking would be "unbearable." If in her adolescence she sought any book that might articulate what she intuited but could not express, in her marriage she chooses "junk" deliberately to avoid that understanding. The novel's critique of marriage thus turns on the reading Mira is willing to take up: reading allows Mira to evade what she "suspects" but does not want to know. Her return to adolescent fare signals less a decline in readerly taste than a retreat from a socially interested mind. The stakes of this retreat are high, for by the time reading makes its next appearance in the novel, its capacity for inciting Mira's thinking has dissolved. With her two children now past infancy, Mira returns again to voracious reading, checking out from the library "stacks of books, all by one author" and consuming "popular and scholarly books on psychology, sociology, anthropology" (68). For the narrator, however, this return is hardly salutary. For Mira can only read "uncritically, making no distinctions," forgetting "most of what she read, having no context to put it in" (68). It is not explicitly asserted, but the point is clear: reading without a purposeful context cannot be meaningful.

The logic that reading needs context for it to be useful—that reading ought to be useful at all—belongs to the narrator, who resists the reading life that leaves women capable of "making no distinctions." Just who is this narrator, then, and what does it mean that her sensibilities should be attached to Mira's? Her first words address the reader with an image of Mira, crouched in a university basement bathroom at Harvard, terrified by the decision she has made to begin graduate studies (3). Coupled with the novel's retrospective organization, this perspective yields a critical sympathy: the narrator regards Mira from a distance even as she makes clear her intimate understanding of her. This balance is pointed when she interrupts the narrative, and even more so when her comments focus on the reading life she shares with Mira. Familiar with the literary canon, her references to "female Bildungsromane," Lear, Hamlet, Romeo and Juliet, Camille, Tristan and Isolde, Antigone, Hester Prynne, and Dorothea Brooke are keenly critical that "the great literature of the past . . . doesn't tell you how to live with real endings" (137). These fictions tell lies anchored in a "dramatic sense" that she resists with endings ridiculously realistic and mundane. Her Lear does not die mad of grief for his lost Cordelia, but lives on, "a babbling old fool drooling over his oatmeal and happy for a place by the fire in Regan's house in Scarsdale" (137). Her Camille is no tragic and virtuous heroine but the owner of "a small popular hotel in Bordeaux," wearing "a shiny pale blue pantsuit" (137). Writerly, these revisions insist that literature has failed women and, in so doing, heighten the novel's metafictional impulse. When the narrator stops to address the reader about Mira, she seeks the reader's identification with Mira—at one point early on she says directly, "I leave it to you to decide on Mira's sanity" (5)—while the latter foregrounds the ways in which reading makes identification almost inevitable and always troublesome for women. Meanwhile, her comments about literature are analytical and, at times, performative. Her claim that Antigone would have been "not only ludicrous but a bore" had she lived disavows the dramatic end requiring "the cave and the rope"—and as a result, displaces the logic that puts Antigone forward as a heroic model (138). And when she writes against Camille's fate, the narrator refuses the interpellative power underlying Dumas's vision of a woman forever-wronged. Her disidentification can proceed because she has no desire to be his Camille, idealized in death. The problem with fiction lies with identification itself.

This is hugely ironic. That *The Women's Room* should find the reading of fiction problematic for women, and that it should finger identification as a particular culprit, flies in the face of the view that identification is essential to understanding the novel's force. What to make of the careful charting the narrator offers of identifications specific to reading? One answer lies with the novel's arc, which takes Mira from her prefeminist life, through her feminist awakening, and to the present. While her narrative begins by identifying her as a reader, its references to reading taper off as Mira's feminist consciousness emerges. The latter coincides with her move to study literature at Harvard, where she meets the women—Val and her daughter Chris, Iso, Ava, Clarissa, and Kyla—who will become her core group of friends, those with whom she is able, incrementally, to imagine a different Mira. Perhaps just as importantly, as *The Women's Room* makes this move, it shifts its account of identification, detaching it from the solitary act of reading and aligning it instead with feminism. Feminism makes identification social and lateral, and Mira comes to feminist consciousness through the relations she develops with the members of her Harvard group. The first inklings of this shift occur, significantly, when she becomes pregnant for the first time. Unplanned, the pregnancy marks the last instance in which the novel refers to Mira reading, "her great belly propped by cushions on either side of her" as she reads *Remembrance of Things Past* (43). The experience prompts neither nostalgia nor self-reflection, but anticipates the detached state she creates during labor, what the narrator calls her refusal "to have anything to do with it [labor]" (47). Mira reads Proust so as not to think about being pregnant, and when she goes into labor, she falls unconscious. What is just as striking, though, is that the end of Mira's reading life also signals her first glimpse of female community. At this point, the narrator turns her gaze to the women in the postdelivery room, noting the simultaneity that makes their conversation go "round and round and round," their sensitivity to one another, their utter focus on their children (50–51). The realization that "they never talked about themselves" taps Mira's conscience, but more than that, it tips over into her consciousness: "for the first time in her life, she thought that women were great" (52).

This first instance of womanly fellow-feeling emerges by random chance, and while the spontaneous exchange might call to mind CR sessions, *The Women's Room* is quick to separate it from the overtly political tenor of those conversations. As if to make this point, the narrative immediately flashes forward, exchanging "the artificial collective" of the hospital ward for its first snapshot of the Harvard group together (51). In this scene, the group discusses Mira's delivery experience, subjecting her claims about women's greatness, as well as their desires to believe in it, to critique and affectionate ribbing. Valerie, for instance, snorts at the notion that childbirth had enabled Mira to arrive "finally, at womanhood" and insists that Mira's revelation about feminine selflessness proves she has been duped to accept her second-class status (52–53). From dissent to prodding and mutual assessment; from personal anecdote to social, historical, and cultural analyses and back again: following this loose pattern, the novel develops the character of CR through the intimacies Mira and her friends come to articulate. Across scenes like these, they discover the specifics of their outrage—at marriage, at the gendered assumptions that underlie social institutions, at the way such assumptions exist even in the most progressive of movements—through one another. The catalyst is precisely the interchange, whether it involves the entire group or a subset of it. Indeed when the narrator focuses on Iso's relationship with Kyla, or Clarissa's disintegrating marriage, or the history of Val's politics, the shift to these particular stories gives the novel the added force of broader commentary. Both the overlap and differences among the women's lives constitute the larger story of women's oppression *The Women's Room* has to tell.

And as the narrator remarks, the intimacy that fueled the sharing in the first place also describes her telling of the story. "I sometimes think," she writes, "that I have swallowed every woman I ever knew" (8). The metaphor that equates knowledge with consumption is familiar enough, and here it describes both Mira's feminist consciousness—her knowledge of other women is a function of her taking in their experience as hers—and her narrative position. That the novel only hints at this identity, and divulges it rather late, means that Mira remains at a distance from herself for much of *The Women's Room*. And as her narratorial pronouncements increase in number and intensity, they reveal Mira's writerly identification. To her readers, she offers explanations for those writerly decisions—"You think I hate men," she says, shortly after a long discussion of male advantage or, about her depiction of Norm, her husband, "You think I am making him up"—that might make her feminism seem excessive (192, 188). For her, the Norm she represents is a product of his identifications just as Mira, the character, is a product of her reading history, and in other similar comments, Mira paints a despairing picture of readerly identification and its impact on gendered relations. When Mira the narrator looks back at her own reading history—one that includes Schopenhauer, Nietzsche, Wittgenstein, Freud, Erikson, Joyce, Lawrence—she finds in it one source of the view that "the men are the ones who matter and that the women exist only in relation to them" (192). Even more painful is her discussion of Virginia Woolf, whom she "revere[s]" and "love[s]," but faults for her representation of the lives of women (40–42). For her, Woolf's imagination of "a violent . . . apocalyptic end of Shakespeare's sister" is astonishing and profound, but it "isn't what happened" because it does not hold true for enough women (41). However possible, Judith Shakespeare is for Mira less probable and therefore less representative. That she holds Woolf accountable for *her* Judith Shakespeare and then goes on to describe an alternate, more mundane fate reveals Mira's readerly dissatisfaction with Woolf. It also marks her preference (for feminism) for writing. Her vantage point as narrator detaches Mira's sympathies from (feminist) reading in order to attach them to the feminist history she is writing. By the end of the novel, Mira the author has displaced reading doubly from her feminist history.

Feminism Closely Reading

Reader, writer, feminist: Mira Ward might have met Kate Millett when in 1968 she began writing the dissertation that eventually became *Sexual Politics*. Like Mira, Millett entered graduate school as second-wave feminism began to make its impact felt, and like Mira, Millett chose the study of literature (at Columbia). From her position as narrator, Mira's literary analyses of Camille and Lily Bart are as furious as Millett's critique of the works of D. H. Lawrence, Henry Miller, and Norman Mailer. And just as Mira finds during her graduate studies a group of feminist-minded women, so too did Millett participate in the Downtown Radical Women, a group she recalls in the introduction to *Sexual Politics*: "I had their support and companionship, their intellectual energy running through me so actively I felt I composed it for all of us, was the scribe of many" (xvii). If these parallels are pleasing, that is because they echo the profound relief women reported about their experience of reading Betty Friedan's *Feminine Mystique*, a text that with *Sexual Politics* and *The Women's Room* forms something of a feminist triangle. These correspondences are powerful because they turn on identification as a structuring principle. And while literary criticism has come to see fictional correspondences like these as proof of aesthetic simplicity or political naiveté, and while *The Women's Room* makes similar judgments, there is something to be learned from them about the identifications that took root in the feminist literary criticism emerging at the moment.[10] For as that discourse gathered steam, steeping itself in textuality in order to expose the workings of literary patriarchy and assert the signatures of female authorship, it turned on a view of reading that mingled personal with textual closeness (or indeed the closeness of the personal with the textual).

Less a codified or deliberate method than a sensibility, this view of reading has one significant beginning in *Sexual Politics*, which augured a form of criticism Millett called "an anomaly, a hybrid, possibly a new mutation altogether" (xx). For Millett, the hybridity of *Sexual Politics* lies in its departures from literary history *and* New Criticism, and in its interest in "the larger cultural context in which literature is conceived and produced" (xx). Yet this broader scope is also sustained by an insistence on the textuality that harbors her own identifications. From the opening chapter to the long "Literary Reflections" section that concludes it, *Sexual Politics* trains its eye on the textual manifestations of sexual politics, building a case that the textual and the political are inseparable. Text by text, scene by scene, Millett's claim that sex means dominion proceeds by accretion: the first chapter accumulates "Instances of Sexual Politics" drawn from *Sexus* (Miller), *An American Dream* (Mailer), and *The Thief's Journal* (Genet) as if in anticipation of the "Theory of Sexual Politics" that follows. Meanwhile her attention sharpens to a point when she pauses on a turn of phrase, or examines at length the impact of one word. In gestures like these, Millett considers, for instance, what she calls "the locution 'muff'" in a scene from *Sexus*: "it is a clue to the reader that the putative humility of the action and the stance of petition it implies are not to be taken at face value. 'Muff' carries the tone, implicit in the whole passage, of one male relating an exploit to another male in the masculine vocabulary and with its point of view" (5). From one word Millett derives action, tone, and dissimulation—all constituting the homosocial address the narrator implies in describing his so-called seduction of his friend's wife. Her analytical move is as aggressive as the narrator's is; she counters his "locution" by unpacking it, and she counters Miller's readerly address with one of her own. As Nancy Miller puts it, the boldness of this gesture lies less in "starting her book in medium coitum with a woman's pubic hair viewed at eye level" and more in her daring to "invoke [*sic*] the existence and reaction of a female reader" (63). For with that invocation, a reference Millett makes about what the female reader knows and what Henry Miller gets wrong (that one rarely wears stockings without garters), she reaches out to the female reader, drawing *her* in to damn the fantasy Miller shares, knowingly or not, with his narrator.

Thus when Millett observes, sidelong, that both Miller and Mailer write themselves into their narrators, she broaches an identification in which she inhabits the act of reading. Unlike French, who invests identification in Mira's writerly self, Millett does not locate her identification with female writers or their protagonists—not for her Woolf, whom she says is "argumentative, yet somehow unsuccessful, perhaps because unconvinced, in conveying the frustrations of the woman artist" (139–140); or Eliot, whose Dorothea "is an eloquent plea that a fine mind be allowed an occupation; but it goes no further than a petition" (139). The figure of the writer/artist, the thinking and expressive woman, appeals, but does not satisfy, and Millett's cursory comments on Mrs. Dalloway, Mrs. Ramsay, Rhoda, Lily Briscoe, and Dorothea, mostly glosses, index her disinterest. But she does devote time to a sustained analysis of Bronte's *Villette* and to Lucy Snowe, who, more than any other character, draws Millett's interest because she approaches the world by watching those around her, men and women both, and the ways in which "men look at women." This last renders Lucy as a figure for Millett, who has in *Sexual Politics* been "studying [*sic*] the image of woman in her culture" (143). Millett regards Lucy in the same readerly terms that she casts her project in *Sexual Politics*, that hybrid in which texts and people intermingle. If her tactics in *Sexual Politics* feature texts in relation to the culture in which they are made, then the intensity with which Lucy studies means that she also understands "the image of woman he [man] would foist on the woman herself" (143). When she goes on to say of Lucy's "most genuine trial" that her world offers "no adequate figures to imitate," Millett makes clear that Lucy's gaze results in disidentification; "having surveyed the lot" (of women), she "prefers to be like none of them" (143). This, too, is Millett's lot. In her survey of the ways in which "men look at women," she finds "no adequate figures to imitate" except for Lucy, to whom Bronte has given the capacity to watch and read.

All this makes sense, intuitively, not institutionally, by the time Sandra Gilbert and Susan Gubar meet in 1973, in an elevator at Indiana University: "We were," Gilbert writes, "two new teachers in the English Department—we'd read Simone de Beauvoir and Betty Friedan, Kate Millett and Gloria Steinem" (Federico loc. 95). In Gilbert's memory of that meeting, and of those that followed as she and Gubar planned a course in "this field that barely existed" (loc. 99), what women knew about the conditions of their lives, and what place literature had in articulating those conditions, was not explicit, but no less felt. That knowledge was present, though, in their shared reading, and became vitally so in the inaugural class that inspired *The Madwoman in the Attic*—and when Gilbert reports on the "click" moments that suffused the class, her turn to align it with CR indexes the sense of closeness that thinking and working together brought to reading. The collaboration that transformed the two young assistant professors into Gilbert and Gubar was already at work in their familiarity with feminism and feminist thought, and would only intensify into consciousness as they launched the team-taught course.[11] It matters, then, when Gilbert looks back—in the foreword to a retrospective essay collection on *Madwoman*—she writes of "ecstasy" to describe not only the experience of teaching and writing in which she and Gubar "were taken out of ourselves," "transported" out of the familiar scripts of profession and life, but also the intense communion of planning the class, teaching it, and turning it into the book. For her emphasis on ecstasy registers the closeness of reading that made *Madwoman* through the intuitive: the two were, Gilbert repeats, struck that what became *Madwoman*, while astonishing in its novelty, still felt like something they had always known.

This is an approach to reading that like Millett's maintained and revised the rather more objective textual closeness prized by New Criticism (in which Gilbert and Gubar were trained).[12] For if the ground upon which the argument of *Madwoman* is based is metaphor, and its action is a careful tracing of the network of metaphors at the heart of the literary tradition it seeks to describe, *Madwoman* takes a distinctly personal view of metaphor and its significance. As early as the preface to the first edition, Gilbert and Gubar begin from the premise that metaphor and experience are mutually constitutive, that where there is experience, there is metaphor (and vice versa), and that that relation informs their critical practice: "Reading metaphors in this experiential way, we have inevitably ended up reading our own lives as well as the texts we study, so that the process of writing this book has been as transformative for us as the process of 'attempting the pen' was for so many of the women we discuss" (xiii).[13] This assertion explains the sense of personal investment that runs throughout *Madwoman*, articulating a line of thinking that echoes the CR account of novel-reading. Just as striking is the place Gilbert and Gubar accord metaphor, which in their hands becomes a figure for (female) subjectivity. Like Millett, for whom even a single locution deserves attention, Gilbert and Gubar understand the reading of texts as careful, meticulous activity—a fact borne out by the host of metaphors with which they describe reading. *Madwoman* is full of figures for reading, ranging from digging, decoding, and unveiling to mapping and resurrecting, as if to emphasize the sheer activity their argument associates with reading.[14] And while these metaphors were themselves not new to the critical imagination, they were fortified by Gilbert and Gubar's insistence that they mattered differently now that they described a feminist reading practice. When they claim for women's texts "palimpsestic subtexts," they offer the parallel personalization that "our mothers' lives" possess "submerged plots," and when they write of *Madwoman* as "a dream of the rising of Christina Rosetti's 'mother country,'" "an attempt at reconstructing the Sibyl's leaves," they signal the work their own reading entails (introduction, 2nd edition xii–xiv; 101–102).

That work, it is worth noting, involves an extrapolation that CR sessions encouraged individual women to make. For in asserting that close readings of Bronte's novel provided them "a paradigm of many distinctively female anxieties and abilities," Gilbert and Gubar articulate an affinity—a conceptual and political one—between conceptualizing Bronte's Bertha as a figure for female artistry and calling on women to know themselves as women (preface, 1st edition xii).[15]

As a feminist figure, Bertha recalls Mira, and *Madwoman*, like *The Women's Room*, displaces reading in favor of writing. If the goal of deriving a feminist poetics depends on reading, a "dissection" that anticipates an eventual "murder" of those angels and monsters that have haunted women, the strategy of feminist reading itself remains instrumental, rather than primary (17). As a result, the arc of *Madwoman* is "the Story of the Woman Writer," with Gilbert and Gubar the "spinners of tales" (Jacobus 517), and however much *Madwoman* acknowledges the impact literary patriarchy has had on women readers, it privileges those readers who responded by writing. By contrast, an emphasis on feminist reading drives Judith Fetterley's *The Resisting Reader* (1978).[16] In a series of analyses of works by Faulkner, Fitzgerald, Hawthorne, Hemingway, Irving, James, and Mailer, Fetterly places readerly experience at the forefront and argues that American literature produces nothing but pain for women readers. For her, the political nature of American literature resides in the way it has compelled women readers to identify with a maleness figured as representative. That this immasculation "burns away" [*sic*] "the merely personal, the purely subjective" creates in the woman reader a "confusion of consciousness" (xi). Bereft of feeling, the woman who reads is left with disidentification, self-division, and even schizophrenia, all psychic states Fetterley defines as reading formations specific to women. This is the insight she turns into a refrain: compelled to read as a man, the woman reads not as herself.

Fetterley objects not to identification, but to its apparently restrictive nature. Much as she damns Hawthorne's Alymer for confining his wife in the prison of his obsession, she damns American literature for confining women readers in its maleness: "Georgiana's situation is a fictional version of the experience that women undergo when they read a story like 'Rip Van Winkle'" (32). And she points to two contemporaries, Lee Edwards and Elaine Showalter, both of whom argue that that dynamic debilitates women students because it gives them no room to think, much less thrive. That she calls immasculation confining suggests something additional, though, something almost prior: that identification entails closeness, here figured as an aggressive occupation of space. Even as she exposes the restrictive maleness of American literature, even as she mourns the toll it exacts on women readers, Fetterley proceeds with the view that in identification, the reader resides in a condition of closeness. Her view thus follows the CR thinking that prized identification for its political potential: to read was to identify was to be close, both proximally and affectively. The feminism of this moment viewed the identification that occurs in reading in terms of the closeness experienced, say, between feminist activists working together, making flyers in preparation for door-to-door conversations. My point is that this principle is also operative in Fetterley's critique of immasculation. She is blunt in saying that for women readers of American literature, identification hurts. Yet her claims about such pain have as their ground a belief that identification *itself* mandates closeness.

Written in a moment when feminism was seeking to create and foster identification among women and women readers, *The Resisting Reader* argues that for women, the pain of American literature is the pain of identification. And more: citing Keats's complaint that poetry exerts a "palpable design" upon readers, Fetterley fingers American literature for hiding, or making "impalpable," its designs (xi). Women readers fail to recognize this design because they cannot feel how it operates even as its impact hits them with each turn of the page. Calling on women readers to intervene, to resist this hailing, Fetterley calls feminist criticism a political act to "to make available to consciousness that which has been left largely unconscious" (xii) and to "change [*sic*] the consciousness of those who read and their relation to what they read" (vii). Meanwhile, her view of literary patriarchy as a "closed system" describes an interiority that emphasizes just how extreme a practice resistant reading must be (xx). That sense of an interior appears again in another familiar statement: "The first act of the feminist critic must be to become a resisting rather than an assenting reader and, by this refusal to assent, to begin the process of exorcizing the male mind that has been implanted in us" (xxii). Given Fetterley's investment in consciousness, it is not surprising to see exorcism as a figure for resistant reading. When literature's possession of women readers ends, their self-possession can emerge. Thus at the moment when Fetterley first describes what the feminist reader must do, she positions reading's relation to literature in language more extreme, more uncanny than anywhere else in the text. In doing so, she has made resistant reading an act of materialization.

The Resisting Reader is no how-to manual detailing the steps by which readers can come to resist those "impalpable" literary designs. Instead, the analyses that follow the introduction perform the consciousness Fetterley has in mind, and the resistant reader remains a construction of her critical imagination. Concern for the reading practices of embodied women emerged with the publication of *Reading the Romance* (1984), in which Janice Radway contended that any assessment of the genre needed to account for the acts of reading that gave it definition. Indeed in its signature interventions—its commitment to following what women did when they read romances and what they wanted from that reading—*Reading the Romance* wrote against the prevailing view that the genre only "perpetuate[d] patriarchal structures and attitudes" ("Women" 54). And in arguing that feminist scholars could not assume that their reading of romances corresponded with the acts of reading in which romance readers participated, Radway reattached reading to the subjectivity of closeness.[17] Methodologically, ethnography brought Radway closer to the scene of reading: to understand what romances were evidence for, or what purposes romances served for their readers. A more strictly textual analysis would miss this scene and the readerly differences that might offer a fresh angle on the production of meaning. Proximity and the openness it made possible—focused on the Smithton women and their reading practices, her understanding of both derived from observations, interviews, and a questionnaire—emerged as feminist values because they engaged more directly women's reading lives. And when she writes about Dorothy Evans, the bookseller the Smithton women had come to consider an expert on the romance genre, and who provided her entrée into the reading community, Radway acknowledges the force of intimate sociability. This was "a group of regular romance readers," she remarks, "clustered about a bookseller" (53). The Smithton women regarded Evans with trust, and that bond, sealed in repeated visits to the chain bookstore, confirms for Radway that for these readers, these interactions constitute what matters about romance as much as the fantasies the narratives offer. In Radway's turn to Evans as an intermediary, moreover, her ethnographic impulse to know a practice through the subjects and their relations with one another becomes especially clear.

Ethnography constituted a better way to understand what function romances served their readers, a question textual analysis answered in terms Radway could no longer believe. In fact, the significance of belief to critical practice became a refrain in the introduction she penned for the second edition of *Reading the Romance*, published in 1991. There the story she tells—of her developing sense that "reading varied spatially and temporally," and that texts come to life through acts of reading—also includes feminist moments that occurred alongside her realizations about reading. In one such instance, she recalls that a feminist CR group during graduate school made her "curious about feminist scholarly writing" and informed her interest in the gothic romance "as a way to engage with this literature" (6). And when she glosses her dissertation, focused on "the differences between popular and elite literature," Radway links it to her desire to "bring together my feminist 'personal' life with my supposedly nongendered academic work which, until that point, had not focused on women" (6). This "decision" becomes the catalyst for the politicization that yields *Romance*: it "set into motion a slow, imperfect, often painful process of transformation that only really gathered steam in the actual writing of *Reading the Romance*" (6). Her language an echo of CR language, Radway articulates the convergence of personal politics with critical practice. From this convergence, she derives answers to her colleagues' questions about literature and, perhaps more importantly, an unexpected identification with the Smithton women, whose act of romance reading she characterizes as a "declaration of independence" (7). Circularity is here productive. For as the "eloquence" of this declaration fuels Radway's identification with the Smithton women, it also generates "a more intense and personal engagement with feminist theory" (6–7).

Retrospection and Close Reading

In 1978, at The Scholar and the Feminist Conference at Barnard, Nancy Miller compared the feminist critique of "men's texts" to the peeling of an artichoke: "I slowly and systematically remove the leaves, cut away the prickly choke, until I arrive at the heart. This patient removal of layers is rewarded by the overdetermined discovery of the core. What could be more gratifying? Once the artichoke is dismantled, you can see what you have, and you can describe it: textual politics" (35). "What could be more gratifying?" Reading as a feminist, "slowly and systematically," with close attention, Miller arrives at the political core. Yet as she goes on to observe, this method works less well on women's texts, which leave her feeling "that my artichoke has turned into an onion" (35). The difference of women's texts, here represented by the onion's absent center, requires "accepting a radical decentering and reorganization of pleasure" (36). But what would that look like? Unhappily, Miller confesses, she has not discovered a metaphor that would describe either women's texts or the kind of reading she believes those texts demand.

Speaking in 1978, at a panel with *Heresies* cofounder Harmony Hammond and poet-playwright Eve Merriam, Miller was also asking, I think, about the kind of closeness women's texts demand. She, like those activists whose print efforts spread the word about feminism, had put her faith in the experience of texts through reading. And she, like other feminist literary critics at the moment, sought out metaphor to capture the difference of women's texts and women's reading. Not for her the New Critical confidence that objective closeness guarantees truth, nor the intellectual immasculation that accompanies that critical posture. Instead, even as Miller admitted that no metaphor had occurred to her, and even if that admission harbored a broader concern about metaphor and its mediations, she held to her belief that sexual difference manifested itself in ways that reading could touch. In this way, her recourse to a classroom scene echoes the balance of this belief, for with it she insists that together, she and her students "had a *close* encounter of the third kind: we all felt that something was out there . . ." (35, emphasis mine). This gesture to an ineffable still within communal reach is so telling as to be uncanny. And that must matter to Miller, because she returns to it when she includes the Barnard talk in *Getting Personal: Feminist Occasions and Other Autobiographical Acts*, a collection of essays written in the more narrative voice that a number of feminist scholars—many of whom came of political age during the second wave—tried on in the 1990s. In the headnote, Miller acknowledges that the piece is "dated," but goes on to locate its value in that temporality, saying that she thinks now that "I'm moving backwards in time to join it" (31). Writing in 1990, by which time the second wave was iconic but distant, she counterposes her nostalgia for the closeness of that moment with the occasion of the present, in which she hopes for a voice for feminist critique that would be readable.

Notes

1. Describing this conflict, Jane Gallop asserts that close reading "has been, for many advocates of diversity, guilty by association" with its history.

2. On this score, it is also worth noting that a good number of the articles in *Sisterhood Is Powerful* originated in the left alternative press as well as the new radical feminist periodicals. See Adams 117.

3. For a summary of the *Ladies Home Journal* sit-in, see Brownmiller 83.

4. Brownmiller reports that *Ms.* even approached Sarachild about writing a book to explain CR (233).

5. The Berkeley paper *It Ain't Me, Babe* offers an interesting case of what I am trying to understand here. Adams rightly observes that the paper, like so many other feminist print ventures of the time, was driven by "the assumption that given the necessary information, women would come to understand and resist their oppression" (120). She goes on to argue that the paper performs its CR work in two ways: on the one hand, in specific features that mention CR groups, and on the other, over time, "accretively" [*sic*]. This latter constitutes the newspaper as "a movable, news-print CR group" (121). In this way, Adams considers what I cam calling the performance of CR, localized here to *It Ain't Me, Babe*.

6. *Quest* itself made this process a topic in the last two issues of its second volume (1976), in which it published a "Report to Readers." In an interview with Brownmiller, Marilyn Webb, founder of *off our backs*, describes a similar "informal hierarchy" in which "jobs were never assigned" (Brownmiller 74).

7. For a quick summary of the views swirling around CR, see Carol Hanisch's "The Personal Is Political."

8. Daughters, Inc. makes an appearance in Elaine Showalter's "Feminist Criticism in the Wilderness" as an example of romantic feminist thinking (201). Describing the press as an attempt at an "Amazonian" utopia, Showalter goes on to cite Lois Gould in *New York Times Magazine*: "They believe they are building the working models for the critical next stage of feminism: full independence from the control and influence of 'male-dominated institution' . . ." (Jan. 1977).

9. Loudermilk and Hogeland cover this ground carefully.

10. Lauret explains, for instance, that Women's Liberation novelists, with their "linear realist first person narratives," faced particular derision thanks to two trends: their so-called excessive emphasis on characters' consciousness (rather than their adventures) and a new tendency in American fiction to elevate the metafictional tendencies and emotional detachment of Pynchon, Mailer, Heller, and Vonnegut.

11. A related instance of the collaborative spirit informing *Madwoman* comes in an anecdote Gilbert recounts in the introduction to the second edition. There she refers to reading the dissertation—with her husband Elliot Gilbert as a reader—that would later become Elaine Showalter's *A Literature of Their Own*. "After the scales had fallen from my eyes on the road to *The Madwoman*," she writes, "I immediately went to the library and began to study the campus copy of her bound and signed thesis" (xxvii–viii).

12. Marlene Tromp writes that *Madwoman* "departed" from the New Critical isolation of the text from the world (loc. 1098), while Susan Fraiman describes the "skeptical close reading" that allowed Gilbert and Gubar "to read from the margins, to pull a stray thread and watch the rest unravel, to dwell on the unintended and unsaid" (loc. 973).

13. Citing Bachelard, de Beauvoir, and Hillis Miller, Gilbert and Gubar call this a phenomenological premise (preface, first edition xii–xiii). My point is to emphasize the feminist possibility in that premise.

14. The contemporary reviews of *Madwoman* reinforced the force of these metaphors. In one moment of her *American Literature* review, Annette Kolodny writes of *Madwoman* that it represents a "skillful joint peeling away of the layers," while in another, she describes how it "quite literally excavates the imputed 'oddity' of women's writing" (129). Meanwhile when Nina Auberach compares *Madwoman* to the feminist literary histories emerging at the moment, she calls Gilbert and Gubar "a sibylline persona, reweaving the threads of a timeless tapestry" (505).

15. Not all readers were convinced by this impulse. In her review for *Victorian Studies*, Nina Auerbach admires its suggestiveness, describing it as "a choric method," but she also reports being disturbed by its "blurring of individual contours" (506).

16. In all fairness, I want to note that Fetterley's work after *The Resisting Reader* has been preoccupied with women writers. She recalls the origin of this shift in plenary remarks at the 2001 meeting of the Society for the Study of American Women Writers, saying that in the aftermath of *The Resisting Reader*, she was considering a sequel, but "had also become interested in the category 'women writers.'"

17. Here Radway refers to the work of Ann Douglas, Tania Modleski, and Ann Snitnow.

Works Cited

Adams, Kay. "Built Out of Books: Lesbian Energy and Feminist Ideology in Alternative Publishing." *Gay and Lesbian Literature Since World War II: History and Memory*. Ed. Sonya L. Jones. Binghamton, NY: The Harrington Park Press, 1998. 113–141. Print.

Auerbach, Nina. Rev. of *The Madwoman in the Attic*, by Sandra Gilbert and Susan Gubar. *Victorian Studies* (Summer 1980): 505–507. Print.

Brownmiller, Susan. *In Our Time: Memoir of a Revolution*. New York: Dell Publishing, 1999. Print.

Bunch, Charlotte. "Building Feminist Theory: The Story of *Quest*." In *Passionate Politics: Feminist Theory in Action*. New York: St. Martin's Press, 1987. 230–239. Print.

———. "Reading and Writing for a Feminist Future." *Passionate Politics*. 217–221. Print.

———. "Women's Publishing: An Interview by Frances Doughty." In *Passionate Politics*. 222–229. Print.

Federico, Annette R., ed. *Gilbert and Gubar's The Madwoman in the Attic after Thirty Years*. Columbia: U of Missouri P, 2009. Digital.

Fetterley, Judith. "Plenary Remarks." *Legacy* 19.1 (2002): 5–9. Digital.

———. *The Resisting Reader: A Feminist Approach to American Fiction*. Bloomington: Indiana UP, 1978. Print.

Firestone, Shulamith. *The Dialectic of Sex*. New York: Farrar, Straus and Giroux, 2003. Print.

———. "When Women Rap about Sex." In *Notes from the First Year*. New York: New York Radical Women, June 1968. 8–11. Duke University Libraries Digital Collections. http://library.duke.edu/digitalcollections/wlmpc_wlmms01037/. Accessed 5 June 2012. Web.

Fraiman, Susan. "After Gilbert and Gubar: Madwomen Inspired by Madwoman." In Federico. Loc. 843–1001. Digital.

Freeman, Jo. "The Women's Liberation Movement: Its Origin, Structures and Ideals." Pittsburgh: KNOW, Inc., 1971. *Duke University Libraries Digital Collections*. http://library.duke.edu/rubenstein/scriptorium/wlm/womlib/. Accessed 5 June 2012. Web.

French, Marilyn. *The Women's Room*. New York: Ballantine Books, 1977 and 1993. Print.

Friedan, Betty. *The Feminine Mystique*. New York: Norton, 2001. Print.

Gallop, Jane. "The Ethics of Reading: Close Encounters." *Journal of Curriculum Theorizing* Fall (2000): 7–17. http://cindykopp.weebly.com/uploads/1/2/9/3/12938517/gallop_2000.pdf. Accessed 15 June 2012. Web.

Gilbert, Sandra. "Conversions of the Mind." Foreword to Federico. Loc. 75–166. Digital.

Gilbert, Sandra, and Susan Gubar. *The Madwoman in the Attic: The Woman Writer and the Nineteenth-Century Literary Imagination, 2nd ed*. New Haven, CT: Yale UP, 2000.

Greer, Germaine. *The Female Eunuch*. New York: Harper Perennial Modern Classics, 2008. Print.

Hanisch, Carol. "The Personal Is Political." 2009. http://www.carolhanisch.org/CHwritings/PIP.html. Accessed 20 April 2013. Web.

Hogeland, Lisa Maria. *Feminism and Its Fictions: The Consciousness-Raising Novel and the Women's Liberation Movement*. Philadelphia: U of Pennsylvania P, 1998. Print.

Jacobus, Mary. Rev. of *The Madwoman in the Attic,* by Sandra Gilbert and Susan Gubar, and *Shakespeare's Sisters: Feminist Essays on Women Poets,* by Sandra Gilbert and Susan Gubar. *Signs* 6.3 (Spring 1981): 517–523. Print.

Kolodny, Annette. Rev. of *The Madwoman in the Attic,* by Sandra Gilbert and Susan Gubar. *American Literature* 52.1 (March 1980): 129. Print.

Lauret, Marie. *Liberating Literature: Feminist Fiction in America.* London: Routledge, 1994. Print.

Loudermilk, Kim. *Fictional Feminism: Representing Feminism in American Bestsellers.* New York: Routledge, 2004. Print.

Miller, Nancy. "Untitled Work, Or, Speaking as a Feminist." *Getting Personal: Feminist Occasions and Other Autobiographical Acts.* New York: Routledge, 1991: 31–37. Print.

Millett, Kate. *Sexual Politics*. Urbana: U of Illinois P, 1990. Print.

Morgan, Robin. *Sisterhood Is Powerful: An Anthology of Writings from the Women's Liberation Movement.* New York: Vintage Books, 1970. Print.

Radway, Janice. *Reading the Romance: Women, Patriarchy, and Popular Culture*. Chapel Hill: U of North Carolina P, 1984 and 1991. Print.

———. "Women Read the Romance: The Interaction between Text and Context." *Feminist Studies* 9.1 (Spring 1983): 53–78. Print.

Redstockings. Redstockings Manifesto. 7 July 1969. *Redstockings*. http://www.redstockings.org/index.php?option=com_content&view=article&id=76&Itemid=59. Accessed 5 June 2013. Web.

Sarachild, Kathie (Amatniek). "A Program for Feminist Consciousness-Raising." In *Notes from the Second Year*. Ed. Shulamith Firestone and Anne Koedt. New York: Women's Liberation Movement, 1968. 78–80. http://library.duke.edu/digitalcollections/wlmpc_wlmms01039/. Accessed 20 April 2013. Web.

Steinem, Gloria. *Revolution from Within: A Book of Self Esteem*. New York: Little, Brown, and Company. 1993. Print.

Tromp, Marlene. "Modeling the Madwoman: Feminist Movements and the Academy." In Federico. Loc. 1002–1657. Digital.

Part II

Chapter 5

"The Element That Shaped Me, That I Shape by Being In"

Alternative Natures in Margaret Atwood's *Surfacing* and *The Edible Woman*

Jill E. Anderson

> Man seeks the Other in woman as Nature and as his peer. But Nature inspires ambivalent feelings in man, as has been seen . . . Both ally and enemy, it appears in the dark chaos from which life springs forth, at this very life, and as the beyond it reaches for: woman embodies nature as Mother, Spouse, and Idea; these figures are sometimes confounded and sometimes in opposition, and each has a double face.
>
> —Simone de Beauvoir, *The Second Sex* 1949

The title of this chapter is an excerpt from an unnamed poem in Margaret Atwood's 1971 collection, *Power Politics*. The collection is made up almost entirely of poems written in the second person, singular and plural, allowing Atwood to explore the relationship between her female narrator and her male counterpart, forming the "power politics" of the collection's title. This particular poem is from an unusual first-person singular perspective, and the children the narrator "intended" are the only others in it (41). The children could be human or they could be the "foxes and strawberries" and "fur seeds & burrows" that the narrator attempts to give a space in her garden to. The children are made ambiguous, not clearly human, and the narrator plays with an accepted, naturalized perception of woman as distinctly maternal and inherently connected to the natural world. The narrator's relationship with nature is fraught, and she eventually drowns in the "element that shaped/me, that I shape by/being in." Thus, the narrator articulates a position of simultaneous disempowerment and vulnerability as well as capacity and potential. In her immersion in water, she shapes and is shaped by, is manipulated as well as manipulator. Her embodiment is multifaceted, subject both to the social and natural environment and to her own inclinations.

As a feminist poet and novelist, Atwood challenges the accepted social conventions of what is considered "natural." She contests the conventions placed upon and absorbed by women, refiguring naturalness to outline trajectories attached to women's victimhood and individual license. Atwood claims she read two classics of second-wave feminism—Betty Friedan's *The Feminine Mystique* (1963) and Simone de Beauvoir's *The Second Sex* (1949)—"behind closed doors."[1] These covert readings might seem contradictory to the feminist purpose of consciousness-raising, but it was apparently an important step in the construction of Atwood's vision. The consciousness-raising novel, as Lisa Maria Hogeland explains, fused the personal with the political (as the mantra of second-wave feminism goes) by implementing "a transaction between character, author, and reader" and by being "testimony to the absent member" (24). The consciousness-raising of the female protagonists in Atwood's first two novels—Marian in *The Edible Woman* (1969) and the unnamed "Surfacer" in *Surfacing* (1971)—takes the form of a critical engagement with their private situations that gets projected onto larger, political discourses.[2] Marian and Surfacer imagine and enact narratives that examine how nature can and should function within a feminist liberatory politics.

In this chapter, I argue that a fully feminist reading of these two novels must address how each contributes to the emerging discourse of queer ecology and to its examination of naturalization, or the process by which various behaviors, ideals, and conventions are accepted and legitimated, often to the detriment of their subjects. I employ the terms *naturalized* and *natural* in two distinct ways. First, I use them as a means of identifying dictates and expectations that have shaped women and caused their oppression throughout specific historical periods. Elements that are assumed to be "natural" for women and that are often used against them in order to subjugate and disempower them are elements that have been "naturalized." That is, that term *natural* has been applied to many practices, behaviors, and lifeways (i.e., the most commonly invoked notion about naturalization is the idea that homosexuality is "against nature" or that women's "natural" state is one of chaos and disorderliness) in order to cast them outside of social sanction. Second, I use them to indicate the method by which

Atwood reverses this primary process of naturalization in order to redefine the terms and construct feminist rebellion and consciousness-raising in the novels. Marian and Surfacer rebel against their prescribed roles by rethinking the way nature is used to imprison them and how it can, instead, transform to liberate them. While withdrawing from social expectations and conventions, Marian and Surfacer are empowered to create their own narratives that inscribe a new form of the natural.[3]

One way this new form is enacted is by an amorphous embodiment that emerges as the women react to environments and construct oppositional identities to answer to codes of naturalization. Dynamic change or reshaping—whether forced, voluntary, or a combination of both—is essential to Atwood's feminist vision because it signals the rejection of womanhoods and femininities that have relied on the twofold dominance of women and the natural world. Here I call on E. L. McCallum and Mikko Tukhanen's concept of queer becoming (which is a play on Delueze and Guattari's rhizomatic becoming), because they articulate situations outside corporeal or societal directives that normalize meanings of the natural. Female bodies in both novels undertake and endure changes, fluctuations, reactions, renderings, and becomings that correlate with how each character imagines naturalness in their particular environment. These becomings, however, are not always affirmative or even fully feminist in the strictest sense; they necessarily illustrate the discursive possibilities of disrupting the damage done by cultural definitions of nature. Becoming also envisions, as McCallum and Tukhanen explain, a "rethinking of the modes of temporality queers inhabit . . . for the essence of the performative . . . is the interplay between texts in context, subject and environments, language and meaning" (12). I find the mention of interplay particularly valuable because it illustrates how this concept of a queer becoming can be adapted to fit a feminist project of creating alternative narratives. But I do not wish to suggest that Atwood's vision of queer ecocritical feminist empowerment merely reverses conventional thought; rather, *The Edible Woman* and *Surfacing* work together to articulate a matrix of imaginative recourse, an always evolving practice for the feminist characters that rearticulates cultural assumptions about naturalness.

This evolving practice can only be carried so far. With all the rejection and rewriting of narratives, the two protagonists are finally unable to fully recast their roles and separate out a more "natural" version of themselves. Doing so would run the risk not only of establishing a value-based system in which that natural is more prized than the socially constructed is, but also of reinforcing the idea these are two poles that can and should be separate from each other. Theorists such as Val Plumwood, Simone de Beauvoir, Judith Butler, and Eve

Kofosky Sedgwick have extensively examined the destructive and dangerous dualisms (or "symmetrical binary oppositions," per Sedgwick) that subsume women, nature, and queers. Greta Gaard points out that a major contradiction in these binaries rests on the idea that "on the one hand, from a queer perspective, we learn that dominant culture charges queers with transgressing the natural order, which in turn implies that nature is valued and must be obeyed," while simultaneously seeing "nature as a force that must be dominated if culture is to prevail" (27).The coalition built between queer theory and feminist theory is essential, then, because it articulates just such an alternative to the dualistic thought against which liberatory feminist theory protests.

My readings of both *Surfacing* and *The Edible Woman* pronounce Marian and Surfacer fully realized feminist characters in the sense that they acknowledge their imagined alternatives and their liberatory practices as limited because of their lived experiences. Ultimately, they are encapsulated within their realities and unable to escape the dualistic judgments that shape their relationships to the world.[4] Even in her effort to overturn naturalization, Atwood must finally transmit her characters back to where they "belong." Social realities are inescapable. Duncan, Marian's graduate student friend in *The Edible Woman*, gives us an appropriate metaphor to consider: "Once I went to the zoo and there was a cage with a frenzied armadillo in it going around in figure-eights, just around and around in the same path. . . . They say all caged animals get that way when they're caged, it's a form of psychosis, and even if you set the animals free after they go like that they'll just run around in the same pattern" (101). That is, even after given the possibility of liberty, the animal merely repeats the pattern to which he has become accustomed. While it could be argued the inevitability of this restriction limits their experiences and might also limit their feminist realizations, in the context of conscious-raising, I would argue perhaps it is enough to know and recognize one's limitations. Marian and Surfacer might not experience the revolutionary psychic and physical breakouts we as feminist readers desire, but working within the limitations set before them, small victories and realizations might have to stand for liberation.

The Edible Woman

The Edible Woman centers on Marian, a recent college graduate who works at Seymour Surveys editing consumer questionnaires. After getting engaged to Peter, a young lawyer, she starts to undergo a transformation: she gets strange urges to run away from Peter and she stops eating almost entirely, until she bakes and eats the titular cake at the end of the novel. The genesis of *The Edible*

Woman and Marian's apparent anorexia result from a combination of factors, as Elspeth Cameron points out—Atwood's observation of a high school classmate taking diet pills to lose weight; the "social realism" of the "Age of Girdles" that Atwood saw occurring around her; the cake decorating craze in the early 1960s, which saw people making cakes into strange and impossible shapes; and the idea of "woman as a kind of confection" meant to be "devoured by men" (Cameron 45–46). Marian sees advertisements for girdles and thinks, "The female form . . . is supposed to appeal to men, not to women, and men don't usually buy girdles. Though perhaps the lithe young woman was a self-image; perhaps the purchasers thought of their own youth and slenderness back in the package" (Cameron 98). That being said, the novel's roots are deep in political discourse. All the markers of "natural" and "normal" female behavior are bound up for Marian in images and metaphors of entrapment and predation or consumption, absorption, and dissipation.

Marian's becoming begins as a reaction to her impending marriage and what she sees as the expected role for women, reinforced by how the shape of women's bodies is understood. Marian begins to reject food as a way of controlling her body. If she does not eat, she cannot maintain the curves and bumps that render her female. As countless feminist scholars have articulated, women's embodied experiences are essential to understanding the subjugation of women. In her pivotal work *Volatile Bodies,* theorist Elizabeth Grosz explains that the "(pseudo) biological terms" women experience because of patriarchal oppression arrive through "essentialism, naturalism and biologism" so that "misogynist thought confines women to the biological requirements of reproduction on the assumption that because of particular biological, physiological, and endocrinological transformations, women are somehow *more* biological, *more* corporeal, and *more* natural than men"(14, emphases in original). The "pseudobiological" Grosz invokes is related to the idea that women's lives are ruled by their reproductive and bodily innateness. Atwood challenges constructs of the physical body, particularly how bodies attain shape and cultural meaning through their associations with naturalized gender expectations. These expectations often link women with a natural world that needs to and should be controlled, conquered with social conventions that inhibit and regulate women.

In *The Edible Woman,* women's bodies are messy, in constant flux, and subject to absorption and expulsion. These fluctuations signify for Marian the essentially feminine, the female body in its most natural state. These bodily becomings are not empowering, however, because they arrive from outside influences while Marian is undergoing her transformation, as she is lashing out against her impending marriage and the type of woman her fiancée expects her to be. In a key passage, Marian is surrounded by the other women from the Seymour Surveys at a holiday party:

> She examined the women's bodies with interest, critically, as though she had never seen them before. And in a way she hadn't, they had just been there like everything else, desks, telephones, chairs, in the space of the office: objects viewed as outline and surface only. . . . and the others too, similar in structure but with varying proportion and textures of bumpy permanents and dune-like contours of breast and waist and hip; their fluidity sustained within by bones, without by a carapace of clothing and makeup. What peculiar creatures they were; and the continual flux between the outside and the inside, taking things in, giving them out, chewing, words, potato-chips, burps, grease, hair, babies, milk, excrement, cookies, vomit, coffee, tomato juice, blood, tea, sweat, liquor, tears, and garbage . . . (181)

Observing the women's bodies separate from the office furniture disorients Marian; just as she begins to feel the restriction of her impending marriage, she fixes her gaze upon female bodies more critically. And it is not just their bodily functions Marian finds disturbing, but also the accouterments of being a woman—corsets, makeup, and clothing. Her reaction to being "suffocated by this sargasso-sea of femininity" is to desire "something solid, clear: a man, she wanted Peter in the room so that she could put her hand out and hold on to him to keep from being sucked down" (181). She seems, at this moment, to buy into culturally inscribed anxieties about the natural chaos and instability of the female body. She fears losing control of her own becoming even as she fears stability, fears becoming "inert," a word used throughout the novel. She rejects both of these inhibiting versions of "femininity."

Marian's refusal to eat, a refusal that oscillates between being deliberate and involuntary, is her way of controlling the fluidity and shape of femininity which alarms her. To refuse to be fattened up is to refuse the subjugation that reinscribes gender roles. It is significant, then, that her inability to eat begins with animal products, as she comes to identify with animals that are forcibly being sliced apart, used, and consumed. For example, on a date with Peter, she watches him "operate" on a steak and is reminded "of the diagram of a planned cow at the front of one of her cookbooks: the cow with lines on it and labels to show you from which part of the cow all the different cuts were taken. . . . It stood there quite naturally, not at all disturbed by the markings on its hide" (163–164). She worries that one day scientists will able to breed animals "so that they're born already ruled and measured," causing her to empathize with the other-than-human world and align herself with cattle, raised and killed purely for the pleasure of man. It is a move that invokes a "cycle of objectification, fragmentation and consumption, which links butchering and sexual violence in our culture" (Adams 47). Her attempt to justify eating her own steak fails: "Everyone eats cows, it's natural; you have to eat to stay alive, meat is good for you, it has lots of proteins and minerals" (164). The appeal to natural human behavior does not work for Marian because she is already actively rejecting it. She grows increasingly aware of the subjugation of the surrounding environment and the pseudobiological terms that work to control women as well as animals, turning them into *only* bodies.

Consequently, pregnancy is fraught in this novel because it changes the physical shape of a woman's body and creates the illusion of severing the mind from the body; culturally, this dangerous divide magnifies the idea that woman are "more biological, more natural" than men are. When Marian's roommate, Ainsley, declares pregnancy liberating and a symbol of "true womanhood," she replicates the accepted social convention constructing woman as mere child-bearer and reinforcing the notion of the child as somehow more than the woman who bears it. As Ainsley *chooses* her pregnancy and carefully plans its fulfillment because it "fulfills your deepest femininity" and seemingly avoids "either/or" in favor of "wholeness," she is invoking the most capacious version of womanhood she can envision (39). She invokes the "Creative Life Force," and, as Sofia Sanchez-Grant points outs, "She *is* performing her maternal destiny, though in all her 'naturalness' the pregnant woman must remain within culturally-defined boundaries" (83). In her frenzied attempts to possess power over her own body, Ainsley constructs a chaotic and ambiguous sort of becoming that relies on her biological functioning as much as her intellectual operations. Ainsley, then, represents one way that an alternate becoming can be destructive for a feminist vision.

Ainsley's "natural selection," which could be interpreted as an empowered attempt at ruling her own biology, involves carefully choosing and pursuing the father of her child, Len. She justifies this by explaining, like a true eugenicist, "We know the human race is degenerating and it's all because people pass on their weak genes without thinking about it, and medical science means they aren't naturally selected out the way they used to be" (41). She combines the socially sanctioned image of the sexually innocent woman, dressing herself as a doll-like child, with calculated "inert patience," that "of a pitcher-plant in a swamp with its hollow bulbous leaves half-filled with water, waiting for some insect to be attracted, drowned, and digested" (78). Later, she accuses Len of "uterus envy" when he rejects their unborn child, but she buys into pop psychology that says a male child with too much coddling from his mother will be "ho-ho-ho-homosexual," as Ainsley laments. She states finally that she does not need a man to complete her family and or her life, but ultimately takes on Fischer, Duncan's roommate, as her partner. Ainsley's attitude toward pregnancy reflects how its biological functions have been so acutely normalized and absorbed that both women assume pregnancy is the most deeply natural thing a woman can experience.

While Ainsley appears to choose her position in the world, Marian's friend Clara sees herself as living in "a kind of exile" as she and her growing family reach toward "the real suburbia of modern bungalows and station-wagons" (27). Her home is a jumble of "scattered obstacles," the signifiers of family life and consumption gone awry: "We negotiated the stairs of the back porch, which were overgrown with empty bottles of all kinds, beer bottles, milk bottles, wine and scotch bottles, and baby bottles" (27). Her pregnancies signify all that is restrictive to women and their individuality, while her children are troubling, perverse, and unruly. The constantly pregnant Clara is a state of "inertia" in which she is reminded of her "lack of room and time, her days made claustrophobic with small necessary details" (29). The use of *inertia* for all three women's situations is important. In a novel where imaginative recourse relies on a fluid becoming, to be inert suggests passivity and an inability to change. Marian labels Clara "vegetative" with a "grim and inert fatalism" (33). Tellingly, Marian "had tended to forget that Clara had a mind at all or any perceptive faculties above the merely sentient and sponge-like, since she had spent most of her time being absorbed in, or absorbed by her tuberous abdomen" (140). To Marian, Clara is a "queen ant, bulging with the burden of an entire society, a semi-person—or sometimes, she thought, several people, a cluster of hidden personalities that she didn't know at all," a woman so absorbed by and involved in her own "nature" and socially mandated role of mother that she loses her selfhood (122). Clara's life happens *to* and around her, and she describes her children and pregnancies as parasitic and perverse—leeches, an octopus "all covered with suckers," barnacles, "galls on a tree," a "huge bunion," a "stinking little geyser." The fact that she is educated means she is doubly aware of her biological subjugation, according to her husband, Joe: "I think it's harder for any woman who's been to university. She gets the idea that she has a mind, her professors pay attention to what she has to say, they treat her like a human being; when she gets married, her core gets invaded . . . The centre of her personality, the thing she's built up; her image of herself, if you like" (259). Clearly, Joe and Clara reinforce the mind/body, culture/nature division and the idea that woman overcome by her biological renderings cannot function intellectually.

Marian, then, comes to equate pregnancy, marriage, and the consumerism of suburban family life with danger to her own selfhood. They lead to a static and confined identity. Taking the shape of a real woman threatens to bring on the inertness from which both Clara and Ainsley suffer. So Marian rejects the "time of reproduction" or "repro-time," which is "ruled by the biological clock for women and by strict bourgeois rules of respectability and scheduling for married couples" (Halberstam 5).[5] Any attempt to break from this pattern of repro-time entails a concomitant rejection of consumerism, waste, and practices destructive of the natural world; it rejects the by-products of middle-class family life, with their link to environmental degradation.

This rejection of repro-time plays into the way Marian encounters her environment. Even as she flees marriage and spurns the biological implications of her female body, she is oppressed by the hazy pollutedness of her environment. Modern Toronto is a dusty and hot city, and walking around in it is "almost like moving underwater" (26). Duncan says it is like "being in a fishbowl full of dying pollywogs" (285). When Duncan takes Marian to his favorite place in the city (in fact, they escape to it, as he says), it turns out to be a "field of tall weed-stalks whose stiff dried branches scraped against them as they passed: goldenrod, teazles, burdocks, the skeletons of anonymous grey plants" (287). Everything is "so thick with green leaves and stuff you can't see three feet in front of you" (288). The place is also a refuge for the winos: "They're beginning to fill this place up with junk too, you know," laments Duncan, "beginning with the creek, I wonder why they like throwing things around all over the landscape . . . old tires, tins cans" (288). Duncan, in his role as "changeling," offers Marian insights into how the natural world creates a discourse with the human body and waste, or with the endless cycle of "production-consumption," as he calls it: "You begin to wonder whether it isn't just a question of making one kind of garbage into another kind. The human mind is the last thing to be commercialized but they're doing a good job of it now; what is the difference between library stacks and one of those used-car graveyards?" (155). He goes on to describe his home, a denuded mining town. The thing he likes about it, he says, is that "there isn't much of anything in it but at least it has no vegetation. A lot of people wouldn't like it. It's the smelting plants that do it, tall smokestacks reaching up into the sky and the smoke glows red at night, and the chemical fumes have burnt the trees for miles around, it's barren, nothing but the barren rock, even grass won't grow on most of it, and there are the slag-heaps too; where the water collects on the rock it's a yellowish-brown from the chemicals" (155). Duncan sees the paradigm of progress as clearly tied to destruction. Consequently, his invocation of commercialization, barrenness, and waste only contributes to Marian's growing anxiety. This sort of progress is the same force that equates women and nature and encourages productivity and accumulation at the cost of individual freedoms. Duncan explains that the complete stripping of what could be considered the natural environment in his hometown is the logical end to the narrative of progress. Interestingly, though, his hometown is just another environment in the novel, an environment that better reflects Marian's becoming at this point in the narrative. She, too, is "barren" in the sense that she has closed herself off to the imaginative possibility of becoming a mother. It is with Duncan, though, that Marian is able to express her fears and gesture toward more liberatory practices. While some critics have suggested that Duncan is actually just another aspect of Marian's subconscious, I would argue that their interactions signal the *start* of Marian's feminist realizations.

Surfacing

Unlike Marian, Surfacer does not close herself off to the possibility of becoming a mother. Surfacer turns the association between women and nature to her own purposes, reclaiming the landscape as a form of becoming that can release her from the restrictive gender roles to which she has been forced to adhere. She begins the novel in a position of subjugation but takes on elements of the natural world in order to wield control over both herself and her environment, a control that eventually drives off the destructive elements that would thwart her; hers is the opposite of the trajectory of Marian's interplay with her environment.

The novel follows Surfacer as she takes two friends, David and Anna, and boyfriend, Joe, on a journey from the city to her parents' isolated home in the French Canadian bush. She is attempting to discover what became of her missing father while she grapples with several personal issues, including a marriage that has fallen apart, a forced abortion, an unwanted child, and another rocky relationship. While in the untamed Canadian bush, Surfacer transforms the "natural" process of subjugation women and nature experience, "defined as passive, as non-agent and non subject, as the 'environment' or invisible background conditions against which the 'foreground' achievements of reason or culture take place" (Plumwood 4). Surfacer's becoming takes her from being an introspective and deliberate illustrator of children's books to recognizing the "natural domination" of women, to a near complete rejecting of human-centered society as she is absorbed into the wild landscape around her. In her article about the Surfacer's internalization of landscape in the novel, Danielle Schaub argues that "she controls otherness, refusing societal norms of identity definition, preferring to respect the land and to become one with its spirit" (92–93). Stories about landscape and female subjectivity "delineate not so much the physical landscape as its integrative interaction with an internal geography; in such novels, landscape symbolizes the female geographical imagination" (85). Surfacer embraces the physical landscape in her becomings. Her imaginative transformation incorporates both her corporeal reshaping and her reexamining of the environment around her.

The natural, then, undergoes a transformation in the novel from the "natural domination" of Plumwood's explanation, with its connections to cultural constructions of gender, to Surfacer's use of the environment surrounding her as a source of power to cast off those constructions, to reject her previous naturalization.[6] This natural domination is what Surfacer comes to feel at the hands of her husband and from the demands of reproduction and family. She reflects that her own parents were disappointed when she left her husband and child, her "attractive full-color magazine illustration, suitable for framing" (25). Magazine clips are referenced again when Surfacer finds the scrapbooks from her childhood featuring illustrations of "proper" kinds of women—keeping house or wearing high heels—whose bodies she has tellingly cut out. A lady, she reflects, was "what you said at school when they asked you what you were going to be when you grew up . . . you said 'A lady' or 'A mother,' either one was safe" (91). The "safety" of these categories reflects their viability as social functions. Claiming either or both is the same as claiming one's naturalized gender role. Surfacer's friend Anna, who has bought into these gender roles, makes herself up every morning because her husband expects it. She is a "pair of boobs" to be abused, verbally and physically, by both Joe and David, a passive victim of sexism and patriarchy. She is, to invoke the magazine illustration motif again, "a seamed and folded imitation of a magazine picture that is itself an imitation of a woman who is also an imitation, the original nowhere, hairless lobed angel in the same heaven where God is a circle, captive princess in someone's head" (169). Anna is all artifice and emptiness to Surfacer, a pure incarnation of all that is considered natural for a woman in contemporary culture.

Surfacing's critique of pregnancy, as in *The Edible Woman*, involves how naturalized biological functions are used against women, but, unlike Ainsley, Surfacer claims that reproduction can and must be recognized by women inside a realm of the natural that pointedly excludes patriarchy and the construction of family life. Thus, *Surfacing*'s use of nature and naturalization differs from Atwood's first novel in that it carries becoming into another practice: while Marian sees the fluctuation of the female body as a source of control over both the woman and the environment, Surfacer takes that control and shapes her involvement in a deep embrace of the material natural world.

This novel has a more clearly defined ecocritical message, as Surfacer is continually horrified by the environmentally destructive actions and attitudes of others. But that ecocritical message is coupled with a critique of socially imposed gender roles. Surfacer's three pregnancies—one culminating in a forced abortion, one imposed upon her by her husband, and the final deliberately begotten in an effort to reclaim her essential naturalness—build toward Surfacer's famous and oft-quoted declaration: "This above all, to refuse to be a victim. Unless I can do that I can do nothing. I have to recant, give up the old belief that I am powerless . . . withdrawing is no longer possible and the alternative is death" (197).

Her revulsion of the ways of "Americans"—an all-encompassing label she uses to describe people who destroy the natural environment for their own profit—is aligned with her recognition of her own victimhood at the hands of restrictive social roles. Cinda Gault explains that Surfacer's illegal and forced abortion is an example of how national politics often control and suppress the female body. Gault explains, "In a society where women have sexual and reproductive autonomy, this protagonist would not have had to face such a distinction [of being a criminal]. Without discounting the controversy attached to medical and moral concerns of human intervention in the natural world, the protagonist's relationship to her own reproductive capacity would exist outside national moral hierarchy" (17). According to Gault, Surfacer is doubly damned and subjugated after her abortion; she is a criminal because her actions are illegal, but whether or not her actions are voluntary seems to matter little since she has no control over her own body or sexuality.

It should not be surprising, then, that the abortion represents Surfacer's breaking point as well as the revelatory imperative that sets her becoming into motion. Patriarchy, in the form of the medical profession and the government, forces her to finally recognize that she is playing within the safety of the roles of wife and mother. The still-living child produced of her marriage, then, is an imposition: "I never identified it as mine; I didn't name it before it was born even, the way you're supposed to. It was my husband's, he imposed it on me, all the time it was growing in me I felt like an incubator. He measured everything he would let me eat, he was feeding it on me, he wanted a replica of himself; after it was born I was no more use" (30). Like Clara in *The Edible Woman,* Surfacer feels she is a vessel whose only function is to divorce her mind from her body and to reproduce.

Pregnancy, the emblem of naturalized, true womanhood, is clearly an agent of patriarchy here. Surfacer sees childbirth itself as another instance of women being stripped of their power: "After the first I didn't ever want to have another child, it was too much to go through for nothing, they shut you in a hospital, they shave the hair off you and tie your hands down and they don't let you see, they don't want you to understand, they want you to believe it's their power, not yours. They stick needles into you so you won't hear anything, you might as well be a dead pig, your legs up in a metal frame, they bend over you, technicians, mechanics, butchers, students clumsy and snickering practicing on your body, they take the baby out with a fork like a pickle out of a pickle jar. After that they fill your veins up with red plastic, I saw it running down through the tube" (79). The clear split between Surfacer and an uncaring "they," as well as the invocation of penetration, deletion, binding, and butchering (reminiscent of Marian's fears) work to dehumanize women even as they fulfill their supposedly natural roles as baby-makers. There is nothing natural about this hospital scene. Plastics, metals, and technicians collude to entrap the shaved and defeated woman. Keeping women ignorant of their own strength is also essential in this equation. Surfacer reveals that these forms of control over women's bodies are intimately bound up in what is described as natural about them.

Her empathy with animals is particularly telling of this position of victimhood. Surfacer is shaped by the environmental degradation and violence she sees occurring around her parents' home. Identifying with the decaying body of a murdered heron that the foursome finds hanging by its feet from a tree, she realizes it was killed "to prove they could do it, they had the power to kill" (118). She classifies it as "food, slave, or corpse, limited choices," a true victim like herself. The association between subjugation and consumption turns Surfacer against certain foods, particularly foods she must kill and process herself: "Thud of metal on fishbone, skull neckless headbody, the fish is whole, I couldn't anymore, I had no right to" (121). Questions about Surfacer's sexuality are also bound up in the idea that she is somehow "inhuman." When she refuses to have sex with David, he flippantly explains, "She hates men . . . either that or she wants to be one" (155). The accusation of lesbianism leads Surfacer into a musing in which all men, or "the Americans, the human beings, men and women both" are eliminated by "a machine that could make them vanish, a button I could press that would evaporate them without disturbing anything else, that way there would be more room for the animals, they would be rescued" (155). Later, she imagines her child, the one she deliberately produces with Joe, as the answer to and replacement for her aborted child, as an animal born of a pure experience of childbirth, the opposite of her first: "This time I will do it by myself, squatting, on old newspapers in a corner alone; or on leaves, dry leaves, a heap of them, that's cleaner. The baby will slip out easily as an egg, a kitten, and I'll lick it off and bite the cord, the blood returning to the ground where it belongs; the moon will be full, pulling, in the morning I will be able to see it: it will be covered with shining fur, a god, I will never teach it any words" (165). This recovery from victimhood, however, requires for Surfacer (and her imagined child) a withdrawal from "evil," or from all of the human constructs that have served to subjugate woman- or animal-kind.

Described by some critics as a descent into madness, Surfacer's transformation toward the end of the novel is actually a deliberate and discernible becoming into a metaphorical body and space that is more sustainable for her vision of naturalness. As the "plant-animal" she carries grows inside, her body undergoes a physical and imaginative change. She loses her name, that marker of humanness, and replaces herself with "a place": "I lean against a tree, I am a tree leaning. . . . I am not an animal or a tree, I am the thing in which trees and animals move and grow" (187). She flees from her friends and rejects anything human-made, from the trail through the woods cleared by human hands to food that is "forbidden," put into cans. In her other-than-human form, she sees herself as a "new kind of centerfold": "They would never believe it's only a natural woman, state of nature, they think of that as a tanned body on a beach with washed hair waving like scarves; not this, face dirt-caked and streaked, skin grimed and scabby, hair like a frayed bathmat stuck with leaves and twigs" (196). Surfacer's version of the "natural woman" is a response to the body of an idealized centerfold. She reimagines beauty and sex appeal as deeply connected to living outside, both literally and metaphorically.

But these visions of becoming and their rejection of the naturalized versions of womanhood can be carried only so far. Hogeland also argues that the consciousness-raising novel asks readers to "envision what happens after the novel, by asking us to participate, through our own newly-raised consciousness, in creating their unfinished futures" (44). Ultimately, the futures of both Marian and Surfacer entail becoming penned in by the reality of their lives, the parameters of their experience. In the famous conclusion of *The Edible Woman,* Marian carefully constructs and eats a sponge cake shaped like a woman but realizes that "as a symbol it has definitely failed" (300). As she returns in the third section of the novel to "thinking of myself in the first person singular again," she also returns to eating and to Duncan. "What does it matter, you're back to so-called reality, you're a consumer," he concludes as they share the cake she has baked (309). Surfacer's fate is a little more doubtful, although after Joe and the others have gone away from the island and left her to her natural state, she realizes that her isolation cannot last. She simply does not know how to live off the land, and the "Americans" will continue to encroach on the environment. Because "no firm recipe for an ideal process of individuation is offered," as Schaub indicates, Surfacer "proves to be a product of her upbringing, inescapably cultured" (92).

I would also argue that their final becomings, their last attempts to convert and reformulate their own internalized, naturalized elements, leave them both looking back toward what they had attempted to escape in the first place. Surely, one could read these imagined alternatives as *enough* empowerment in themselves. Even though in the end both characters have enacted rebellions—Marian attempts to throw off Peter by constructing and eating the woman-shaped cake, and Surfacer carries the child of her choosing alone in the Canadian bush—each must accept the limitations of their alternatives. To try to discard systems that invoke the natural is to simultaneously acknowledge one's victimhood at the hands of these systems. Or, as Elizabeth Grosz argues, "In short, we need to understand the body, not as an organism or entity in itself, but as a system, or series of open-ended systems, functioning within other huge systems it cannot control, through which it can access and acquire its abilities and capacities" (*Nick of Time* 3). The female body and all that is bound up with it—nature and systems of naturalization, along with feminist practices—should be considered within a scope of lived experience. Surfacer and Marian cannot discard their bodies just as they cannot completely cast off the discursive outcomes of naturalization. They can only imagine alternatives and seek embodiments that signal their fluidity and adaptability.

Notes

1. The assertion shapes the view that *The Edible Woman* is a refiguring of Friedan's thematic issues. Coral Ann Howells examines Marian's response to the restrictive social roles in 1960s Toronto through Friedan's study, explaining the novel "is an imaginative transformation of a social problem into comic satire as one young woman rebels against her feminine destiny" (*Margaret Atwood* 20–21). Howells further asserts *The Edible Woman* fits into a specific historical moment, namely early second-wave feminism, "in its resistance to social myths of femininity," but it is ultimately about one woman's failed rebellion (20). The novel circles around, Howells explains, keeping women within their prescribed gender roles, making babies and cakes and "leaves unresolved the issue of women's attempts to establish themselves as independent subjects" (35).

2. While some of the general themes in both novels relate to Atwood's critique of the roles that the privileged and empowered classes inscribed upon women's bodies and identities, critics tend to separate the two novels along political lines. Fiona Tolan's feminist readings of Atwood's work articulate this stance, as she sees *The Edible Woman* as an introductory "dialogue with feminism," while *Surfacing* expands on that as well as "introduces issues of ecology, nationalism, spirituality, and ancestry to Atwood's canon of political focus" (35). Ellen McWilliams calls upon the conventions of the *bildungsroman* to explore "the splitting and unraveling of identity" in *The Edible Woman,* a move that

allows her to explore the "systematic revolts against the dismal choices open to" Marian (89, 76). She also separates out *Surfacing's* nationalistic tone as a way of examining how "the interior voyage of the unnamed narrator is conflated with the search for a meaningful national identity" (61). Both critics invoke a pointed engagement with the political climate of the late 1960s and early 1970s, linking the characters' private struggles with a very public debate over the role of women.

3. Stacy Alaimo's insistence that "no central metaphor, concept, or narrative could rein in the diverse, contradictory, but often overlapping ways in which North American women have written themselves into, out of, and through nature" is apt here (*Undomesticated Ground* 21). Her work on the refashioning of natural spaces as feminist explores the idea that "feminist conceptions of nature do not stand outside of dominant cultural views; they stage dialogues, protests, and contests with the meaning of 'nature' and the 'natural.'"

4. In fact, Marge Piercy critiques both novels by labeling Marian and Surfacer's journeys as "an entirely solitary battle. Their only allies are the dead, the forces in nature and the psyche, their own life energies. Yet they must live among others. Somehow the next step is missing. I don't believe one woman can single-handedly leave off being a victim: power exists and some have it" (65).

5. J. Jack Halberstam sees repro-time as intrinsically linked to "the time of inheritance" within which "values, wealth, goods, and morals are passed through family ties from one generation to the next." Elizabeth Freeman labels a similar temporality as "chrononormativity, or the use of time to organize individual human bodies toward maximum productivity" (3). Freeman also introduces a "chronobiopolitics," defined by "having a life" that is "event-centered, goal-oriented, intentional, and culminating in epiphanies or major transformations. The logic of time-as-productive thereby becomes one of serial cause-and-effect: the past seems useless unless it predicts and becomes material for a future" (5).

6. Sharon Hengen argues that *Surfacing* "hints at the search for faith in primitive gods as antidote to current psychic malaise, that faith being one of humankind's 'saving graces' . . . The most natural version of the self must often be discovered under layers of culture and then the split halves of the self rejoined in these tales" (78). The problem with Hengen's argument is that it splits nature/culture, a dichotomy not so easily separated. Yes, Surfacer's attempts to seek out and engage with the natural world are her method for throwing off a purely constructed "natural" role as a woman. But Hengen's assertion that the "split halves of the self [are] rejoined" is problematic because Surfacer always feels a pull from various sides—the other-than-human world as well as the human.

Works Cited

Adams, Carol J. *The Sexual Politics of Meat: A Feminist-Vegetarian Critical Theory*. New York: Continuum, 1990. Print.

Alaimo, Stacy. *Undomesticated Ground: Recasting Nature as Feminist Space*. Ithaca, NY: Cornell UP, 2000. Print.

Atwood, Margaret. *The Edible Woman*. 1969. New York: Anchor, 1998. Print.

———. *Power Politics*. 1971. Toronto: Anansi, 1996. Print.

———. *Surfacing*. 1972. New York: Anchor, 1998. Print.

———. *Survival: A Thematic Guide to Canadian Literature*. Toronto: Anansi, 1972. Print.

Cameron, Elspeth. "Femininity, or Parody of Autonomy: Anorexia Nervosa and *The Edible Woman*." *Journal of Canadian Studies* 20.2 (1986): 45–69. Print.

Freeman, Elizabeth. *Time Binds: Queer Temporalities, Queer Histories*. Durham, NC: Duke UP, 2010. Print.

Gaard, Greta. "Toward a Queer Ecofeminism." *New Perspectives on Environmental Justice: Gender, Sexuality, and Activism*. Ed. Rachel Stein. New Brunswick: Rutgers UP, 2004. 21–44. Print.

Gault, Cinda. "'Not Even a Hospital': Abortion and Identity Tension in Margaret Atwood's *Surfacing*." *Atlantis* 32.1 (2007): 14–24. Print.

Grosz, Elizabeth. *The Nick of Time: Politics, Evolution, and the Untimely*. Durham, NC: Duke UP, 2004. Print.

———. *Volatile Bodies: Towards a Corporeal Feminism*. Bloomington: Indiana UP, 1994. Print.

Halberstam, Judith. *In a Queer Time and Place: Transgender Bodies, Subcultural Lives*. New York: New York UP, 2005. Print.

Hengen, Shannon. "Margaret Atwood and Environmentalism." *The Cambridge Companion to Margaret Atwood*. Ed. Coral Ann Howells. New York: Cambridge UP, 2006. 72–85. Print.

Hogeland, Lisa Maria. *Feminism and Its Fictions: The Consciousness-Raising Novel and the Women's Liberation Movement*. Philadelphia: U of Pennsylvania P, 1998. Print.

Howells, Coral Ann. *Margaret Atwood*. 2nd ed. New York: Palgrave MacMillan, 2005. Print.

McCallum, E. L., and Mikko Tukhanen. "Becoming Unbecoming: Untimely Mediations." Introduction. *Queer Times, Queer Becomings*. Ed. E. L. McCallum and Mikko Tukanen. New York: SUNY P, 2011. 1–21. Print.

McWilliams, Ellen. *Margaret Atwood and the Female Bildungsroman*. Burlington, VT: Ashgate, 2009. Print.

Piercy, Marge. "Margaret Atwood: Beyond Victimhood." *Critical Essays on Margaret Atwood*. Ed. Judith McCombs. Boston: G. K. Hall & Co., 1988. 53–66. Print.

Plumwood, Val. *Feminism and the Mastery of Nature*. New York: Routledge, 1993. eBook collection. *EBSCOhost*. Web. 13 Apr. 2013.

Sanchez-Grant, Sofia. "The Female Body in Margaret Atwood's *The Edible Woman* and *Lady Oracle*." *Journal of International Women's Studies* 9.2 (2008): 77–92. Print.

Schaub, Danielle. "'I Am a Place': Internalised Landscape and Female Subjectivity in Margaret Atwood's *Surfacing*." *Mapping Canadian Cultural Space: Essays on Canadian Literature*. Ed. Danielle Schaub. Jerusalem: Magnes Press, 2000. 83–103. Print.

Tolan, Fiona. *Margaret Atwood: Feminism and Fiction*. New York: Rodopi, 2007. Print.

Chapter 6

The Second-Wave Sandbox

Anne Roiphe's Monstrous Motherhood

Lisa Botshon

> What is a monster? A being whose duration is incompatible with the existing order.
>
> —Denis Diderot, *Elements of Physiology* (1774–1780)

> The weak, plastic, developing cells of the brain are twisted, distorted, and a perverted psychic growth promoted by the false examples and teachings of a discontented mother.
>
> —New York Medical Journal (1900)

In today's parlance, a sandbox is a digital testing zone, a restricted environment where we play with new ideas, but where certain functions are prohibited. While this concept would have been foreign to second-wave feminist writers, an earlier idea of the sandbox as an area where we cordon off young children to play safely in the dirt would have been all too familiar. Both definitions speak to the idea of a contained area for testing possibilities—whether in digital tools or nascent human relationships. And it is this set of ideas that is relevant to my exploration of Anne Richardson Roiphe's 1970 work *Up the Sandbox!* In this chapter, I look at the vexed idea of motherhood experienced in a patriarchal world through Roiphe's experimental narrative. Her title *Up the Sandbox!* is notable in itself—the reader is unclear if, with its unique phrasing and punctuation, Roiphe is issuing a directive, uttering an exclamation or an expletive, or even, as some of the content might allude, suggesting an explosion.[1]

The work revolves around a late-twenty-something mother of two, Margaret Reynolds, who is married to Paul, a graduate student in history at Columbia University. She has defied her family's expectations by settling down in what was then gritty New York City instead of the New Jersey suburbs where she was raised. Yet she suspects that she has not met her own potential as a college graduate and someone who is interested in the social transformations taking place in the late sixties. The tension between her domestic life and the more public life she might be living, indeed the revolutionary activity in which she might be engaging, is manifest via a cleaved narrative and a nascent sense of the "monstrosity" of motherhood.

Up the Sandbox! was Roiphe's second novel, and it launched her writing career. Upon its initial publication, it was widely reviewed in mainstream media outlets, became a national best seller, and was made into a feature film starring Barbra Streisand. The novel is frequently listed as a classic of second-wave feminist fiction, but it rarely receives much scholarly attention beyond this.[2] The few critics who have looked at it more closely are not particularly approving, finding its overall ideology too conventional. Part of my project in this essay is to contest this condemnation. The politics of motherhood are especially difficult to parse—this was so in 1970 and remains so today—and while even contemporary critics may find Roiphe's ostensible embrace of motherhood and marriage too pat, I suggest that this novel emblematizes some of the conflicts present in the second wave, and, in particular, the challenges of a white middle-class feminist motherhood.

Roiphe's novel is structured in series of twinned chapters, describing six weeks in the narrator's life from a first-person perspective. Each set of chapters explores Margaret "in" the week—the quotidian events as lived with her husband and children on the Upper West Side—and "out of" the week—exploring her potential in the public sphere, where she blows up the George Washington Bridge with black separatists, interviews and beds Fidel Castro, and tries to discover the gendered secrets of an isolated Amazonian tribe, among other adventures. The story of this New York wife and mother is transformed in the paired chapters that describe the other socially significant identities she embodies. Writing in a realist style, Roiphe refuses to distinguish between Margaret Reynolds's two sets of lives—neither life is privileged over the other in the narrative—nor does she call any attention to the fact that the two stories coexist. And, while most reviewers read the chapters detailing Margaret's world adventures as a fantasy, the narrative does not cue the reader to do so. Overall, this novel challenges the status quo in its form and message, as it queries the roles that women, particularly mothers, might play in society; it blurs the lines between domesticity and public life.

Margaret is a compelling character for a number of reasons, including her desire to participate in both motherhood and radical sociopolitical change. Early in the novel, she anticipates with "mingled terror and joy the apocalypse, the day of judgment, the confrontation of poor and rich, black and white, and I envision the American redemption . . . I am not an observer, a reader of *The New York Times*, a sympathizer with tender thoughts—I have put my body into the fight and am prepared to sacrifice everything that may be demanded" (27–28). She is also very honest with herself about the privileged positions that she occupies. During the "out" chapter in which she has joined a black separatist cell she confesses, "Despite my concern for civil liberties, for equality, for justice in Mississippi and freedom in Alabama and school busing in Massachusetts—I am blond and blond is still beautiful, and if I have one life to lead it will be as a white, and I am a mass of internal contradictions, all of which cause me to finally attempt some rite which will bring salvation, save me from a system I despise but still carry within me like any other of my vital organs" (27). What bell hooks calls the white supremacist capitalist patriarchy has afforded Margaret Reynolds some magnificent privileges, but it has also disabled her and rendered her a servant to the very system that creates her subordination.

Margaret sees herself as an unruly subject, especially during the "in" weeks, which depict her domestic self; this life is often "out of order, in irregular and unmanageable places" (19). She acknowledges that "things [are] in continual disorder I can't really control" (45). In contrast, her husband Paul, who in the "in" weeks does not participate in childcare or housekeeping (although he does more of this work during the "out" weeks), "has become a scholar of disorder" (43), controlling the chaos through his knowledge and authority. Roiphe demonstrates that the conventions of motherhood in a patriarchal society marginalize women, rendering them both monstrous and capable of creating more "monsters"—bodies that are perceived to be unmanageable, frightening, and out of sync with the norm. Margaret's unruly subjectivity is evident in the way she occupies multiple times and spaces simultaneously; each week she is at once a wife and mother working her way through a domestic life and an activist striving for civil rights, peace, and medical breakthroughs. Because these coexisting selves conflict with one another, Margaret is haunted by the possibility of failing as both a mother-wife and as an actor in society. Physical manifestations of her anxiety take various "monstrous" forms: dwarves, "morons," encephalitic babies, and others outside of what Rosemarie Garland-Thomson would call the "normate."[3]

David Mitchell would deem her representations of disabled bodies "narrative prostheses." He has argued that "disability . . . serves as a metaphoric signifier of social and individual collapse" (16). In other words, bodies that are disabled violate social norms; they can seem dangerous or threatening because they are perceived as disruptive, out of control. Mitchell explains that "the concept of narrative prosthesis evolves out of "a narrative issues [*sic*] to resolve or correct—to 'prostheticize' . . . a deviance marked as abnormal or improper in a social context" (20). If, as he argues, "narratives turn signs of cultural deviance into textually marked bodies," then we have to wonder about the many deviant bodies that populate this novel (21). Margaret's failure to measure up, her irregularity, her resistance to certain forms of white capitalist patriarchy mandate that she birth monsters, signifiers of her deviance. These monsters demonstrate narratively how the mother who wants to create social change is consistently corralled against doing so.

CR Fiction and the Mad Housewife

The late sixties and early seventies were replete with fiction that focused on the female condition, and scholars of the second wave have noted the centrality of fiction to the women's movement. In her influential 1998 work *Feminism and Its Fictions*, for example, Lisa Maria Hogeland asserts, "The belief that feminist literacy was feminism—that women's interpretive strategies were equivalent to social change—privileged literature and literary criticism not only as means but in some sense as ends in themselves" (13). This literature was, in turn, fed by the liberationist politics of the movement. Maria Lauret comments, "Not only did writing promise the freedom of self-definition in the search for a female authenticity, not only would feminist writing liberate its reader to recognize the real conditions of their existence, but it might also serve to liberate literature itself from restrictive and prescriptive male-determined standards of good and serious writing" (77). Hence, contemporary scholars often view second-wave literature as producing the movement and concomitantly being produced by it. This at least partially accounts for the ways in which texts that fall under this umbrella are scrutinized and judged for their ideological content as well as their narrative form. How was the literature of the moment helping to create social change? And how were feminist politics transforming literature? Because of the stakes involved, critics want to draw a line in the sand(box!?)—one text is authentically feminist, performing the work of the movement, the other not so much.[4] *Up the Sandbox!* has often landed in the second category. And even though Roiphe herself has said that she did not consider herself a feminist before the publication of this novel (personal interview 2014), the work's preoccupations are intrinsically political, and it lends itself to feminist analysis.

The novel falls into two interrelated subgenres of feminist fiction, both of which were fairly popular and published by mainstream and feminist presses alike: the consciousness-raising (CR) novel and mad housewife novel. While these forms became ubiquitous in the seventies, and they were maligned almost instantly for their lack of radical feminist content (perhaps in part because they were so popular, as Harker and Konchar Farr note in the introduction), it is easy to forget that they were new and groundbreaking in the era in which they appeared, and that they helped transform the cultural landscape. Maria Lauret reminds us that much of the dominant American literature of the seventies written by men such as Norman Mailer and Joseph Heller was "self referential, preoccupied with the problems of representation and autonomous fictionality rather than asserting, as women writers did, the necessity of a literature rooted in the social" (78). Women's realist writing during this period performed an important role as it brought women's life issues into the public sphere for consideration and comment. Nicci Gerrard observes, "Fictional women sitting at kitchen tables drinking peppermint tea and discussing their problems is not a mundane literary event if real women see through that conversation a commentary on their own lives" (112). Amy Kaplan has famously asserted that nineteenth-century American literary realism was a "strategy for imagining and managing the threats of social change" (ix).

Arguably, a century later, women's realist fiction is involved in parallel cultural work. A substantial portion of second-wave-era fiction relied on the confessional form, featuring first-person women narrators ambivalent about female identity trying to make sense of the tensions and contradictions in patriarchal society. These works, according to Imelda Whelehan, "dutifully record and describe menstruation, abortion, childcare, and sexual desire. . . . [F]or readers of the time these stories of urban isolation and self-doubt allowed them to feel less cut off from the world and . . . allowed for the experience of a shared reality which suggested that these feelings . . . were actually a justified reaction to being positioned as unequal to men" (*Feminist Bestseller* 66). This seemed true for the writers as well. In a 1993 interview, Anne Roiphe recalls, "When 'Up the Sandbox' came out and it was recognized as a feminist novel, I was rather surprised . . . It didn't come out of a political frame, it came out of an observational, deeply felt frame—which happened to be political" (Nobel).[5] In other words, the personal became political in these works, even if neither the writer nor the reader was specifically seeking it. Hogeland sees in CR novels "a form of feminist consciousness often imagined as a split or duality" (31), where "the protagonist moves from feeling somehow at odds with others' expectations of her, into confrontations with others and other institutions and into a new and newly politicized understanding of herself and her society" (23). In Hogeland's understanding, CR women are always second-guessing themselves because of the patriarchal world in which they cannot be fully realized.

A related category of feminist fiction (some would say a subset of CR fiction) is the mad housewife novel, where, as Imelda Whelehan explains, women protagonists seem "in danger of losing their hold on rationality in face of the ways domestic duties threaten to rob them of all sense of self" (*Feminist Bestseller* 67). The central protagonists of novels such as Sue Kaufman's *Diary of a Mad Housewife* (1967) and Sheila Ballantyne's *Norma Jean the Termite Queen* (1975), not to mention *Up the Sandbox!,* are generally well educated and creative; their marriages are "based on the solid foundation of compatibility and companionship. They freely enter into these partnerships, secure in the knowledge that this is a new era of equality and self-definition and that their marriage will be different to [*sic*] that of their parents," as Whelehan observes (*Feminist Bestseller* 75). This combination of factors results in what Betty Friedan, in *The Feminine Mystique* (1963), famously calls "the problem that has no name," a malaise that affects white middle-class wives and mothers who are virtually absent in the public sphere and have little sense of self outside of the domestic. The protagonists of these novels seek freedom and autonomy; they speak of finding something new. Scholars have been of two minds about this fiction, finding it, on the one hand, able to "give literary expression to the female sphere in a way that is unprecedented" (Greene 60). On the other hand, as Gayle Greene argues, it does not, "for the most part, make the connections—between individual and social, personal and political, past and present—that might enable [its authors] to challenge the situations they depict" (60). Greene offers, pessimistically, that Roiphe's *Up the Sandbox!* "actually reiterate[s] rather than challenge[s] the clichés of the culture" (71).

Those familiar with the 1990s controversies over Anne's daughter Katie Roiphe's postfeminist textual turns[6] may be interested to know that Roiphe *mère* has had her own lasting (albeit significantly smaller) group of feminist detractors. In 1977, for example, Arlyn Diamond fumed, "*Up the Sandbox* exhibits a spurious and marketable concern with the subject of liberation" (19). Diamond reads the private-public split in Roiphe's novel as one that subverts the protagonist's fantasies and ambitions, defusing "their power through Margaret's realization that love and motherhood are really her proper goals," rather than challenging this split or offering serious alternatives to domesticity (19). In 1980, Elizabeth Fox-Genovese bristled, "Anne Roiphe . . . self-proclaimed happy mother, sang the praises of wifedom and motherhood in *Up the Sandbox.* Ominously, Roiphe, a smart lady, acknowledged the pull of independent roles for women, but cast them as daydreams, improbable fantasies, not options" (204–205). If, like Greene, Diamond, and Fox-Genovese, one reads Roiphe's novel as a split narrative that considers alternatives to domesticity only to cast them aside out of convention or, as Diamond suggests, fear (20), then *Up the Sandbox!* may be a disappointment. But it is worth looking at Roiphe's novel as a challenge to the status quo. The narrative structure itself responds to the split inherent in the white middle-class educated woman's knowledge that she can/should/might transcend social expectations at the same time that she finds no way to refuse those expectations. This structure also corresponds to Hogeland's assertion that CR novels deliberately "provide multiple, even contradictory readings" (47), which is useful to consider, especially in light of some of the disappointed critics' appraisals of *Up the Sandbox!*

Arguably, Roiphe not only deploys but also defies many of the conventions of the social realist novel, the CR narrative, and the mad housewife genre. In postmodern fashion, the protagonist, Margaret, appears to live multiple lives simultaneously. Via a narrative structure that presents two versions of each week, Margaret can be a full-time mother and wife *at the same time* that she is a medical researcher, an Amazonian anthropologist, and a member of a black separatist group. Moreover, Margaret begins her narrative with revolutionary ideas, deliberately casting herself out of her "tribe" of New Jersey suburbanites, and recognizing that her racial and class position means that when the revolution for social and political equality occurs, her "head will roll" with other privileged white people (106). Unlike the protagonists of other CR novels, Margaret's consciousness is raised from the get-go; it is not something she achieves at the end of a novel's worth of reckoning. Additionally, if one does not read the double narrative as a sign of "madness," whereby the "out" weeks are representative of the excesses of an underused mind, but rather as a unique portrayal of coexisting multiple selves, *Up the Sandbox!* resists mad housewife categorization. Casting off the expectations of codified genres opens up this novel to a broader consideration of its feminist politics, particularly as it simultaneously addresses the challenges of white middle-class motherhood and acknowledges the ideological constraints of that subject position.

Second-Wave Motherhood

In her 1996 memoir *Fruitful: A Real Mother in the Modern World*, which was a finalist for the National Book Award, Anne Roiphe relates that becoming a mother was "the beginning of [her own] feminism" (11). Criticism of this idea lies at the heart of most of the judgmental analyses of *Up the Sandbox!*, but an examination of her representation of motherhood, together with a consideration of her twinned narrative structure, demonstrates that this novel limns some of the most potent conflicts in second-wave liberal feminism. As is clear in Fox-Genovese's disapproval, one of the biggest criticisms about the novel is that the protagonist is a "self-proclaimed happy mother," but this assessment is difficult to comprehend, not least because anxiety and fear about motherhood are pervasive throughout the work.

Second-wave feminists understood the entrenched nature of motherhood and how our society has held it up as an ideal while simultaneously subverting it economically, politically, and socially. Imelda Whelehan reminds us, "From the late 1960s, motherhood as a concept was under renewed political scrutiny, particularly by feminists . . . Writers of the period foregrounded the artificiality of the social expectations that accompanied motherhood" ("Shit and String Beans" 148). Adrienne Rich, for example, decried the way that "maternal power has been domesticated," and how the womb, "the ultimate source of the power—has historically been turned against us and itself made into a source of powerlessness" (68). From a more contemporary standpoint, Andrea O'Reilly asserts that motherhood, as a patriarchal institution, has operated "to constrain, regulate, and dominate women and their mothering" (37).

The postwar era rendered the middle-class white woman's body more ornamental than productive, repeating the pattern of the previous century when middle-class white women were removed from their work and mandated to become consumers. But Roiphe's protagonist exists in a transitional moment, one in which middle-class white women were throwing off the mantles of domesticity and (re)entering the public sphere. The paradigms for empowered white middle-class motherhood were still nascent, and such mothers were caught between competing sets of cultural demands: that they prove themselves their husbands' intellectual and public equals, and that they commit themselves fully to what Rich would call the "powerless responsibility" of mothering, sans agency or authority. Roiphe's bifurcated narrative, with its seemingly unconscious focus on the "monstrous," encodes a resultant anxiety and ambivalence about mothering under such circumstances.

Up the Sandbox! begins with a common scene of domesticity complete with repetitions, annoyances, entrapments. While her graduate student husband is researching his dissertation, Margaret is meant to take care of the house, a cramped New York City apartment, and their two young children, one of whom is an infant. She reveals, "After the children's nap, I repeated the morning's chores in an abbreviated fashion . . . Suddenly, I am in a hurry to get out of the apartment. The brick way behind the kitchen window lets in no light. The dishes in the sink seem unbearable, and the spilled orange juice on the counter surface seems a defacement . . . The early June heat and the garbage, not entirely contained within the aluminum can, combine in a terrible odor" (9). Margaret is beleaguered by the requirements of domestic work, and she is unable and unwilling to be the paragon of housewifery that her suburban mother and her husband expect her to be. She confesses, "The chores each day, if I faced their demands, were overwhelming, and only by laxity, a certain bohemian looseness, was I able to keep us all together" (19–20). In a passage that is paradigmatic of mad-housewife fiction, she relates, "Eat, eliminate, prepare food, clean up, shop, throw out the garbage . . . Despite computers and digit telephone numbers, nuclear fission, my life hardly differs from that of an Indian squaw settled in a tepee on the same Manhattan land centuries ago" (18). Strangely, some critics read this as embracing of her role as domestic.[7] It seems obvious, however, that this comparison, albeit primitivist, is meant to be an objection; with all of the progress that the twentieth century has brought, patriarchal motherhood is still a sentence of servitude.

Roiphe's protagonist has graduated from Barnard College and begun a master's degree in literature with a focus on Jane Austen, but at the playground with her children, she feels "nothing challenges wit or demands a fine performance" (125). Margaret knows that her husband is worried that she'll "grow stupid and dull" in the confines of her domestic life if she does not return to graduate school. She implies that the motivation behind Paul's suggestion is his own self-interest rather than concern for her well-being: he requires regular stimulation from a highly educated wife. This is just one of many signs of Paul's self-absorption, which is evident during the "in" weeks only. During these chapters, he also takes over the small apartment, requires her attention when afflicted with a mild summer cold, has little interest in childcare or housekeeping above the "helping" level, and employs his wife as a typist and sounding board for his dissertation. However, Margaret is also keen for her own stimulation and growth: "I know Paul has experiences away from me that he keeps private, uses to enrich himself. His mind; his soul is only partially the sum of our united life. I want the same separateness. I want to grow strong and older with more than age. I want to learn something myself" (57). Margaret, as the person in this partnership whose identity comes solely through her domestic work, here expresses an oft-iterated desire for autonomy and an identity in the public sphere. This yearning becomes manifest in Roiphe's "out" chapters.

Roiphe articulates a rebellious, subversive subjectivity in these chapters. Here, Margaret is an agent of her own and, ostensibly, others' liberty, attempting to expose and undermine dominant institutions. In the first "out" week, for instance, Margaret has joined a cell of PROWL, a black separatist group intent on blowing up the George Washington Bridge in order to isolate Manhattan and claim it in the name of black liberation. This action, like each of the other "out" chapter adventures, departs widely from the domestic content of the "in" chapters. But it shares a number of qualities with the other "out" chapters. In each one, Margaret has worked out a way to reassign her childcare and other domestic duties with some combination of Paul, her mother, and a housekeeper; this assistance is generally nonexistent during the "in" weeks. And in each case she embarks on an experience that is meant to generate social change. One week, for example, she is a journalist who journeys to Cuba to report on the status of women there and unexpectedly meets Fidel Castro. Another week she is a medical researcher. In yet another week, she becomes a pacifist organizer and travels to Vietnam to campaign for peace.

Each of these "out" weeks contains a dark core of humor as well: in Cuba, for example, Fidel Castro turns out to be a woman in drag who seduces her. As a doctor in New York City in yet another chapter, Margaret treats a child with stigmata and, unable to explain them with science, is about to declare her bleeding palms a sign of Mary when the girl's brother rushes in claiming that she has imbibed orange juice containing his methadone and is hallucinating. In Vietnam protesting violence, she witnesses a convent ceremony in which a nun sacrifices herself to a bathtub of piranhas. The black humor in these chapters is tied to the ultimate failure of Margaret's public actions for change. If Fidel Castro cannot come out as a woman as part of the revolution, then how egalitarian can Cuba be? If the nuns are engaged in violent, self-destructive behavior, then how will the pacifists promote peace among the soldiers on the front lines of war?

Yet Roiphe is explicitly engaged with the possibility of revolution, of social transformation throughout *Up the Sandbox!* It is significant that Margaret's husband is writing his dissertation, titled "Bloody Revolutionaries, or Idealists Turned Murderers—An Historical Survey," on the ways in which revolution will always fail because at least one revolutionary leader will betray the cause and grab power in the end. His thesis is that "revolutions have always been betrayed, that idealism has turned inevitably into dictatorship, and that humanitarianism, when believed in passionately, has resulted in cruelties beyond the imagining of dispassionate moderates . . . The human being is too corrupt, too greedy, too hungry, for revolution to succeed" (102). In contrast, Margaret consistently asserts her belief in social transformation. Early on, she directly disagrees with Paul: "I still think that someday things will change" (44). When she embarks on her journey to Cuba, she reflects, "I wanted to believe that greed, exploitation, hopelessness, religious excess, could all be put to sleep by the people working together . . . I looked forward to visiting Cuba to see for myself the world created anew" (58).

Despite the fact that Cuba ultimately disappoints, she continues to reiterate her hope for radical change: "Some day there will be a revolution with genuine heroes and the way of life for that country will change and the air will be clean" (104). While the novel's twinned chapters allow Margaret to explore a wide variety of potentially transformative activities such as black liberation and pacifism, a common interest running throughout her adventures is the condition of women and children. And it becomes apparent in the aggregate that Roiphe is invested in an exploration of motherhood as métier.

Roiphe's Monstrous Motherhood

Throughout her novel, Roiphe evidences the anxiety, boredom, and even violence of modern parenting. In the playground, in her first "in" week, Margaret confesses ambivalence about mothering: "I pick up my baby and hold him on my lap . . . I could starve him—or leave him behind me, dropping him on the cement, crying in the park until the police come and assign him some nameless future" (11). Similarly, she also worries that she is not fully equipped for the job of mothering: "Sometimes I think perhaps it's wrong, morally wrong, to have children, when I am so uncertain whether or not I am a good person, enough of a person to create another" (55). The act of mothering inspires a query of selfhood, and the "success" of her children, their ability to achieve "normalcy" becomes one of her ongoing obsessions. Early in the novel, she expresses a desire to join the "student revolutionaries" but for the intensive schedule of childcare that has been delineated for her: "the baby must have what the books call consistent mothering or his small soul will warp and bend in strange directions" (13). The possibility that she will fail as a mother and that her children will become warped pervades the entire text, and her own body, as well as other bodies, become unruly in response.

For Margaret, mothering creates a division of her selfhood, mirroring the narrative structure of the novel, only in a more disorderly fashion. Her children are parts of her; once they are in the world, she is no longer "in and of myself . . . complete" (51). She says of her daughter that she is "my child, not yet another person, but a limb of mine, struggling like all the other limbs" (46), as though motherhood produces a kind of polyploidal identity. She has become a generator of limbs, of clones, of something sometimes monstrous. She recognizes that being a mother requires her to be "devoted to a replica of myself, now slave, now master" (54), a relationship that is painful and full of conflict. Toward the end of the novel, Margaret confesses, "what I really want, what I'm after, is an extension, a selfish extension of my being into more life than I can contain in one—singular—body. I want to expand myself not merely in time, but in space, out toward other connections, to be a multiple person, to experience as much as possible" (151). Margaret's desire to expand, to be multiple selves, looks very much like the novel's structure, in which she inhabits many selves through narrative mitosis. However, this idea of motherhood is strikingly chaotic, even grotesque.

From the very beginning of *Up the Sandbox!*, Margaret grimaces under the weight of her domestic role, which in turn results in the presence of monstrosity. This is evident from the outset. In the first few pages of the first chapter, in a hurry to leave their small, hot and untidy New York apartment, Margaret rushes her children down to the street. She has already disclaimed the dishes in the sink and guiltily admits that she has yelled at her daughter for deflowering the geranium. All she wants to do is escape. Notably, the first person they encounter once they emerge is "the dwarf lady" who lives in their building. Even though Margaret is familiar with her as a neighbor of four years, she relates, "each time we pass my skin crawls." Moreover, she comments, "Despite all the humane teachings I have of course heard, I still feel not considerate, compassionate or easy in the company of cripples. I hold to the medieval conviction that someone has been criminal, perhaps in bed, or maybe only in imagination, but someone has committed a crime, perhaps the victim herself" (11). As only the first of many such encounters, the "dwarf lady's" presence becomes an embodiment of the monstrosity of motherhood, a displacement of Margaret's precarious selfhood. The criminal, then, is Margaret.

Marie-Hélène Huet reminds us that in the Middle Ages "no theory was more debated, more passionately attacked or defended, than the power of the maternal imagination over the formation of the fetus" (6). She explains that into the eighteenth century, "monstrous births were understood as warnings and public testimony; they were thought to be 'demonstrations' of the mother's unfulfilled desires. The monster was . . . seen as a visible image of the mother's hidden passions" (6). *Up the Sandbox!* is filled with both maternal desire (sexual, political, social) and "monstrous births," and although the latter are not Margaret's biological progeny, they are her narrative progeny, populating all chapters of this first-person novel. She notices them in every corner of her many lives—in the playground and on the street in New York City, and in the hospitals of Cuba and jungles of the Amazon. They are physical manifestations of her unruly desires: her desire to escape domesticity, her desire for her husband's touch, her desire to simultaneously nurture and leave her children, her desire to engage in revolutionary activity in a manner that is counter to her husband's theories.

Sarah Trimble argues that the ideology of the "good mother" shifts to keep up with the needs of social reorganization, "ensuring that women's time, energy, and capital are disciplined and the status quo is upheld" (179). Similarly, Andrea O'Reilly notes that in the West the requirements for "good mothering"—for example, great investments of time with children, putting children's needs and desires before their own, the insistence that mothers find exclusive fulfillment via mothering, etc.—are amplified along with "women's increased social and economic independence: increased labor participation, entry into traditionally male areas of work, rise in female-initiated divorces, growth in female-headed households, and improved education" (43). Roiphe's Margaret falls into this paradigm. With her half-finished master's thesis on Jane Austen and inclination to join the student revolutionaries at nearby Columbia University, her time must be even further regulated by childrearing experts who, through the pages of popular guides, recommend that mothers conform to time-consuming standards of nurturance and cleanliness. When Margaret's mother unexpectedly visits, she sees "all the toys in the living room I had not yet cleaned up and the dishes in the sink, and the unmade bed," and she refuses to sit down anywhere before spreading a newspaper on a chair; she becomes livid, finally insisting on sending for a housekeeper (48). Margaret comments, "I felt guilty because she was right, the house was a garbage dump" (48–49). Margaret realizes that she is a failure at one of her essential roles, and this results in an even greater unconscious buildup of monstrous bodies in the narrative.

More than two and a half decades after publishing *Up the Sandbox!,* Roiphe revisits her concept of motherhood in *Fruitful* and confesses, "I understand perfectly what Adrienne Rich meant by 'the invisible violence of the institution of motherhood . . . the guilt, the powerless responsibility for human lives, the judgments and condemnations, the fear of her own power, the guilt, the guilt, the guilt'" (72). In 1970, Roiphe had perceived that maternal guilt, in a moment in which mothers are set up to fail, results in monstrosity. Belgian psychoanalyst Maud Mannoni, also writing in the seventies, forwarded the idea that "the child's past is always the story of parental failure and its future is the explosion in their faces of their own guilt . . . There will be payment exacted from these failed parents, payment in the form of a monstrous progeny" (qtd. in Blum 177–178). Margaret is shown to "pay" as a failed parent through her myriad monstrous progeny.

A mere paragraph after Margaret's disastrous guilt-ridden visit with her mother, she discusses "the moron" who frequents the same playground as her children: "He looks . . . like a cartoon monster, and the ladies on the benches turn their eyes away from him—a catastrophe" (49). While she adds, "Thank God, someone else's [catastrophe]," it is not a coincidence that the "moron" appears immediately after Margaret's mother confronts her about her domestic failings. Like the dwarf lady, who appears in the shadow of Margaret's initial domestic failings, the moron belongs to that same mother who has not succeeded in keeping her floors swept and desires in check. Despite her claims to the contrary, the moron belongs to Margaret, a manifestation of her failure. In the same scene, while another mother in the playground distracts and pacifies the moron with a pretzel, Margaret's daughter Elizabeth trips over a toy truck and falls, blood pouring from her mouth. Margaret is certain it is a superficial wound, but she had not been paying attention to Elizabeth and now erupts: "My life is not my own any more, it belongs in part to her. I have committed myself to taking care of her and I must not fail" (59). Failure will result in the monstrous progeny occupying her womb and her home, not just the playground or the street.

In the "out" version of this same week, Margaret is a journalist contracted to write an article on women in Cuba. She interviews "the female chief of the Havana Main Hospital, Dr. Maria Lopez," whom she thinks will be "an excellent example of the new Cuban woman" (63–64). Instead of the "political speech" she expects, however, the doctor explodes into an emotional declaration, imploring Americans to donate to medical research that will "discover the cause and cure of mental retardation" (64). Behind this outburst is the doctor's own experience; her son is one such "damaged child" (65). Margaret is disappointed with Dr. Lopez. Instead of being "cool and rational, like the chief surgeons in New York hospitals," she is "simply a mother who was hurt. A doctor, an administrator—all these facets of her accomplishments did not protect her from crucifixion on the cross of motherhood" (65). Dr. Lopez is disappointing to Margaret the New York journalist because this Margaret, an independent thinker seeking a socialist solution to patriarchy, wants to discuss how "the women in Cuba have improved their lot since the revolution" (66). Dr. Lopez, though, complicates this idea, as she embodies the curse of the desirous mother; the nonnormative child has been marked by his mother's ambition and drive, desires that have been cultivated by the socialist state.

The disabled child, the moron, and the dwarf neighbor all function as nonspeaking subalterns either needing to be saved and cured or as objects of horror. Margaret cannot see these bodies as autonomous subjects, and the use of disabled bodies as narrative prostheses for white middle-class maternal anxiety becomes even more evident as the chapters continue. In "out" week three, Margaret is a medical intern specializing in pediatrics. The first case she references is "the mongoloid born that morning on the OB ward," a baby she wishes she could transform into a "normal" infant (87). In the same paragraph, she comments, "I intend to be a pediatrician, and have worked now for ten years toward that end, ten years because I took time out for Paul and the children, but Paul has understood. I always have to return, however little of myself I could give to him and Elizabeth and the baby . . . They want more of me at home, arranging flowers, cooking in big pots, but I have forced myself to be ruthless and leave at my appointed time. I am a woman determined to be of value, of social use, a skilled and particular tool" (87). Here Margaret betrays the anxiety she feels in every "out" week when she leaves her family to live her public life. The narrative issue that wants "correcting" in this passage is the idea of the working career mother, a woman who does not necessarily have to work for financial reasons, but who, selfishly, wants to be "of social use," "correcting" disabled babies through eugenics-like medical experiments, and is, as a consequence, absent from home.

The parallels between the domestic corrections imaginatively aimed at Margaret and the medicalized ones directed at the disabled are striking. The difference, however, is that Margaret is aware that she functions like an "assistant god" in contrast to others, as she is "healthy and clean and white" (90). In other words, then, despite her subordinate position as a woman and mother in a patriarchal world, she recognizes that her class, race, and physical statuses are privileged. And each of her various selves is able to employ this privilege in some way or another, unlike the disabled bodies that she creates to represent the fragility of her social power.

In "out" week five, Margaret pursues anthropological research documenting an Amazonian tribe. She is uncommonly successful until one of the young tribeswomen she has befriended gives birth to a nonviable baby born with severe deformities. As a result, Margaret "must be punished" (146); she is pursued by poisoned arrows until she—just barely—makes it to the safety of her colleagues. Unfortunately, she has also been pierced by one of the arrows and, for a time, it is unclear if she will live. The only remedy, it seems, is for her to never leave home again and reinvest in domesticity: "I will learn to bake bread and make chocolate mousse," she writes to her husband (147). The deformed baby in this chapter is another symptom of unruly maternal desire, and the only antidote is the reinstatement of patriarchal control.

Ultimately, one might read *Up the Sandbox!* as a comment on motherhood as a disability in a patriarchal system. Women and the disabled are both embodied subjects; both represent deviations from the normative male body; both, as Marjo-Riitta Reinikainen asserts, "have been regarded prisoners of the body and biology, which do not confirm the norm. This, in turn, has been taken as a justification for their otherness and inferior social status" (19–20). Rosemarie Garland-Thomson observes that even in our own cultural moment, the general American public associates femininity with disability, noting, "a recent study on stereotyping showed that housewives, disabled people, blind people, so-called retarded people, and the elderly were all judged as being similarly incompetent," incomplete and vulnerable ("Integrating" 19). It is then no wonder that Roiphe's novel is so heavily populated with nonnormative bodies. They remind Margaret only too well of her own deviance from the white educated male norm embodied by her husband, a man who is allowed to pursue his own interests regardless of others' needs and desires, while her own desires are clearly fraught.

Motherhood only underscores the unruliness of the female body. Rosemarie Garland-Thomson comments, "The disabled body stands for the self gone out of control, individualism run rampant; it mocks the notion of the body as compliant instrument of the limitless will and appears in the cultural imagination as ungovernable, recalcitrant. . . . Even more troubling, disability suggests that the cultural other lies dormant within the cultural self . . ." (*Extraordinary* 43). Similarly, Margaret's maternal self is out of control and ungovernable, always teetering on the possibility of failure amid rotting garbage and cluttered living rooms, unable to prevent the children from falling and bleeding or scribbling on Paul's master/work, ruining it. Her desires to achieve racial justice in New York, spread the word of the Cuban revolution, bring an end to the Vietnam War, also occupy nonnormative and contestatory spaces on the fringes of white patriarchal society. In comparison to Paul, the graduate student who has been embraced by society's elite institutions, Margaret is out of sync, embodying Garland-Thomson's definition of a disabled body: "incongruent both in space and in the milieu of expectations" ("Integrating" 33). And yet, as mentioned, Margaret's self-confessed privileges as "healthy and clean and white," an "assistant god," place her much closer to white patriarchal power than to others who seek liberation.

Notably, critics who are disappointed with this novel are generally most dissatisfied with its ending. While the "in" chapter of week six concludes with Margaret's reiteration that she has "not given up all hope for a revolution that will not be corrupt" (154), the "out" chapter is a single paragraph in which Margaret confesses that she is pregnant with her third child. In chapter six, the two narratives that have remained separate thus far—domestic Margaret and radical Margaret—finally merge. Gayle Greene and Arlyn Diamond read this as a return to convention, that "feminist rhetoric is enlisted to reinforce the old boundaries: feminist aspirations are childish stuff and to 'grow up' is to step back within bounds" (Greene 73). But Roiphe is neither suggesting that Margaret has been childish in her activist pursuits, nor that an additional pregnancy will help her reach her true potential as a wife and mother. Rather, Margaret remains ambivalent. She may be an Austen fan, but she is not sealing off her story with a socially beneficial marriage. Moreover, during the "in" section, Margaret worries about the pregnancy producing a monstrous offspring, evidencing once again the presence of her unruly desires: "Mutations do happen: intrauterine second-month development of fangs, green skin, scales. Third intrauterine month, gills, longer fangs, pop eyes, hair on hands, nails sharp, in fact claws, a monster growing in me—a comic book terror building strength from my blood system, and suddenly tearing with its pointed fangs at my uterus . . . it would leap on to the bed, the embodiment of all that is vicious and ugly within me" (150–151). The last line of the novel is the most indicative of her state of mind: "I hope the baby will be healthy and undamaged" (155). Knowing that she departs from the expected, the controlled, and the normative, however slightly, and knowing the ways her transgressions could result in monstrosity, Margaret fears that her fetus will bear physical marks of its mother's intemperance and depart even further from the requirements of "normalcy" within the privileged position of the able-bodied white middle class.

In *Narrating Mothers: Theorizing Maternal Subjectivities*, Brenda Daly and Maureen Reddy posit that "the hybrid forms of writing that women authors often produce are textual symptoms of the effort to reformulate the subject (maternal or otherwise)" and suggest that "in the process of redefining mothering it is also necessary to redefine genres and their conventions" (12). In *Up the Sandbox!*, Roiphe creates a set of twinned narratives that explore the cultural minefields plaguing mothers who attempt to come to grips with patriarchal oppression and political struggle. Far from capitulating to patriarchally defined ideology, then, Roiphe ends her book with the same ambivalence with which she begins: anxious over the expectations of motherhood and the ways in which the role disables women, rendering them monstrous and productive of monstrous others. In this double-narrative novel that parallels two lives—the private and the public, the mother and the activist—Roiphe provides a nuanced consideration of the conditions of white liberal feminist motherhood. In her portrayal of the monstrous cleaved self of the mother, Roiphe attempts to wrestle mothering from its patriarchal moorings and set it loose in the playground. What would a feminist mother look like in 1970? Roiphe experiments in the sandbox.

Notes

This paper would not have existed but for the herculean efforts of my stalwart writing group: Melinda Plastas, Siobhan Senier, Robin Hackett, Eve Raimon, Monica Chu, Rebecca Herzig, and Lisa Walker. Thanks are also due to Lisa Maria Burgess Noudehou and Jaime Harker, both of whom provided essential comments.

Epigraphs. The first epigraph is quoted in Huet (89) and the second in Ladd-Taylor and Umansky (10).

1. Usually one finds oneself "in" a sandbox. "Up the sandbox" is difficult to visualize and does not correspond to any known idiom. I have found no explanatory references to Roiphe's title anywhere in print, including in the novel itself. However, in a personal interview, Roiphe mentions that the title was the creation of her editor and publishing house and was meant to parallel the colloquial expression "up yours" (2014).

2. Roiphe appears to be of greater interest to contemporary scholars as a Jewish writer, as these references attest: Carol McKewin Weaver, "Tasting the Stars: The Tales of Rabbi Nachman in Anne Roiphe's *Lovingkindness*," in *Mother Puzzles: Daughters and Mothers in Contemporary American Literature*, ed. Mickey Pearlman (New York: Greewood P, 1989); Naomi Sokoloff, "Imagining Israel in American Fiction: Anne Roiphe's *Lovingkindness* and Philip Roth's *The Counterlife*," *Studies in American Jewish Literature* 10 (Spring 1991): 65–80; Jay L. Halio, "Anne Roiphe: Finding Her America," in *Daughters of Valor: Contemporary Jewish American Women Writers*, eds. Jay L. Halio and Ben Siegel (Cranbury, NJ: Associated University Presses, 1997); and Melanie Levinson, "'My Own Design': Finding Identity in Anne Roiphe's Writings," in *Modern Jewish Women Writers in America*, ed. Evelyn Avery (New York: Palgrave Macmillan, 2007).

3. In "Integrating Disability," Garland-Thomson defines *normate* as "the corporeal incarnation of culture's collective, unmarked, normative characteristics" (23).

4. Clearly, the "second wave" and the "women's movement" are hardly homogenous or ideologically unified. These terms are useful, though, to stand for the trends of the era in which people worked for the betterment of women in society. Of course, that meant many different things to different people.

5. In a *Publishers Weekly* interview with Roiphe in 1993, Sybil Steinberg says, "Remarried in 1967 to psychoanalyst Herman Roiphe, she was then pregnant with her second child and wondering what her life would have been like had she not chosen marriage and motherhood. . . . '[*Up the Sandbox!*] came out just when a lot of other feminist books were starting to appear. Suddenly I realized: so *that's* what it is! I had identified the problem without the political scaffolding'" (236 emphasis original).

6. Katie Roiphe's 1994 book, *The Morning After: Sex, Fear and Feminism on Campus*, posits that young women should resist radical feminist misandry and take more responsibility for their sexuality. Upon its publication, it was both lauded and lampooned in the media.

7. See Greene, for example.

Works Cited

Blum, Virginia. *Hide and Seek: The Child between Psychoanalysis and Fiction*. Urbana: U of Illinois P, 1995.

Daly, Brenda O., and Maureen T. Reddy, eds. *Narrating Mothers: Theorizing Maternal Subjectivities*. Knoxville: U of Tennessee P, 1991.

Diamond, Arlyn. "Flying from Work." *Frontiers: A Journal of Women Studies* 2.3 (Autumn 1977): 18–23.

Fox-Genovese, Elizabeth. "Female Literary Culture." *Antioch Review* 38.2 (Spring 1980): 193–217.

Garland-Thomson, Rosemarie. *Extraordinary Bodies: Figuring Physical Disability in American Culture and Literature.* New York: Columbia UP, 1997.

———. "Integrating Disability, Transforming Feminist Theory." *Feminist Disability Studies.* Ed. Kim Q. Hall. Bloomington: Indiana UP, 2011. 13–47.

Gerrard, Nicci. *Into the Mainstream: How Feminism Has Changed Women's Writing.* London: Pandora, 1989.

Greene, Gayle. *Changing the Story: Feminist Fiction and the Tradition.* Bloomington: Indiana UP, 1991.

Hogeland, Lisa Maria. *Feminism and Its Fictions: The Consciousness-Raising Novel and the Women's Liberation Movement.* Philadelphia: U of Pennsylvania P, 1998.

Huet, Marie-Helene. *Monstrous Imagination.* Cambridge, MA: Harvard UP, 1993.

Kaplan, Amy. *Social Construction of American Realism.* Chicago: U of Chicago P, 1992.

Ladd-Taylor, Molly, and Lauri Umansky. *"Bad" Mothers: The Politics of Blame in Twentieth-Century America.* New York: NYU P, 1998.

Lauret, Maria. *Feminist Fiction in America.* New York: Routledge, 1994.

Mitchell, David T. "Narrative Prosthesis and the Materiality of Metaphor." *Disability Studies: Enabling the Humanities.* Ed. Sharon Snyder et al. New York: MLA, 2002.

Noble, Barbara Presley. "AT LUNCH WITH: Katie and Anne Roiphe; One Daughter's Rebellion or Her Mother's Imprint?" New York Times 10 Nov. 1993. http://www.nytimes.com/1993/11/10/garden/lunch-with-katie-anne-roiphe-one-daughter-s-rebellion-her-mother-s-imprint.html. Accessed 24 Jan. 2014. Web.

O'Reilly, Andrea. *Rocking the Cradle: Thoughts on Motherhood, Feminism and the Possibility of Empowered Mothering.* Toronto: Demeter, 2006.

Reinikainen, Marjo-Riitta. "Disablistic Practices of Womanhood." *NORA Nordic Journal of Feminist and Gender Research* 16.1 (March 2008): 19–32. http://www.tandfonline.com/doi/full/10.1080/08038740701772790#.VR1K8vzF-So. Accessed 24 Jan 2014. Web.

Rich, Adrienne. *Of Woman Born: Motherhood as Experience and Institution.* 1976. New York: Norton, 1986.

Roiphe, Anne (Richardson). *Fruitful: A Real Mother in the Modern World.* New York: Houghton Mifflin, 1996.

———. Personal interview. 22 Jan. 2014.

———. *Up the Sandbox!* New York: Simon and Schuster, 1970.

Steinberg, Sybil S. "Anne Roiphe." *Writing for Your Life #2.* Ed. Sybil Steinberg. 2 Aug. 1993. New York: Publishers Weekly, 1995.

Trimble, Sarah. "(Un)usual Suspects: Mothers, Masculinities, Monstrosities." *Feminist Mothering.* Ed. Andrea O'Reilly. Albany, NY: SUNY P, 2008. 177–190.

Whelehan, Imelda. *The Feminist Bestseller: From Sex and the Single Girl to Sex and the City.* New York: Palgrave Macmillan, 2005.

———. "'Shit and String Beans,' Boredom and Babies: Bad Mothers in Popular Fiction since 1968." *Mediating Moms: Mothers in Popular Culture.* Ed. Elizabeth Podnieks. Montreal: McGill-Queens UP, 2012.

Chapter 7

Desire and Fantasy in Erica Jong's *Fear of Flying*

Jay Hood

At the time of its 1973 release, *Fear of Flying*, with its unabashed presentations of the female body, and indeed all bodies, was widely considered controversial and risqué. One reviewer wrote that *Fear of Flying* was a "dull and dirty book" (*Best Sellers* 425). Another noted that it was "difficult to review in a gentlemanly manner"; then, apparently finding the strength to do so, he concluded that "everyone and everything Miss Wing describes with enthusiasm is disagreeable, and whatever she sneers at is generally pleasant" (*Times Literary Supplement* 813). Among the "disagreeable" depictions are, the reviewer suggests, the nude male and female body: what they look like, feel like, smell like. Cutting through the disdain, his criticism nonetheless raises questions about why Erica Jong was so invested in depictions of material bodies.

In this chapter, I argue that these representations of the body are directly tied to the novel's attempts to mediate the flow of desire between fantasies of fulfillment and the difficult realities of human relations. The main character and narrator of the novel, Isadora Wing, embodies both culturally inscribed fears regarding the limits of bodily self-control and sexual desire and also the possibility of getting outside these limits. For this reason, *Fear of Flying* is perhaps the most famous of the consciousness-raising (CR) novels of second-wave feminism—texts that were defined by a "utopian project of total social transformation" and often by explorations of alternatives to traditional thinking about happiness, desire, sexual relations, and propriety (Hogeland 12). Within this context, Jong's CR novel is more than a utopian fantasy full of personal and social transformation; *Fear of Flying* undertakes a fuller renegotiation between the protagonist and her world, and thus becomes a kind of bildungsroman, striking a compromise between desired fantasies and achievable realities.

The novel, in the CR tradition, attempts to promote a specific female conceptualization of the body, cultural prescriptions and all. Isadora's anxieties about her body and how others perceive it exemplify a feminist project that directly confronts patriarchal attempts at circumscribing female experience within a private sphere, one in which female bodies are regulated by masculine desires and anxieties. This being the case, Jong's project is ultimately exhibitionistic in its unregulated, uncensored, and distinctly unflattering representations of the human physical form and in its mobilization of the body to achieve individual pleasure. If such a project can be understood in any one sense, it is perhaps best understood as establishing a counternarrative to what Susan Bordo describes as the "determinist fantasy" of the female body. Such a fantasy, Bordo writes, is a fantasy of constant physical change, albeit within a limited and static framework of representation. "Fantasies of rearranging, transforming, and correcting, an ideology of limitless improvements and change," an order based upon top-down arrangements and hierarchical power, marks the determinist fantasy of patriarchal society (Bordo 245). These improvements directly coincide with the marginalizing of nonnormative experience and of the slow destruction of variation among culturally acceptable physical body models. Jong's work recuperates a way of conceiving bodies as loci of desire, rather than loci of individual power. Indeed, bodies in Jong's texts frequently serve to deconstruct notions of physical power and personal agency. For Isadora, the body is too open to the world, too easily influenced by the desires depicted in the media and consumer culture around her, yet also too limited in the options such depictions provide for managing fantasies and desires. The fantasies and desires in Bordo's world of "improvements" reduce the significance and ubiquity of bodies in the world, not only through limiting representations of individual bodies, but also through representing individual bodies in terms of how they differentiate from preexisting models or ideals (Bordo 278).

Contrasting with the programmatic fantasies of consumer culture are the countercultural productions of CR novels. Although Jong's *Fear of Flying* was wildly successful in the U.S. cultural mainstream, the text itself is a part of a mode of expression that has its roots in underground political action. The countercultural effort of second-wave feminism, Rhodes contends, was defined by "a radical feminist emphasis on written texts disseminated through an underground publication network" which "served as a loose, superficially stable organization for the movement" (26). These roots of *Fear of Flying* are not always apparent within the text, but a larger history of the movement reveals how feminist writers worked to generate alternative visions of power and unconventional cultural discourse. Perhaps the most significant of these visions for Jong's novel is the fantasy of sexual intimacy and happiness both outside of and in opposition to the institution of marriage.[1]

The opening chapters of *Fear of Flying* place Isadora's well-known fantasy of the zipless fuck within an ironic context that deconstructs the fantasy itself. Isadora describes this idealized sexual encounter as "a platonic ideal. Zipless because when you came together zippers fell away like rose petals, underwear blew off in one breath like dandelion fluff. Tongues intertwined and turned liquid. Your whole soul flowed out through your tongue and into the mouth of your lover" (17). Isadora also insists that this ideal encounter must be brief; spending too much time with a person would inevitably lead to overanalysis and to his becoming little more than "an insect on a pin, a newspaper clipping laminated in plastic" (18). Isadora links her fantasy to a memory of an Italian film in which a "tall languid-looking soldier, unshaven, but with a beautiful mop of hair, a cleft chin, and somewhat devilish, lazy eyes," seemingly forces himself upon a widow in a "tight black dress which reveals her voluptuous figure" (19). Initially the soldier massages between the legs of the crying widow, engaging in full sex only when the train, all too symbolically, enters a long, dark tunnel.

This scene could easily be described in terms of hegemonic masculinity and sexual aggression—the encounter can easily be read as an act of public rape, a sexual aggressor taking advantage of a woman in mourning. Yet, the scene's significance within the novel is best understood in the context in which it is appears. Isadora is on an airplane flying to Vienna with her husband, literally surrounded by psychoanalysts—many of whom have psychoanalyzed her. While her fantasy of the zipless fuck is innately malleable—a train can easily be replaced by an airplane, and a nameless soldier can easily be replaced by a captain, male flight attendant, or any other fellow passenger—the reality of her surroundings highlight the problematics of the fantasy itself. The eroticism of the fantasy suggests the possibility of wordless passion, but the immediate presence of dozens of psychoanalysts drowns the fantasy in discourse.

Almost simultaneous to informing the reader of Isadora's fantasy, the narrative also informs us of the cultural conditions that resist its materialization. The culture of which she is a part has, as Foucault might say, talked desire to death, and produced as delinquent or pathological those who attempt to make such desires real: "'I knew my itches were un-American,' laments Isadora, '—and that made things *still* worse. It is heresy in America to embrace any way of life except as half of a couple. Solitude is un-American. It may be condoned in a man—especially if he is a "glamorous bachelor" who "dates starlets" during a brief interval between marriages. But a woman is always presumed to be alone as a result of abandonment, not choice'" (17). Significantly, what seems to define the fantasy for Isadora is its representation of female sexuality outside of the context of an established or defined relationship. What is unusual about the fantasy of the train is not the public exposure of sexuality (since, after all, marriage "exposes" sexuality within specific confines), but rather the woman's desire for an autonomous sexuality that is not defined by her partner's sexuality.

"For the true, ultimate zipless A-1 fuck, it was necessary that you never get to know the man very well," proclaims Isadora (18). Such a statement further emphasizes the relationship between the fantasy and the conditions of Isadora's life. Isadora is trapped in a loveless marriage, a fact that gives the train scene more significance, particularly the detail of the woman being a recent widow, someone, in effect, permanently free of her husband. While the fantasy itself is devoid of dialogue, it is not devoid of meaning and signification. What Isadora attempts to depict as an act of intense physical desire between two individuals may be better described as a fantasy of the possibilities of desire outside of the confines of marriage. Indeed, marriage is in many ways depicted as anathema to the definition of the zipless fuck.

Moreover, Bennett and Isadora's marriage is filled with mutual disdain, annoyance, and constant overanalysis: "Wise up Bennett, old boy . . . you'd probably marry someone even more phallic, castrating, and narcissistic than I am," Isadora taunts him (13). Such an experience of physical pleasure as she describes in her fantasy of the zipless fuck cannot exist in this marriage, largely because of the limitations Isadora and Bennett place on one another. For example, Bennett's response to Isadora's implied request for oral sex is met with the question, "Why don't you buy yourself a little dog and train him," suggesting Bennett's own sexual neuroses at the possibility of being rendered sexually subordinate (or, to follow the dog theme to its natural conclusion, obedient) to his wife while simultaneously devaluing Isadora's sexual desires as a superficial cry for dumb affection (35). Given the nature of the relationship between Bennett and Isadora, it is no wonder that Isadora's fantasies suggest that to be a part of a couple is not to grow as a person, but to be limited, to be a component part of something else and fundamentally incomplete.

This notion of the zipless fuck as a fantasy of liberation is, however, just as readily contradicted by the construction of the fantasy itself. While the primary conflict and topic of the text is Isadora's affair with another man, what ultimately develops from the fantasy of the zipless fuck is her effort to find happiness within her marriage to Bennett. The seeds of this are in the setting of the zipless fantasy and in its nature as a diegetic space. It is diegetic in that the fictional train scene was constructed as a specific scene, as a story. Isadora's fantasy is also innately carceral, or prison-like, in the setting of this imagined film scene. It takes place in the restricted, public, and paradoxically private confines of the train car. According to Wolfgang Schivelbusch, the train itself is a carceral space, a space that is highly regulated, both in reality and in our imaginations. "The conductor," Schivelbusch writes, "was the civilian equivalent of the prison guard who controlled the cells from his central tower" (196). Indeed, given the nature of the scene itself, a train seems hardly a "free" space at all, as the confines of the compartment and the proximity of other passengers serves to limit any one given person's physical mobility. The depiction of the train entering the tunnel, while on one level symbolic, also obfuscates the difficulty inherent in producing sexual pleasure between two bodies when the bodies are confined by their immediate conditions and surroundings. The moment of pleasure that seems to be the defining aspect of the fantasy itself is deconstructed by the very nature of the fantasy. The fantasy of the zipless fuck, it would seem, offers far fewer promises than Isadora initially perceives, merely trading the confines of one relationship for the confines of another.

In light of the problematics of her marriage, Isadora attempts to find the zipless fuck in her actual life, to mobilize her fantasy in a material approximation of a consequence-free relationship, devoid of her usual neuroses and relationship anxieties. She attempts to make the psychoanalyst Adrian Goodlove into her ideal: "Sweet Jesus, I thought, here he was. The real z.f. The zipless fuck par excellence" (38). That Isadora would immediately latch onto Adrian is rather obvious, considering the various parameters of the fantasy of zipless fuck, for example, how the participants are identified. The man in the Italian train fantasy is a soldier, presumably on leave. To be a soldier is to be a part of a "workplace that was homosocial and apart from 'civilized' heterosocial society" (Taillon 40).[2] Standard rules of decorum as a part of "polite society" do not operate in the same way in fantasy notions of such occupations. Because Adrian operates in a similarly heterosocial sphere, his language, the consistent use of words like *cunt*, implying a degree of superficial, racist sexual interest ("it's actually more Chinese *girls*, I fancy—but Jewish girls from New York who like a good fight strike me as dead sexy") and his lack of shame towards bodily processes ("he farted loudly to punctuate" a comment about his parents, and Isadora energetically responding with "You're a real primitive . . . a natural man") suggest an unrefined, anti-intellectual crudity (39, 40; Jong's emphasis).

Adrian has, superficially at least, the potential to satisfy some of the elements of the fantasy Isadora envisions. The reliance on superficial crudity to attract her is telling, considering the problems Isadora later faces in navigating Adrian's sexuality. Indeed, Adrian's superficiality is what eventually deconstructs Isadora's fantasies, as he is far from "natural" in the terms Isadora desires. His heterosexual desire and hypermasculine presentation, we come to see, are altogether simulated, and his crudity turns out to be of the type commonly worn by men in an effort to hide femininity and sexual ambiguity (Plummer 182). The brilliant irony of this affair is that Adrian is almost completely sexually impotent, at least toward Isadora (or, perhaps, all women). The reason for this is perhaps biological, but much more likely is the suggestion that Adrian is a closeted homosexual.

The most useful element of this failed zipless fuck, then, is that Isadora is forced to encounter the signification of the fantasy itself. As a fantasy, the zipless fuck exists within a potential conceptual vacuum—a fantasy heterotopia. To mobilize such fantasy in reality is to deny the reality of action and consequence, of overdetermination and signification. When Isadora is forced to deal with Adrian's impotence, she confronts the failure of her fantasy and the inherent problematics of a fantasy defined by its refutation of more complex forms of relationships and by its rejection of the dialogic in sex. The closest Isadora gets to her ideal zipless fuck actually comes as a result of a pseudo-ménage-à-trois, as Bennett invades Adrian and Isadora's shared hotel room. Bennett, Isadora recalls:

> fucked me violently right there on the cot adjoining Adrian's. In the midst of this bizarre performance, Adrian awoke and watched, his eyes gleaming like a boxing fan's at a particularly sadistic fight. When Bennett had come and was lying on top of me out of breath, Adrian leaned over and began stroking his back. Bennett made no protestation. Entwined and sweating, the three of us finally fell asleep . . .
>
> The whole episode was wordless—as if the three of us were in a pantomime together and each had rehearsed his part for so many years that it was second nature. We were merely going through the motions of something we had done in fantasy many times . . . In the morning we disowned each other. Nothing had happened. It was a dream. (197)

This scene serves as an intriguing evolution of Isadora's fantasy. Indeed, the elements of the encounter suggest the zipless fuck: silence, violent sexuality, performativity, and the absence of any acknowledgment of the event. As with the sexual liaison between the soldier and the widow, there is an act of a taboo sexuality, one the participants never verbally acknowledge or give consent to. As in Laura Mulvey's film theory, there is an extreme visual and observational element to this event, a to-be-looked-at-ness in which the participants and observers are hyperconscious of one another.

The possible revelation of this scene is that Isadora's relationship with Adrian is impossible because he is more interested in the kind of fantasy Isadora entertains for herself—of being the recipient of violent, penetrative sex—rather than the role he plays, the ultramasculine performer of such carnivorous male sexuality. And the tragedy of this scene is that it performs the function of the zipless fuck all too well. Any progress to be made on an interpersonal level with either Adrian or Bennett is subsumed in the segregation of this fantasy heterotopia from the rest of their respective worlds.

In his essay on *Fear of Flying,* Timothy Aubry asserts that the Italian train fantasy of the zipless fuck "makes this scene the closest thing to a feminist fantasy in the entire text" through the sexual independence of the female participant (424). Yet, this later liaison among Adrian, Bennett, and Isadora suggests a collision between the fantastic and the actual that may be more liberating for Isadora. It is the closest we see her come in the text to achieving her fantasy as she conceives of it. She gets her zipless fuck, a seemingly no-strings-attached, highly visceral, potentially uncomfortable, but still satisfying sexual encounter. It even exists within the confines of her marriage—Bennett does exactly what Isadora had wanted; here their desire is not subordinated to the ambiguities of language and interpersonal power, as so much of their relationship seems to be. But what is most significant is that the encounter does *not* get talked about the next day: "confronted with a real event in their own lives they [Adrian and Bennett] couldn't even discuss it" (199). The reality of the fantasy, as it evolves in this second iteration, is one in which the fantasy exists not only in the doing, but in Isadora's later retelling. Isadora's fantasy comes to encompass her vision of herself as a writer, as someone for whom the fantasy, while fun for what it is, is most important for what it does. In much the same way the Italian film inspired her original fantasy, so, too, does Isadora's meta-fictional fantasy influence the creation of feminist fantasies for her readers.

This second event also represents a significant shift in Isadora's conceptualization of her ideal fantasy. Where before she seems to lament the constant belaboring of desire and sexuality within the construct of psychoanalytic discourse, this scene demonstrates the failure of desire through silence. Perhaps the most significant reason for this is that Isadora's initial fantasy of the zipless fuck can only operate within the confines of film (or more broadly, fiction) and the technical aspects of the medium in which it is deployed. Film and fiction have historically made extensive use of stock characters or character types. Such a narrative mode is based on the idea that a character's value to a story is in that character's ability to function according to certain conditions. Film has historically relied on stock characters for entertainment and narrative efficiency. Likewise, Isadora's fantasy is one in which the male character enters as lothario, rake, seducer of women, and effectively dissolves after his usefulness is fulfilled. Yet the characters in Jong's novel refuse to dissolve. The men with whom she seeks sexual satisfaction refuse to enter and exit her life at her convenience. Their bodies persist, problematically, even as she tries to rid herself of them. Here, rather than proceeding like the tryst between the widow and the Italian soldier, Isadora's night with Adrian is interrupted by a very alive Bennett, a character not so easily "killed off" or forgotten.

Such physical protestation and the eventual rejection of discourse between the two men about the evening leaves Isadora annoyed; she eventually describes them as "Siamese twins joined at a crucial but invisible spot on the side of the neck." Yet more important, Isadora has now, at the very end of the chapter, cast herself as character type in relation to both of these men. She is "Pandora and her evil box," the box implying her body, or, more specifically, her vagina (199). The passive and powerfully mysterious widow has been replaced by a chaotic and active female sexuality. The night shared by Isadora, Bennett, and Adrian alters the significance not only of the male characters in the fantasy but of the central female character as well.

Rather than a female body as pure locus of sexual desire, waiting to consume and be consumed by pleasure as the script dictates, the female body at the end of this scene is recast as an expulsive source of chaos and change through its sexuality. The significance of this expands Isadora's personal agency. She has, at last, achieved some form of change in her life, but only through action. The fact that she is dissatisfied with the nature of the change is essential to the further production of fantasies, new fantasies embedded in the physicality of her writing instead of merely in the immateriality of her thought. Isadora as Pandora seems to reflect Hélène Cixous's sentiment that "I, too, overflow; my desires have invented new desires, my body knows unheard-of songs. Time and again I, too, have felt so full of luminous torrents that I could burst with forms much more beautiful than those which are put up in frames and sold for a stinking fortune" (876). Cixous's call for women to produce and to create through the body is answered by Isadora and affirmed in later instances in the novel where the body is both exposed and full of productive energy.

Following the night with Adrian and Bennett, Isadora leaves with Adrian to explore Europe and attempt to discover, however that might be, a true fantasy of sex and desire. This trek, however, is also couched within Isadora's remembrance of her youth in an upper-middle-class New York home, a part of a family of failed and bitter artists. This middle section of the novel traces the origins of many of Isadora's anxieties about being a woman and an artist, a product of a family that practiced a reserved prudishness toward sex while superficially endorsing the ideals of "free love." The origins of her quest for her zipless fuck are, Isadora suggests, partially the fault of D. H. Lawrence, whose Lady Chatterley served as Isadora's introduction to sexual knowledge and was also a model by which to measure her own capacity, or lack thereof, for ecstatic sexuality. "At fourteen all I could see were the disadvantages of being a woman," laments Isadora. "I longed to have orgasms like Lady Chatterley's. Why didn't the moon turn pale and tidal waves sweep over the surface of the earth?" (217). For a young Isadora, the constructedness of female desire is too much to comprehend, as she is forced to hunt for pleasure that is meaningful and good not because of the feeling itself, but because it triggers the production of some external phenomenon. What Isadora comes to fear most in this imagined quasi-impotency is that her sexuality and her capacity for desire and pleasure are nonproductive, that she is creatively and physically barren and unable to be a "true" artist, and only truly suited to domestic slavery. Ultimately, these dueling images—of a barren, failed, lonely artist, and of a Pandora-like demigod of creative energy—compete in the production of Isadora's further fantasies.

One of the most significant ways in which these dueling images manifest themselves in Isadora is through these fantasies, her rampant production of desire and her frustration in being unable to ever fully sate her appetites. Perhaps the most embodied desire Isadora expresses is in her desire to have a child. "Suddenly I wanted a child with my whole heart. Adrian's child. Bennett's child. My child. Anyone's child. I wanted to be pregnant. I wanted to be *big with child*" (348). Pregnancy is a significant desire, largely because it is the biological phenomenon that most directly represents productive desire. It is a literal symbol of nonvirginity, of having been desired physically by another. More importantly for Isadora, it is a symbol of her nonaloneness. For Isadora, pregnancy and childbirth also signify a means to produce an end to her aloneness, the ultimate incarnation of "turning to an analyst, to a lover, to a husband, a parent" for solace and understanding (348). Pregnancy is a bodily form that makes a stark declaration of the fecundity of one's body and an exposure of "the inner body . . . indeed its entire inner economy" to the rest of the world (Laqueur 121).[3] Pregnancy for Isadora attests to essential qualities of one worth desiring, of having a lover and of having had meaningful connections with that lover. This discussion of children and childbirth needs to be understood within the context of the failure of Isadora's past relationships,

relationships that proved more destructive than productive and which never lasted long enough to have children come of them. Isadora perceives her lack of children as a signifier of her inability to truly be loved by another and of her body's hunger for new sensation, but also of its inability to fully realize the expectations of her desires.

After relating her family history and her own fears about herself as a person and artist, Isadora has a dream that serves as another powerful, complimentary example of the evolution of the fantasy of the zipless fuck. Isadora experiences a series of dreams related to her anxiety over her difficulty in discovering the ideal partner; in the first, she has to "walk a narrow plank between two skyscrapers to save someone's life," whose life is never certain, but it is clear that failure to save this person's life would ultimately lead to the ruin of her own. Following this is a dream in which she is back in college, where she "walked up a long flight of steps . . . teetered on very high heels and worried about tripping over [her] gown" (398). She is handed her diploma and told that she is allowed three husbands simultaneously, but that those who are awarding her the diploma hope she will decline the allowance in favor of picking one. Isadora gives an impassioned defense of her right to all three. Afterward, "I was picking my way down the steep steps, half crouching and terrified of falling. I looked into the sea of faces and suddenly realized that I had forgotten to take my scroll. In a panic I knew that I had forfeited everything: graduation, my fellowship grant, my harem of three husbands" (398). In the final dream sequence, the most important for my purposes, Isadora is back at graduation, making her way to the lectern, encountering the French novelist Colette, who acknowledges that Isadora's first novel was, at the very least, a beginning, albeit a "shaky" one. After this, Colette undoes her blouse, and, Isadora says, "I understood that making love to her in public was the real graduation, and at that moment it seemed like the most natural thing in the world. Very aroused, I moved toward her. Then the dream faded" (225–226).

The first two dream sequences involve a lack of mobility on Isadora's part. Awkwardly walking a plank between two skyscrapers, afraid of falling, becomes walking in high heels, afraid of tripping over her gown, to receive her diploma. In each dream, Isadora lacks control over her body and her surroundings. She is all too conscious of the physical danger of falling in the first, and all too conscious of the embarrassment of falling in the second. Her physical instability in each reflects the unhappiness her pursuit of a culturally prescribed and acceptable male partner, or set of male partners, has brought her. Ultimately, it is in the model of Colette that she finds satisfaction and, ultimately, this final dream sequence is the only one that brings about any kind of narrative or individual progress in Isadora's constant concern for her sexual and romantic happiness. This final dream sequence most clearly demonstrates a reorganization of priority and desire for Isadora. While the dream fades before Isadora can engage in sex with Colette, the discursive potential of this scene has already been realized: within the framework of this final dream, Isadora realizes that stability is an illusion and that a teleological endpoint for relationships and for one's desires is equally intangible. Even the dream ends on a cliffhanger, never quite realizing the sexual act itself, but moving inexorably toward it. Isadora comes to realize that personal satisfaction is found in expression rather than in the silence of her once ideal film fantasy, expression in both her creative works and in her pursuit of desire and pleasure.

This dream scene figures as the final evolution away from her previously expressed anxieties about a woman entering the active, public world. Having lost both Adrian and Bennett, Isadora laments her affair, not for any kind of moral violation of trust between partners, but for the tragic impotence she believes her pursuit of the zipless fuck has cost her partners. As Isadora says: "I knew what I had done wrong with Adrian and why he had left me. I had broken the basic rule. I had pursued him. Years of having fantasies about men and never acting on them—and then for the first time in my life, I live out a fantasy. I pursue a man I madly desire, and what happens? He goes limp as a waterlogged noodle and refuses me" (377). Her Collette dream reconfigures the impotence of female sexual desire into a procreative power of self-representation, one that locates female expression as the natural, generative seed of culture. The public nature of the event is similarly significant in the way that it mobilizes a fluid fantasy of desire, as Isadora engages in the same kind of voyeuristic fantasy as with the zipless fuck. The "naturalness" of the scene is embodied both in its homoeroticism and in the public nature of the encounter. The zipless fuck as initially outlined by Isadora is significant partially because of its mediated voyeurism: it is an encounter of which Isadora is aware precisely because of its filmic—and intentionally public—nature.

In terms of scopic power, Isadora is both an exhibitionist and voyeur in this final dream sequence. There is a consciousness of being observed, but also an implied awareness of observing. The naturalness of the scene encompasses the social relations, the being watched and the conscious awareness of being watched, that define that brief, potential moment of homoerotic pleasure. Jong recovers a feminist fantasy by defying the normalized institutions of sexual relations in favor of a more fluid—the second dream melts into and becomes the final, third dream with Colette—fantasy of pleasure, even if the fluidity of that fantasy allows (or perhaps necessitates) it to be public.

If the patriarchal ideal of the woman is one of less-ness, or of limiting the occupation, especially public, of the female body and its discursive abilities, then we can also understand a counternarrative to this ideal as one that understands masculine fear of the female body in the female body's ability to violate these set cultural boundaries. Indeed, the public female body could be understood in this sense to be a contaminating agent for patriarchy, one that explicitly highlights its fundamental lack of control over the female body. Approaching the end of her novel, Jong conceives of a menstrual experience for Isadora so intense that the floor of her hotel room "was beginning to look like the aftermath of a car wreck" (402). So profuse is her bleeding that Isadora, who has always welcomed her period for its proof of her being not pregnant, for the first time regards it as part of the overall hassle of female body management, complete in her memory alongside training bras and the various half-understood facts of sex gleaned from late-night television. Her period takes on special significance in the context of patriarchal conceptualizations of female menstruation, ranging from understanding periods as "unabashedly . . . failed production" to viewing them as signs of the contaminating influence of female bodies on public spaces (Martin 92–94).

Yet, while Isadora regards her body's corporeality with marked disdain, she perceives her period as something of a mark of freedom, of the potential for independence from a purely reproductive act of femininity. In some sense, this reconceptualization of the period, perhaps the most intense symbol figure possible for the reality of female sexuality and materiality, demonstrates a clear evolution from Isadora's once gilded conceptualization of the zipless fuck. The heterotopic fantasy has been overcome by this crisis, a state in which Isadora must successfully mediate her own bodily needs and desires with her own surroundings, compromising and improvising (even making herself a make-shift diaper). Jong humorously recounts Isadora's attempts at disposing of her Kotex pad in a French commode, an act that clogs the drain, both literally and figuratively, of Western society.

Isadora's period also marks the end of this transformative period in her life. She comments that "Leaving Bennett was my first really independent action, and even there it had been partly because of Adrian and the wild sexual obsession I had felt for him" (390). The zipless fuck, a model of a potentially unachievable ideal—all sex carries with it some burden of consequence, even if left unspoken—has served a useful purpose in a journey of self-discovery.

The novel ends with Isadora finally acting out a fantasy. While she was never able to truly find comfort or pleasure with her own body, here we finally see her relax and take pleasure in being alone, even if it is only for as long as it takes

Bennett to return to the hotel room. The ending depicts a fantasy that may be less about sexual temptation than it is about self-acceptance, particularly bodily self-acceptance. And it is also fundamentally uncertain: "Perhaps I had only come to take a bath. Perhaps I would leave before Bennett returned. Or perhaps we'd go home and work together and work things out. Or perhaps we'd go home and separate. It was not clear how it would end" (424). Readers are never privileged to see what fate lies ahead for Isadora's relationships. Yet, to emphasize the plot in this instance would be to ignore Isadora's final warning to the reader: "Life has no plot . . . At least it has no plot while you're living" (424). The plot is immaterial to the ending, but what is material is Isadora. Naked, exposed, and still self-evaluating, Isadora looks over her body and decides, for the first and only time in the novel, that it is "a nice body."

Fantasies are, for Isadora Wing, a critical way to develop a more complex relationship with both her own body and her own desires. A number of critics have read Isadora's return to Bennett's hotel room to wait for him in the bath as a mark of defeat, of Isadora sacrificing her independence to return to the relative security of patriarchy. Such a reading, however, ignores the nature of the narrative—a story of an individual's development, of her exploration of desire in the face of the unknown. Essentializing desire, a central element of human sexuality, as a lesser form of sexual experience and reducing the novel to a story of Isadora's succumbing to cultural and hegemonic narratives fails to recognize the capacity her fantasies have for subversion of those narratives. As Walter Benjamin says, the actor masters the apparatus, demonstrating the capacity for individuals to act as free agents in relation to norms and systems of power that go far beyond their capacity to affect on an individual basis. Indeed, actors grow in different roles to expand their power over the apparatus. Isadora's fantasies evolve from a longing for a brief, consequence-free bout of physical intensity to a desire for true, lasting satisfaction. Isadora may never get what she wants. We have no guarantee returning to Bennett will provide her the happiness she is looking for, but the importance of the action lies in the acting: to pursue one's fantasies is not a sign of insanity, but rather the only sane thing to do.

Notes

1. Prison and marriage, two of the institutions most readily analyzed by Michel Foucault across his intellectual career, operate according to established formulas and are intimately related to the construction of society. Much like the construction of gay or female identity, Jong's text also highlights the constructedness (or, perhaps, nonnaturalness) of the institution of marriage and its similarity to the formal parameters of modern prisons.

2. Paul Taillon in his essay "To Make Men out of Crude Material" writes specifically of American railroad culture as a model for the masculine homosocial in labor-intensive occupations in the United States in the early twentieth century. Regardless of the difference, his analysis of certain modes of masculine labor is applicable to Isadora's fantasies.

3. Thomas Laqueur discusses models of body and their significance in the early modern period, particularly emphasizing Mikhail Bakhtin's discussion of "grotesque bodies," which he identifies as reproductive bodies, largely open to the world, with their interiors exposed for the full view of the public. As a model of signification, one can argue that the pregnant body is one that is still labeled or categorized as grotesque or pathological in some way. For further explication on the topic, please see Zillah Eistenstein's *The Female Body and the Law.*

Works Cited

"Altitude Sickness." Rev. of *Fear of Flying,* by Erica Jong. *Times Literary Supplement* 26July 1974. 813.

Aubry, Timothy. "Erica Jong's Textual Bulimia: *Fear of Flying* and the Politics of Middlebrow Consumption." *Journal of Popular Culture* 42.3 (2009): 419–441.

Benjamin, Walter. *The Work of Art in the Age of Its Technological Reproducibility.* Cambridge: Belknap P of Harvard U, 2008.

Bordo, Susan. *Unbearable Weight.* 10th anniversary ed. Berkeley: U of California P, 2004.

Cixous, Hélène. "The Laugh of the Medusa." *Signs* 1.4 (1976): 875–893.

Eisenstein, Zillah. *The Female Body and the Law.* Berkeley: U of California P, 1988.

Foucault, Michel. *The History of Sexuality.* Vol. 1: *An Introduction.* New York: Vintage, 1990.

Hogeland, Lisa. *Feminism and Its Fictions.* Philadelphia: U of Pennsylvania P, 1998.

Jong, Erica. *Fear of Flying.* New York: Holt, Reinhardt, and Winston, 1973.

Laqueur, Thomas. *Making Sex.* Boston: Harvard UP, 1990.

Martin, Emily. *The Woman in the Body: A Cultural Analysis of Reproduction.* Boston: Beacon Press, 1987.

Plummer, Ken. "Male Sexualities." *Handbook on the Study of Men and Masculinities.* Ed. Michael Kimmel, Jeff Hearn, and R. W. Connel. London: Sage, 2005. 178–195.

Rev. of *Fear of Flying,* by Erica Jong. *Best Sellers* Dec. 1973. 425.

Rhodes, Jacqueline. *Radical Feminism, Writing, and Critical Agency.* New York: State University of New York Press, 2005.

Schivelbusch, Wolfgang. *The Railway Journey.* Berkeley: U of California P, 1977.

Taillon, Paul. "To Make Men out of Crude Material." *Boys and Their Toys.* Ed. Roger Horowitz. New York: Routledge, 2001. 33–54.

Chapter 8

Coming Out and Tutor-Text Performance in Jane Chambers's Lesbi-Dramas

Jaime Cantrell

> Politics is theater. It doesn't matter if you win. You make a statement. You say, "I'm here, pay attention to me."
>
> —Harvey Milk

> It is perfectly meaningless to "come out" as a heterosexual.
>
> —Michael Warner

Exploring lesbian hypervisibility, or the blatant, surface representation of explicit lesbian topics and themes in second-wave feminist and Southern literary productions, I turn to Jane Chambers's considerable contributions to lesbian theater history as exemplified by lesbi-dramas *A Late Snow* (1974), *Last Summer at Bluefish Cove* (1980), and *My Blue Heaven* (1981). Through a combination of surface and close readings, I assert that these plays function as especially explicit tutor-texts, because instances of lesbian hypervisibility in these works, are, in fact, performed.[1] In this way, the plays concretize visually and aurally what the script conveys, and, in so doing, they require the audience to process and understand codes and meanings at a moment's notice—while, perhaps, calling into question the theatergoer's beliefs or values (Davy 44). Through the performance of these plays a sort of visual imaginary is communicated to the audience: discourses within the scripts advocate for lesbian social justice at the national level, intersecting with social politics and public identification.[2] Representations of positive lesbian relationships, friends and lovers, combine to produce a critical and visible message to audiences, an unabashed and discernible demand for equality, tolerance, and solidarity. There are infinite possibilities for performance and reperformance in these works, which in turn, nightly set the stage for progressive political claims.

In dialogue with one another, Chambers's plays evidence robust engagements with lesbian sexuality, sociality, and political intersectionalities. These vibrant works are significant, even central, to the burgeoning national story of feminist politics and creation of a lesbian historiography. As dramatic performances, *A Late Snow, Last Summer at Bluefish Cove,* and *My Blue Heaven* would have generated palpable energy, creating liminal space where the politics of being and coming "out" was both a performed and performative gesture. Chambers's writing, and the performance of her works, all but beg the audience to come out—as allies, as lesbians, as activists, and as feminists—placing her work at the center of the late 1970s-era gay and lesbian movement in terms of disclosing one's sexual identity publicly for the purposes of achieving social justice. At the heart of Chambers's plays is a drive toward imagining a new normativity into existence, a different worldview where lesbians who had entered into heterosexual marriages at one time could keep custody of their children (Rae and Annie in *Last Summer at Bluefish Cove*), where being out as a lesbian at a university was not a risk to one's career (Ellie in *A Late Snow*), and where two women could legally get married (Molly and Josie in *My Blue Heaven*). Chambers creates a world of love between women, where love "makes the world go round, resolves all problems, conquers all," a place where love is related to hope in some wonderful and obscure way that is as yet undetermined, but which inspires change (*My Blue Heaven* 83).

Thinking Lesbian Theater and Performativity

While it is not my intention to provide a sweeping chronicle of lesbian theater in America or lesbian-themed drama in Southern literature, I do seek to explore trends in these plays that parallel and engage with major changes in American culture at the time they were written and produced on stage, as twentieth-century gay and lesbian life increasingly marked plays, playwrights, and performers. I also seek to acknowledge the importance of lesbian playwrights occupying a double minority position in terms of sex and sexuality—complicated further here by Southern regional identities and contexts. As Gary Richards noted in a 2013 Modern Language Association Convention panel on "The South and

Sexuality," "theater and performance studies have been notoriously uninterested in regional identity."

Beyond the scope of mid- and post-mid-century literary productions, contemporary playwrights negotiating sexualities and working within (global) Southern contexts include Jim Grimsley, the much-publicized Tony Kushner, Cuban-American 2003 Pulitzer Prize winner Nilo Cruz, and Alfred Uhry (often recognized for his 1987 Off-Broadway play *Driving Miss Daisy*, later the 1989 Academy Award for Best Writing Adapted Screenplay). The large-scale success of *Driving Miss Daisy* as a film adaptation, for example, would have shaped and framed understandings of the region in the mainstream, however stereotypical and racially fraught they were. Within a landscape of Southern writers producing works of drama, it is particularly striking that scholarship on post-midcentury Southern female playwrights depicting non-normative sexualities neglects to engage dramatists including Carolyn Gage, Sharon Bridgforth, and Shay Youngblood.

Chambers's plays are examples of what I call non-Southern Southern writings; more precisely, these works lean toward nuance and intricacy when representing Southernness. Chambers avoids overtly Southern settings in an effort to foreground her tutor-text messages through lesbian hypervisibility. Moving her characters into Southern locations would shift the focus from lesbian issues of political importance to overwhelmingly regional ones. We understand her non-Southern Southern writing, that is, her strategic inclusion of Southern (literature) allusions, when considering it within the framework of more explicitly, self-consciously Southern writings, and, most importantly, alongside other works of lesbian drama in Southern literature. Reading the surface allusions to Southern drama in her plays allows us to imagine these works operating in and accessing the South across a temporal and geospatial divide. Lesbian schoolteachers in *A Late Snow, Last Summer at Bluefish Cove,* and *My Blue Heaven* are reminiscent of Karen and Martha in Lillian Hellman's *The Children's Hour,* for example. As I will demonstrate, these instances of energetic intertextuality elicit an odd sense of *déjà* or *presque vu,* a sense of details already or almost seen, as precise representations of space and place, settings, vocations, and small textual references within the plays align Chambers's lesbi-dramas with other key works of Southern lesbian drama, in effect producing a non-Southern Southern context.[3] These three Chambers plays are crucial but understudied lesbian literary productions of the period that evidence a sizeable awareness of the national feminist movement and concretize the formidable, vitalizing role that Southern lesbians had in it.

Chambers was born in Columbia, South Carolina, and grew up in Florida, although as a writer, she is "not usually associated with the South" (Flora 429).

After attending Rollins for a year, Chambers studied acting at the Pasadena Playhouse before becoming a full-time writer. Her literary oeuvre is sizeable. Her output can be attributed to a myriad of job experiences: she worked as a staff writer for a television station in Maine from 1964 to 1966, as a literary agent, television soap opera writer, and theater critic in New York City, and before she began writing plays, she acted in them. "I got out of college and tried to participate in the coffee house theater Off Off-Broadway," Chambers recalls, "but at that time it was even harder than today for a woman to get anything done. Primarily I worked as an actress and I also wrote" (Hill 520). Chambers wrote over twenty novels under various undisclosed pseudonyms and at the age of forty-six, at the height of her career as a playwright, she died of brain cancer.

Before her death, her twelve plays garnered considerable national attention, awards, and grants; they were performed in lesbian theaters Off-Broadway and "even in regional theaters" (Faderman 596). Chambers got her break when her civil rights play *Christ in a Treehouse* aired on Connecticut Educational Television in 1971 (Haggerty 156). Each following year saw some success: her plays *Random Violence* (1973), *Mine!* (1974), and *The Wife* (1973) were first presented at the Women Interart Theater in New York City, of which Chambers was a founding member (Hagerty 156). Vexingly, it is extremely difficult to establish whether Chambers's plays had been performed at all in the South, and if so, what their reception might have been. Southernness, then, is not emphasized to the degree that lesbian hypervisibility is, although small, deft references within the plays evidence anxieties surrounding the urban/rural divide, strategically allude to other histories of Southern literature and drama, and subtly connect to the region. As one example, consider how Chambers's *A Late Snow* strands lesbian characters in a snowbound cabin; this deliberate use of snow-as-fate and "out there"-ness is reminiscent of Carson McCullers's *The Member of the Wedding* (1946), where Frankie is obsessed with snow and the new life it represents for her. "One of the most intriguing features of modern lesbian-themed literature," according to Terry Castle, is "its tendency to hark back, by way of embedded intertexual references, to earlier works on the same subject" (Castle 85).

The referential settings Chambers embraces in these plays pointedly set their characters apart from city life—immersing them in women-populated spaces where lesbian sociality fuels the realistic, domestic-comedy dramas. Castle identifies two mimetic contexts in which realistic works of lesbian literature have presented flourishing lesbian plots and characters: the world of adolescence or "the world of divorce, widowhood, and separation" (85). Castle seeks to develop a contextual environment that surrounds postmarital relations, but I wonder if separation, when conceived as a network of spaces mediated through the politics of place, might encompass locales and settings that are exclusive, remote, secluded, isolated, and out of the way. Chambers's *A Late Snow, Last Summer at Bluefish Cove,* and *My Blue Heaven* eschew city-based metro-narratives of lesbian life as they instead favor intimate spaces where women gather to support one another and build lasting friendships and community: an old cabin by a lake, where five women become trapped together during a snowstorm, an island cove that had been "a gay women's haven for thirty years or more," and finally, a dilapidated farmhouse located someplace in upstate New York (*My Blue Heaven* 49). Chambers avoids both urban settings and overtly Southern ones in an effort to foreground her tutor-text messages—moving her characters into Southern locations would actually distract from the hypervisibility of lesbianism because it would inadvertently shift the focus from lesbian sexual issues to regional ones. In a way, these settings are conspicuously non-Southern, and are, in effect, hypovisible examples of Southern literature even as they suggest hypervisible representations of lesbian sexuality and sociality.

It should be noted that Chambers wrote largely for a general audience, and with the exception of the three plays that are the focus of this chapter, she did not usually incorporate lesbian characters or themes (although her 1982 two-character one-act play *Quintessential Image* does).[4] This does not compromise the emotional truth of these works or diminish the universal applicability of their themes—justice, equality, rights, and the right to love; indeed, it suggests that Chambers was keenly aware of the highly charged moment in which she was writing and producing. With these three plays, her contribution to lesbian theater was "monumental, far beyond that which other lesbian playwrights had previously achieved" (Flora 149).

In a *New York Times* review from 1981 titled "Play's Theme: Lesbians With Out Apology," Chambers is heralded as an iconic contributor to contemporary lesbian theater, distinctive in feminist voice and mission: "Jane Chambers is a playwright who speaks for the cause of women in general and lesbians in particular. Ask her which has been the greater obstacle in her life: her gender or her sexuality, and she answers: 'That's easy—judgments are based on seeing; one of the things about being gay that doesn't get in the way is that, most of the time, you can't see it, but being a woman is something you have to deal with every minute'" (Klein). Chambers's response is laden with a feminist consciousness-raising rhetoric characteristic of the 1970s-era Women's Liberation Movement, and it reveals the centrality of her identity politics and personal narrative.

Chambers's three lesbian-centric plays were also a direct response to late 1970s and early 1980s feminisms—particularly in terms of conceiving the politics of coming out as not only descriptive, but also deeply constitutive. As a performative utterance within the field of speech-act theory, coming out is constitutive even though it is made to sound descriptive due to its communicative nature.[5] Each of these plays pioneered positive self-images of lesbians while resisting and dispelling traditional negative stereotypes of lesbians as pathologically ill.[6] Her works resist narratives of lesbian fiction where bonds between women are broken up by heteronormative systems and structures, or where lesbians die, get married, reconcile themselves with celibacy, asexuality, or return to the erotic world of men (Castle 85).[7]

Jane Chambers's own stance on the classifying and categorizing of lesbian plays is important, especially when taking into account tutor-text messages in her works: "The world calls them [lesbian plays], and producers call them that. As far as I'm concerned, they are *plays*" (Sisley 53). As for labeling her own body of work, Chambers remarks, "I'm not a one subject playwright—and there is no reason to believe I will be categorized—at least I hope not" (Klein).[8] This chapter will endeavor to sidestep posthumously categorizing Chambers, while simultaneously establishing these three plays as groundbreaking works representing love between women as nonpathological, and most important, representing relationships between lesbians as deeply invested in community-building and sociality.[9] Chambers's plays intersect with each of Emily L. Sisley's nine working definitions of lesbian theater, especially as they are "dedicated to clarifying points concerning oppression" and practice "consciousness-raising in performance" (47).

Lesbian theater of the late 1970s and 1980s was interconnected with and a product of concurrent U.S. feminisms, and the gay and lesbian theater movement in turn paralleled the Women's Liberation Movement. The bulk of lesbian theater was produced in major metropolitan areas including New York City, Los Angeles, Minneapolis, Chicago, and San Francisco. In an effort to begin cataloging these theater groups, the Gay Theater Alliance was formed in 1978.[10] In a 1981 article written for *The Drama Review*, Terry Helbing, the cofounder of the alliance describes a list appearing in their January 1981 newsletter comprising "28 lesbian and gay theater companies in 21 cities and in 5 countries" (42).[11] Feminist theater groups were also formed at that same time, and many ran lesbian-themed plays and plays written by lesbians—works like Kate Kasten's *On the Elevator*, Holly Hughes's *Lady Dick* (1985), Cherríe Moraga's *teatro, Giving Up the Ghost* (1986), Sheila McLaughlin's *She Must Be Seeing Things* (1987), and Jane Wagner's Broadway hit *The Search for Signs of Intelligent Life in the Universe* starring her partner, Lily Tomlin. These plays, and many others, also fall on the spectrum of Sisley's lexicon.[12] In "Notes on Lesbian Theater," Sisley interviews the artistic director of The Cambridge Lesbian Theater who, in 1980, mentions several lost and forgotten lesbian shows performed between 1977 and 1978 in New Orleans, including such scintillating titles as *Dyke Drama Drag Show* and *Outlaw Music* (55).

Other dedicated lesbian theater companies produced plays that hypervisibly engaged with lesbian themes—ranging from coming-out experiences to "boldly sexual work." These included The Lavender Cellar in Minneapolis, Medusa's Revenge in New York, the Front Room Theater Guild in Seattle, and the Red Dyke Theater in Atlanta, Georgia, which sought to "entertain lesbians and celebrate their sexuality, *not* to educate straight people about lesbian and gay issues" (Sinfield 309). Through archival research, I can ascertain that Jane Chambers's *Last Summer at Bluefish Cove,* her most successful and frequently performed lesbian play, was produced in at least one Southern city, at Red Dyke.[13]

Some theater companies aimed to educate heterosexual audiences by scattering stereotypes and lesbian myths. While Chambers did not gear her work toward that purpose, she acknowledged that personal testimonies and audience reception played a key role in the plays' cultural importance: "Gay people tell me they feel better about themselves, and straight people can suddenly understand a son or a daughter who is gay. I didn't mean for the play to do that, but I'm thrilled that it's helping people" (Klein). While lesbians were disadvantaged with negative representations, silencing, exclusions, and the pressures of conforming, experiencing Chambers's *A Late Snow, Last Summer at Bluefish Cove,* and *My Blue Heaven* yielded a celebratory valuing of lesbians both on and off stage; the plays produced lesbian sociality through their nightly runs, and they resulted in expansive, affectively charged benefits for their receptive heterosexual audiences open to lesbian visibility and social and political acceptance.

Naming oneself a lesbian or identifying one's work or theater company as specifically lesbian during the 1970s and 1980s was, in itself, a revolutionary and semantically revelatory act, because it equated to public visibility. Public, explicit naming was an empowering act, as it signaled a massive shift out of the silence and open secret cultural practices characteristic of mid-century Southern authors to a politics of consciousness, recognition, and acknowledgment. Within the realm of lesbian theater, speaking and performing personal testimony holds the power to transform, as naming oneself "burn(s) at the heart of lesbian feminism" (Zimmerman 672).[14]

Regardless of who Chambers wrote for or how her plays were performed in their various contexts, *A Late Snow, Last Summer at Bluefish Cove,* and *My Blue Heaven* challenged and changed audiences by asserting lesbian hypervisibility and the right to personal fulfillment. They highlighted key issues important to the national feminist movement (solidarity and sociality) and the gay and rights movement (coming out, in particular) in an empowering way. These works framed what was possible—to be seen and to be—at the time.

We Are All Seeing Things: Tutor Texts and Politics of Visibility

A Late Snow

Chambers's *A Late Snow*, billed as "an important play that should be seen by everyone, straight, gay or on the fringe," brings together a small group of women, each grappling with her own relationship to sexual identity (Drama-Logue). They exhibit strength and fear, embarrassment and bravery, and various degrees of out-ness as they struggle to negotiate their complex interpersonal relationships to one another. It was a lesbian romantic comedy about, in Chambers's own words, "five women snow-bound in an isolated mountain cabin: Ellie and her first, last, current and next lover" (jacket cover). The two-act play debuted in 1974 at the Clark Center for the Performing Arts in New York City, produced by Playwrights Horizons and directed by Nyla Lyon.[15] The cast included Susanne Wasson playing Ellie, an esteemed college professor; Carolyn Cope as Quincey, a sincere college student and Ellen's current lover; Susan Sullivan as sassy, alcoholic Pat, Ellie's last lover; Anita Keal playing Margo, a novelist and Ellie's future lover; and Marilyn Hamlin playing the unattainable Peggy, Ellie's first lover. *A Late Snow* employs some features of a traditional romantic-comedy formula that would have appealed to audiences—surprise characters appearing late in act 1, confrontations and confessions, a prism of love triangles, and witty satire. It is a story about romantic love: what love is good for us, what love we must move on from, and how we determine what we need and want from love. Ellie, the central character, struggles to examine her relationships, when a freak, late season snowstorm brings her lovers together for one thrilling evening.

Although the play was destined for success, Chambers encountered great difficulties during the production stage: "beginning with auditions, when women refused to read for a lesbian role, and culminating when a cast member dropped out the day before the opening because her boyfriend convinced her she would not get any more commercials if she appeared onstage as a lesbian. Chambers later described the experience as a 'hideous nightmare,' which abruptly changed when the play was a hit and 'suddenly the cast and crew adored each other.' The Broadway option was dropped, however, after six months when no backers were interested in a play about lesbians" (Peterson and Bennet 73).

The challenges to producing a play representing lesbian hypervisibility were unmistakable, but the radical import of such an endeavor—even in New York at the time—should not be undervalued. As conventional representations of women on stage altered and shifted with the rising tide of cultural mores, images of difference performed aurally and visually focus attention on the lesbian, shifting representation from marginal subject to political being with agency.

In the middle of act 1, Ellie, the professor, and Quincey, her student and current lover, grapple with their disparate views on coming out at their university, and indeed, on speaking and claiming a public lesbian identity. Both are passionate in maintaining their points of view and honest in their emotions with each other, while perhaps not being entirely honest with themselves about their fast-crumbling relationship. In *Publics and Counterpublics*, a study on how the idea of public frames our understandings of modern politics, literary texts, and contemporary life, Michael Warner writes,

> Being publicly known as homosexual is never the same as being publicly known as heterosexual; the latter always goes without saying and troubles nothing, whereas the former carries echoes of pathologized visibility. It is perfectly meaningless to "come out" as heterosexual. So it is not true, as common wisdom would have it, that homosexuals live private lives without a secure public identity. They have neither privacy nor publicness, in these normative senses of the terms. In the United States, the judiciary, along with the military and its supporters in Congress and the White House, has gone to great lengths to make sure that they will have neither. It is this deformation of public and private that identity politics—and the performative ritual known as coming out—tries to transform. (52–53)

The delicate issue of when (or if) to come out would have undoubtedly resonated with 1970s-era audiences, even as it is still under negotiation today, as workplace nondiscrimination policies continue to be a pressing concern. The personal exchange between Ellie and Quincey evidences more than a squabble between lovers, one scared to come out, the other desperate to challenge workplace inequities. It is a call for advocacy that, even then, engaged with issues at the forefront of national politics—1974 marked the heyday of both the gay liberation and Women's Liberation Movements. It was not accidental that such energies on the page and on the stage engaged with real, political forces determining and shaping the professional and personal lives of gay men and lesbian women.

The scene below hypervisibly performs an already public national dialogue, fueled by U.S. Supreme Court decisions on workplace discriminations and by laws that targeted homosexual teachers:[16]

ELLIE: It makes people uncomfortable. They don't understand.

QUINCEY: It's time we made them understand.

ELLIE: Quincey, I know you're right.

QUINCEY: Then, why won't you do something about it? Aren't you proud? Don't you like yourself?

ELLIE: I like being a woman.

QUINCEY: A woman who loves other women.

ELLIE: Quincey, listen to me! When I was your age, "lesbian" was a dictionary word used only to frighten teen-age girls and parents. Mothers fainted, fathers became violent, landlords evicted you, and nobody would hire you. A lesbian was like a vampire: she looked in the mirror and there was no reflection.

QUINCEY: You're scared.

ELLIE: Of course I'm scared. I don't want to be different. I don't want people pointing fingers at me, misguided altruists feeling sorry for me.

QUINCEY: You're a VIP on campus. You could be a figurehead.

ELLIE: I don't have the courage to be a figurehead, Quincey. I'm sorry. (*She starts to leave.*)

QUINCEY: Ellie? I hope I didn't screw things up for you. I don't want to hurt you. I love you. I love you, love you, love you. (*Ellie holds her.*) It's just that I'm so fucking tired of living in a closet. (46)

At the foreground in this exchange are affective resonances stemming from fear and probable backlash. Ellie cannot imagine performing the action required to be a figurehead on campus, because she does not realize that she is already a political subject—an inactive, unintentional one. In "Sexual Indifference and Lesbian Representation," Teresa de Lauretis writes, "the political concepts of oppression and agency developed in the struggles of social movements such as the women's movement, the gay liberation movement, and third world feminism, as well as an awareness of the importance of developing a theory of sexuality . . . takes into account the working of unconscious processes in the construction of female subjectivity" (177).

Ellie's agency, or lack thereof, with regard to coming out publicly as a lesbian, hinges on the discourses surrounding concepts of public and private, publicness and visibility, pathologized sexuality and identity politics. The play's central message as a tutor-text places positive representations of lesbians in the public eye while educating on issues relevant to lesbian-feminists and the national homophile movement. But Ellie, as a character, is deeply enmeshed in the struggles of living in the closet, unable to fully negotiate the paradoxes and possibilities of coming out. In a way, the play holds up a mirror to the audience members, inviting them to reflect on their understanding of community, subjectivity, and visibility.

On the surface, we see not only same-sex desire and partnership between Quincey and Ellen, but also a nonnormative relationship in terms of intergenerational difference. Ellie, the older professor, does not want anyone to know about her sexuality, as she crosses an age-span where articulating one's lesbian identity shifted from not okay to something more normalized, if not a burgeoning new normal. Her position is entirely understandable—as a lesbian, she has been invisible. Quincey, however, a plucky young student, sees the situation from a different perspective. She urges Ellie to engage with the politics of coming out and begs her to reject the invisibility that continues to shape her sexual identity. Quincey wants to exit the closet; she yearns for people to know not only that she is a lesbian and that Ellie is a lesbian, but that they are together in a committed relationship. For Quincey, it is through this visibility that her sexuality—and her taboo intergenerational student/professor relationship—is affirmed, validated, and conveyed.

This question of who produces representations of lesbians, for whom, and to what end grounds de Lauretis's work in theater and performance theory, on homosexual subjectivity and spectatorship. She calls on Elizabeth Ellsworth, who argues "that the struggle over interpretation is a constitutive process for marginalized subjectivities, as well as an important form of resistance" (169). With this interpretive struggle in mind, the dynamics of seeing in the scene presented earlier are multifaceted. Ellie has difficulty understanding (or finding the courage to recognize) how coming out would challenge the invisibility that burdens her. Quincey sees coming out as a deeply meaningful performative act, one that would enrich their individual subjectivities and improve the health of their relationship. To readers, and to the audience, this fraught exchange between Quincey and Ellie visually suggests the emotional labor of remaining closeted, a constant effort that remains unseen but is gestured toward on stage. At stake in not coming out is continued silence and affective upheaval. At stake in coming out would be a near constant repetitive performance, something very much viewed, seen, and witnessed. And yet what Ellie does not consider—something the reader and spectator might themselves not process though it is suggested in the script—is that the risks Ellie fears in coming out will remain whether she speaks or not. Housing discrimination, violence, and fear of unemployment exist in the world beyond the playhouse. This is certain. What is unclear is whether or not Quincey will stay despite Ellie's refusals. The play navigates different registers of the political (no job protections) and the personal (will they stay together?) through a delicate balance of humor and tension.

Offstage, the audience's relationship to lesbian hypervisibility enables them to consider alternative forms of being and moving in the world—sexually, politically, and from a social justice perspective. Considerations of temporality illuminate the tutor-text message conveyed through the performance to the audience. In "Constructing the Spectator," Kate Davy elucidates, "perhaps performance by its very nature has more subversive potential than other venues precisely because the spectator is unable to stop and reread one of its moments. In this sense her perceptions are more easily manipulated and learned conventions can be smashed up against her new imagery and relationships in a time sequence that allows little room for reflection" (52). This interplay of lesbian hypervisibility *performed* versus lesbian hypervisibility *read* concretizes my argument: that the possibilities for performing sociality and lesbian sexuality enable teaching moments for the audience, where key issues might be pulled to the forefront of the aural and visual arena.

Onstage, Ellie acknowledges that with time she began to decipher what she needs and wants most out of a relationship, and how that changed drastically from her position on romance as a young woman. And yet her fiery passion for true love is still there—eloquent, alive, and infectious—despite the succession of her past lovers parading in and out of the rustic cabin. Ellie wants, and she wants badly enough to finally act. There is a usefulness to this temporal aspect of identity. In inhabiting her lesbianism in this way, moving forward through the snow that has trapped her both metaphorically and physically, Ellie can finally move away from her past of failed relationships toward a future that reimagines her public life, where coming out provides points of access to personal and social change.

Last Summer at Bluefish Cove

In *Last Summer at Bluefish Cove,* Chambers again centers the action of the play on a core group of lesbians, best friends who have been visiting a summer getaway together for several years. Eva, a heterosexual woman and newly initiated feminist who arrives at the cove lost, does not know this history. Like Peggy in *A Late Snow,* Eva functions both as a straight outsider and as a point of reflection for the other characters, as each woman explores her own notions and experiences of "the lesbian lifestyle." As hilarity ensues, so too does a generative self-awakening, where Eva yearns to locate herself within both her feminist ideals and the lesbian community. Meanwhile "her presence immediately provokes tension among the group, most notably from Dr. Kitty Cochrane, the best-selling author of a book on women's sexuality who fears being outed by Eva, and from Lil, who worries her attraction to Eva will turn out badly" (Peterson and Bennet 73).

Along with Kitty, Eva, and Lil, the characters compose three couples, each exhibiting a certain diversity within a white, middle-class framework: Sue, a very wealthy older lesbian partnered with Donna, a frequent shopper; Lil, soon to be paired with Eva; Kitty, partnered with Rita, her most enthusiastic supporter; and Anne and Rae, in a stereotypical butch/femme relationship but with two grown children from former heterosexual marriages. To amplify the comedic dialogue, these established partnerships are complicated and enhanced by a crossover pairing: for example, Lil used to date Kitty, although unlike Annie and Rae who are in a nine-year relationship, Lil confesses she is not "a long-distance runner" (22). Unbeknownst to Eva, oscillating just beyond the scene a startling revelation awaits: Lil is dying from cancer after previously successful chemotherapy treatments have stopped working. Her time at the cove is limited, and although she finds love for the first time in her life, she must soon say goodbye.

The play as tutor-text remains focused, celebrating life and love, lesbian sociality, and the call for social justice. Remarkably similar to Ellie in *A Late Snow*, Kitty fears the social repercussions of revealing her sexual identity publicly. Within the first few pages of the play, Chambers constructs a scene where two characters debate the politics of visibility and consequences of coming out, a surface discussion necessitated by Eva's arrival at the cove:

> LIL: She seems like a nice woman. She's all right, Kitty, it's going to be okay. (*Pause.*) Knock, knock, Kitty, can you hear me through the closet door?
>
> KITTY: If this woman blows my cover, if she goes to the media and announces Dr. Kitty Cochrane is a dyke (*She wags her finger at LIL*) do you know how David Susskind would love to get hold of that?
>
> LIL: Deny it, Kitty. Deny everything. You're so good at that.
>
> KITTY: The public is not ready. The public is still trying to accept the concepts of equal rights and the clitoral orgasm. It would be a catastrophe for me to come out of the closet now. It would be as incredible as if—Gloria Steinem announced her intention to marry—Marlo Thomas. The entire Movement would shudder and collapse. (27)[17]

Chambers's direct references to key figureheads in the women's movement and the gay and lesbian movement would have not been lost to audiences reasonably aware of popular culture, and this exchange evidences one of the key moments in the play where intertextuality acts as a springboard for audience interpretation and for the reading process. Gloria Steinem needs no introduction; in the decade prior to *Last Summer's* production, Steinem cofounded the National Women's Political Caucus with other feminist leaders, including Betty Friedan and Fannie Lou Hamer. In an article written for *Time* in 1970, Steinem advocated for lesbian marriages in the context of a utopian future she worked toward as a radical feminist activist.

Kitty mentions David Susskind, a perhaps lesser well-known figure, but important advancer of gay rights. His syndicated *David Susskind Show* ran on New York affiliate stations every Sunday night from 1966 to 1986, and it featured guests who spoke compassionately about homosexuals (see Battaglia). In 1971, Susskind hosted two gay-themed shows, one with a panel of seven lesbians, including activist Barbara Gittings who told him, "Homosexuals today are taking it for granted that their homosexuality is not at all something dreadful—it's good, it's right, it's natural, it's moral, and this is the way they are going to be!" (Tobin and Wicker 220).

Kitty's quip that Susskind would just love her coming out was both hilarious and accurate, as Susskind's talk show in the 1970s "provided more national air time to homosexuals than any other program," according to the *Advocate* (Alwood 40). Such programs indeed had a considerable impact on gay and lesbian audiences, as Susskind's show not only educated the general public—"unusual and controversial topics, including homosexuality, attracted radio and television audiences"—but it also provided a visible means by which gays and lesbians could have a voice in unashamedly constructing their public image, expressing their stance against sexual discrimination and for social justice, and finally, stand as beacons for the closeted homosexual community (ibid.). We might read Kitty's assessment as both a sign of her personal reticence and of her understandably complicated relationship to what would have been a fluctuating public image of the lesbian—complicated by the mediating, "out there" counterpublic space of the cabin, where lesbianism was accepted. But beyond that generative space, nonnormative sexualities carried specific political and civil consequences.

Consider the cove itself as a space of fruitful, positive lesbian community. There, lesbians connected an ability to speak their love of women with the power found in recognizing others like themselves. Building on the concept of language as action, of coming out as a performative act that produces community, and of the transformative social power in conveying lesbian-feminist ideals through her plays, Chambers's writings as tutor-texts evidence a literary step in generating the momentum behind the late 1970s to early 1980s gay and lesbian movement.

My Blue Heaven

The last of her plays that I will examine in this chapter, *My Blue Heaven,* presents *Green Acres*–like television hilarity with a twist: lesbian affirmation and hyper-visibility punctuated by a heavy insistence on the issue of marriage equality. Loosely based on her own partnership with Beth Allen, Chambers's longtime lover and manager since their meeting at Goddard College in 1971, *My Blue Heaven* features a lesbian couple, Molly Sanford and Josie Williams. Chambers, who wrote for television years before, was intrigued by a compelling thought: how might lesbian themes and style function in a mainstream entertainment style characterized by 1970s television, including situation comedies such as the *Mary Tyler Moore Show*? (Williams). Her answer was *My Blue Heaven,* which was produced by The Glines and opened at the Shandol Theater on June 3, 1981, for the second annual Gay American Arts Festival in New York City. Connecting *My Blue Heaven* to *Green Acres,* for example, rewrites a plot where northerners go to the live on a rural country farm, while in this play, the South is recognizable through its absence.

Wisecracks and off-the-cuff glib humor proliferates in *My Blue Heaven.* The play is set in a ramshackle farmhouse in upstate New York—rounding out Chambers's predilection for setting her lesbian plays beyond the scope of traditional city life, a reversal of a stereotype that suggests that gay utopias may not be found within the metropolis after all.[18] Each of Chambers's lesbian plays instead favor backward, rustic, and unfashionable locales for their subversive potential for lesbian sociality. And, continuing her commitment to the politics of coming out, Chambers creates a central scene in which visibility and public awareness are under negotiation:

JOSIE: You sold a book once, a whole book!

MOLLY: And it cost me my teaching job! *Living the Good Gay Life* did not sit well with the New York City School Board!

JOSIE: Well, write about something else.

MOLLY: You're the one who told me to write what I know! You bought that little plaque and hug it over my desk in the city: BLOOM WHERE YOU ARE PLANTED. Well, financially, where I'm planted, the soil sucks.

JOSIE: (Hurt.) There's nothing gay about that column you write for the *Farmer's Journal* now.

MOLLY: Of course there is! I can't help myself, I'm possessed!

JOSIE: Honey, your column is about a heterosexual All-American young couple, homesteading. "The Adventures of Molly and Joe."

MOLLY: I'm Molly and you're Joe. It's the story of you and me. I just change your gender.

JOSIE: I'm not crazy about having my gender changed.

MOLLY: I'm not crazy about having to use your last name as my by-line. This column is the only thing I write that sees print and I'd like to see my name on it!

JOSIE: Well, do it!

MOLLY: I can't. If anybody on the *Farmer's Journal* were to connect Molly Sanford, homespun humor columnist with Molly Sanford, known dyke author of *Living the Good Gay Life* . . .

JOSIE: That's so unlikely, honey. (17–18)

Molly's remonstrative attitude toward their reduced circumstances is palpable and surfaces in this early scene. After having suffered the censure of the New York School Board in the form of the lawful termination of her ninth-grade teaching job on the grounds of homosexuality, Molly's attitude is "once burned twice shy." The book that got her fired, *Living the Good Gay Life*, not only revealed her lesbian lifestyle, but also portrayed a (doubly damning) positive view of love between women. Molly wants to continue to write, but her solution landed both partners in somewhat unfamiliar territory: away from the repressive city, secluded in a farmhouse where their sexuality is uninterrupted by social pressures and standards—including the structures that privilege heteronormativity.

Making a go of the country life, with their reduced financial circumstances, ultimately takes a toll on the vitality of their relationship. Enmeshed in a self-sufficient domestic lifestyle, Josie, who has a master's degree in computer science, tinkers and tries her hand at pioneering earthworm communities, developing a methane generator fueled by chicken shit, and constructing a poorly engineered windmill. In maintaining her relationship with Molly, she wonders aloud, "If we never make love, are we still lesbians?" (27). After nearly a decade filled with the strife and turmoil of city life, both women are struggling to hang on, and Molly's heteronormative "print family," appearing as a column in the local *Farmer's Journal*, is a frequent source of their discontent. It symbolizes their financial dependence on ideals they do not share, creates a public life that is not available to them, and, in turn, impacts the emotional tenor and labor of their relationship.

Complication arrives in the form of two men: religious, disruptive, heavy-handed intruders. The first, Ralph Miller, an ultraconservative editorial executive at the American Way Book Company, seeks to market and capitalize on Molly's relationship—more accurately, the falsely constructed relationship between Molly and Big Joe as exemplified by her column. They are two "independent, individual, courageous, hardworking . . . modern pioneers that people can look up to," or as Ralph says, a family that is "very special in this age of self-serving perversity" (38, 42). In exchange for an advance check of seventy-five thousand dollars, he exclaims:

RALPH: Why, Mrs. Williams, we are going to make your family the most famous family in America! You and Big Joe and little Arnold—your faces will be on cereal boxes and magazine covers, we'll put you on talk shows, we'll make you America's First Family, Mrs. Williams, the real life symbol of good Christian living.
MOLLY: Oh, Josie.
JOSIE: Oh, Molly.
MOLLY: Oh, Mr. Miller. (39)

Little does Ralph know, the traditional family he seeks as a beacon of conservative Christian hope in an increasingly degenerate world is in fact composed of two lesbians, their goat, another litter of kittens in the barn, and "the horniest damned rooster in the western hemisphere," Arnold, who doubles as Molly and Big Joe's son in the *Farmer's Journal* column.

Eventually, Molly confesses her lie (or her hypocritical homestead family, according to Josie) to Ralph, and in a gesture of sheer brilliance, Molly blackmails him by threatening to out herself to the general public and publicize their true lesbian relationship through The American Way Book Company. In this scene, Molly outs Big Joe, or her lover of nine years, Josie:

MOLLY: (*Holding onto contract.*) Mr. Miller, meet Jo Williams.
RALPH: (*Scanning the room.*) I beg your pardon?
MOLLY: This is Big Joe. This is she.
RALPH: Big Joe Williams is your husband.
MOLLY: (*Her arm around JOSIE.*) Josephine Williams is my lover.
RALPH: I don't understand.
MOLLY: Arnold is a rooster.
RALPH: I beg your pardon?
MOLLY: We're lesbians, Mr. Miller. (She sees he doesn't understand.) Gay. (*He still doesn't get it.*) Homo-sex-u-als.
RALPH: You mean you've duped the public?
MOLLY: I only changed the gender of my partner and endowed a rooster with some human qualities.
RALPH: You mean . . . You're really . . . ? (They nod.) The L-word? Lord God, I never met one before. (*He backs away from them.*) (42–43)

Ralph, unable to fathom the depths of sexual depravity he unwittingly sought out, leaves the cabin with a promise to sue the women for misrepresentation. As act 1 draws to a close, the audience and readers are surprised to learn that the scenario was in fact nothing more than a figment of Molly's imagination. Josie wakes Molly, and then there is a blackout to intermission.

The television-like premise of *My Blue Heaven* suggests it is worth dwelling on the seductions of realism in the first act of the play. As readers, we are duped into the construction of reality—articulated through the dreamscape—in effect, fooled about what's really happening, much in the same way that Mr. Ralph Miller is. Compulsory heterosexuality and the intentional framing and marketing of Molly's *Farmer's Journal* column fools Ralph into believing that Big Joe is a man and somewhere just around the corner, off-stage, and out of view (in a pointed reversal of the traditional representation of the lesbian figure in literature). Audience members would have been equally duped, as the action takes place within the realistic performance space of the play.

The bulk of act 1 of *My Blue Heaven* again heavily engages with issues of privacy and identity politics, and the reimagining of a different, better world for lesbians, one in which coming out translates into increased political visibility and equality. Although figured as a dream, in coming out and introducing Big Joe Williams as Josie, Molly risks greatly and is rewarded for it. Reading with the grain, we see three distinctive valences in her coming out to Mr. Miller: initially, she calls Josie her lover; then, she speaks their sexuality as lesbians (thus suggesting public visibility, even within the private space of the cabin); and finally, she solidifies their "perversity" by literally and semantically spelling out the word *homosexuals*. That Ralph struggles to interpret her meaning is not lost on the audience, who do not share his difficulties. In a way, Ralph's inability to grasp their sexuality, that they are lesbians, symbolizes the very closeted space that Molly and Josie flee in favor of their rustic cabin in the woods—where remoteness allows for lesbian possibility. However, in the repeated process of coming out excerpted, we see the constitutive, descriptive nature of the act as well its own important particular form of heteronormative resistance.

My Blue Heaven departs from *A Late Snow* and *Last Summer at Bluefish Cove* in a surprising way—the entire second act centers on the issue of homosexual marriage. Within a conceptual, social, and legal system of heterosexuality at the national level, this degree of consciousness-raising and advocating for lesbian marriage within the context of the play seems surprising as well as strategically planned. Foreshadowing clues lie in the play's title, and a minute reference in the front matter of the script, where the set is described. Both the title, *My Blue Heaven*, and the initial stage direction, "When the audience is seated, a harmonica is heard. It plays 'For Me and My Gal'" (10). This song references previous films and songs of the same name, as does the song "My Blue Heaven," originally recorded in 1928 by Gene Austin, and a cover standard ever since (with notable performances by Fats Domino, Frank Sinatra, and Norah Jones). The lyrics describe a couple together, cozy by the fire, so happy in their blue heaven: "Molly and me, and the baby makes three." That Chambers anthropomorphized the rooster, Arnold, in the play undoubtedly provided many laughs; significantly, this deft gesture again harkens back to *Green Acres* vis-à-vis a pig on the show called Arnold.

Beyond comedic value, and beyond a play's performed verisimilitude, such a direct commitment to envisioning a future where marriage equality exists must have been extraordinary at that time. The majority of act 2 engages with this thematic, one that is introduced by the play's second male intruder, Dr. John. The minister is a past boyfriend of Molly's, a man she could not marry because she was in love with a woman. Ironically, he enters *My Blue Heaven* advocating for visibility, social acceptance, and marriage equality:

> MOLLY: It's not legal for us to get married, Johnny. (*She nervously eats a cookie.*)
>
> DR. JOHN: It's time somebody challenged that. Homosexual matrimony was one of the major topics of our conference.
>
> MOLLY: It was?
>
> DR. JOHN: There are a lot of you now—our statistics say fifteen percent. Everybody's coming out of the closet. There are more of you than there are blacks. You're the major minority.
>
> JOSIE: No kidding?
>
> DR. JOHN: You're an issue.
>
> DR. JOHN: I think we could get the national press.
>
> MOLLY: My mother would have a heart attack. The Ku Klux Klan would ride up here and burn this house down.
>
> JOSIE: It's insured.
>
> DR. JOHN: No change occurs unless somebody's willing to take chances. (*He picks up book from shelf.*) You wrote this book. *Living the Good Gay Life*. You stuck your neck out once.
>
> MOLLY: Once was enough.
>
> DR. JOHN: This book has helped a lot of people, Molly. I use it in my Young Adult group sessions.
>
> MOLLY: You do?
>
> DR. JOHN: It helps the straight kids understand the gay kids and makes the gay kids feel good about themselves. You did something worthwhile here. (73)

Reading with the play, the rhetoric of coming out of the closet echoes throughout Chambers's works, as I have argued. But *My Blue Heaven* is her only play that explicitly references the performative, constitutive act of coming out. Here we see a culmination of the tutor-text messages of social progressiveness sprinkled across her works of drama. Coming out is significant and even central to living a public life. In fact, everyone should be doing it.

John calls homosexuals "a major minority" and places sexuality inside a web of intersectional identity politics, linking nonnormative sexuality and race. Such a move evidences awareness of cycles of salience within the national frame, linking the gay and lesbian homophile movement to a lineage of progressive social movements, exemplified by the fights for civil rights and racial equality begun only a decade or two earlier—in the South. Molly's humorous response belies a very real concern she has: fear of repercussions. Experience with publishing *The Good Gay Life*—speaking as a lesbian and putting her sexuality in print—has taught her that consequences are inevitable. When she incorporates the Ku Klux Klan as censure and threat, it carries a clear association with the South and enforced racial segregation. Here again, we see evidence of Chambers's strategic use of non-Southern Southernness. But the presence of this paradigmatic Southern threat posits a continuum of nondominant identities (not just blacks, but gays and lesbians, too) as possibly vulnerable to house burning. Chambers's hypervisibility postulates the fight for (gay and) lesbian equality as a civil rights issue while deliberating linking it to the South.

If a challenge to the heteronormative institution of marriage seems surprising, it is also because that imagined, progressive future is introduced in the play by a minister. Given our current lesbian, gay, bisexual and transgender, queer political climate, this seems familiar, as pastors in South Carolina just recently petitioned to overturn the state's ban on same-sex marriage, citing their freedom of religion. We might consider the exchange with the minister above with that sensation of déjà vu that I outlined earlier. For the scholar of Southern literature, seemingly recognizable correlatives and associations have contributed to and shaped our understandings of Chambers's use of non-Southern Southernness through deft allusions to other works of Southern drama that incorporate strong lesbian themes. Could such a system of details "already seen" shift and operate in the reverse temporal direction?

Analyzing Chambers's plays through surface reading techniques begs us to place it within a temporal frame that allows for (a) critical examinations across works of Southern drama that were produced before its publication, as in the case of allusions to particular aspects of McCullers's and Hellman's works; (b) conceiving specific, individual examples as part of a process enabled or facilitated through more concurrent texts produced within the same period, say, connecting *My Blue Heaven* with *Green Acres*; and (c) thinking with Chambers in our own temporal moment, that is, aligning her work from the past with events and literatures of special significance in the present. In addition to reading this scene from *My Blue Heaven* alongside recent political stances on marriage equality from South Carolina preachers, we might briefly pause to consider how Molly's book, *The Good Gay Life,* itself functions as a tutor-text (just as each of Chambers's lesbi-dramas does). As John says, it "helps the straight kids understand the gay kids and makes the gay kids feel good about themselves," much in the same way that the nationally visible "It Gets Better" campaign, begun in 2010, works to communicate similar messages of hopeful futurity to gay, lesbian, bisexual, and transgender youth facing bullying and harassment in the U.S. schools and communities.[19] Such is the beauty of incorporating surface reading methods alongside close readings of texts. Chambers's *A Late Snow, Last Summer at Bluefish Cove,* and *My Blue Heaven* each provide exceptionally rich examples through which to not only model these points, but also to utilize them in making a persuasive case for reading her dramas as works of Southern literature produced during an especially rich period of national second-wave feminist writing.

These plays increase spectators' awareness of key issues at the forefront of the lesbian-feminist movement: coming out politics, marriage rights, and workplace equality. Similarly, and at a basic level, these plays taught theatergoers—whether gay, straight, lesbian, queer, allies, supporters, or homophobes—the role of sexual identity in creating and shaping one's subjectivity, even as they actively illustrated that there's more than one way to be (act, perform) a lesbian. The characters in these works are not exemplary. There is no sense of particular exceptionalism, deification, separateness, or natural superiority. Chambers's women are ordinary in their quests for success and love, passion and commitment, and they are everyday in their commonplace woes and worries. What is extraordinary, however, is the unapologetic portrayal of lesbians, lesbian-feminist politics, and most importantly, the repeated, performed representation of lesbians as social beings and political subjects during a remarkably charged period of activism for the larger feminist movement.

Notes

Epigraphs. Harvey Milk (Sean Penn) to Scott Smith (James Franco) in Gus Van Sant's film *MILK* (2008). Michael Warner in *Publics and Counterpublics* (52).

1. See Martina Ladendorf's "Commercialization of Lesbian Identities in Showtime's *L Word*" in *Culture Unbound* 2 (2010), 265–282, for a discussion of teaching moments;

this article posits the television series as a learning text for a heterosexual audience who wonders what lesbians do and how lesbian desire and lesbian sexual possibilities are constructed and embodied.

2. It may be worth briefly mentioning how these plays express their politics. They are not overwhelmingly didactic in, say, the manner of political plays of the 1930s or jarringly experimental, as with modern and postmodern drama. Instead, the dramatic form and style of these plays are realistic: they incorporate social critique and social commentary.

3. Terry Castle calls this sensation "a feeling of outright 'possession' by the ghosts of the lesbian literary past" (62).

4. Chambers's *Quintessential Image* written in 1982 "was published posthumously in a double bill with *In Her Own Words,* a biographical portrait compiled from her writings" in 1989 (Haggerty 156). See her novel *Burning* (1978) and *Kudzu* (1981) for more examples of lesbian representation.

5. For more on performative utterances, see J. L. Austin's *How To Do Things with Words* (Cambridge, MA: Harvard UP, 1962). For gender and speech act theory, see Judith Butler's *Excitable Speech: A Politics of the Performative* (New York: Routledge, 1997).

6. See Ann Fleche's essay "The Lesbian Rule: Lillian Hellman and the Measures of Realism" in *Modern Drama* 39.1 (1996), 16–30, for a discussion of Southern lesbian drama where lesbian characters are ignored, portrayed negatively, or ambiguously represented.

7. For more on celibacy in canonical works of American literature, see Benjamin Kahan's treatment of Henry James's *The Bostonians* in *Celibacies: American Modernism & Sexual Life* (Durham, NC: Duke UP, 2013).

8. Twenty-eight years after Chambers's death, during the Twenty-Third Annual Lambda Literary Award acceptance speech, Edward Albee (best known for his plays *A Zoo Story* (1958), *The Sandbox* (1959), and his 1962 produced/1963 Tony Award for Best Play winner, *Who's Afraid of Virginia Woolf?*) would echo her sentiment, saying, "A writer who happens to be gay or lesbian must be able to transcend self. I am not a gay writer. I am a writer who happens to be gay." In a National Public Radio interview conducted with Rebecca Montagne in 2011, he remarked, "Maybe I'm being a little troublesome about this, but so many writers who are gay are expected to behave like gay writers and I find that is such a limitation and such a prejudicial thing that I fight against it whenever I can."

9. In Klein's "Lesbians With Out Apology," Chambers comments on the troubling representations of lesbians and gays in twentieth-century American theater history, quipping, "The Boys in the Band," the breakthrough play for male homosexuals, "was negative; the characters didn't like themselves," Miss Chambers declared. "Maybe 'Bluefish Cove'"—which has been referred to as "The Girls in the Sand"—"will open the door for lesbian characters," who have previously been depicted as bizarre ('The Killing of Sister George') or suicidal ('The Children's Hour') or simply nonexistent."

10. For more information on the Gay Theater Alliance, and the Gay Theater Alliance list of gay and lesbian theater companies, see Terry Helbing's papers at New York's Lesbian, Gay, Bi, and Transgender Community Center (hereafter, The Center).

11. It is unclear at this time how many of these companies might have toured in the

South, for example, or how many Southern cities might have appeared on the list—such detailed information is buried within an archive, notably Helbing's personal papers in New York at The Center. However, fascinatingly, The Center's online finding aids show four folders within the collection dedicated to Jane Chambers, in box 2, folders 27–30—providing clear evidence that Chambers's work resonated within the highest echelons of the premier gay and lesbian theater organization of the late 1970s and early 1980s.

12. See Phyllis Mael, Beverly Byers Pevitts, and Rosemary Curb's "Catalog of Feminist Theater" in *Crysalis: A Magazine of Women's Culture* 10 (April 1980), and *Feminist Theater Groups*, surprisingly published in Jefferson, North Carolina (McFarland & Co., 1980). For more contemporary sources on gay and lesbian theater history, see James Fischer's *"We Will Be Citizens": New Essays on Gay and Lesbian Theater* (Jefferson, NC: McFarland, 2008) and various chapters in Alan Sinfield's *Out on Stage*.

13. The Red Dyke Theater was established in 1974 by a group of Atlanta lesbians who self-described as "sharing an interest in theater, dancing and boogying, lesbian/feminist politics, and huge egos!" and who had eventually grown tired of "male-identified theater" (Chenault, *Gay and Lesbian Atlanta* 67). According to Fran Pici, one of the co-founders, "The members of RDT were very involved in both the gay and lesbian and women's communities" (Chenault and Braukman 67). For more on the Red Dyke Theater from a Southern sexuality studies perspective, see chapter 17 in James T. Sears's *Rebels, Rubyfruit, and Rhinestones: Queering Space in the Stonewall South* (New Brunswick: Rutgers University Press, 2001), where he mentions the Red Dyke Theater as an aside, "the weekend events included a standing-only-room performance by the Red Dyke Theater Group" (185). Finally, it bears mentioning that the Red Dyke Theater appeared within one of Minnie Bruce Pratt's vignettes in *S/he* (1997) titled "Steam Heat."

14. For examples of lesbian silencing and exclusions in modern lesbian writing, see Terry Castle's *The Apparitional Lesbian*.

15. According to their website, the Clark Center was created in 1959 by Alvin Ailey. It housed a multiracial and multiethnic arts community for three decades before closing in 1989 due to considerable financial struggles.

16. See, as one example, the 1985 Supreme Court case Board of Education v. National Gay Task Force, which challenged a law that allowed schools to fire teachers for homosexual conduct. Also see Anita Bryant's national 1977 "Save Our Children" crusade that began through a successful repeal of an ordinance in Dade County, Florida, which prevented discrimination based on sexual orientation, and Harvey Milk's successful campaign against California Proposition 6 (aka the Briggs Initiative), which would have banned gays, lesbians, and allies from working in California's public schools.

17. The tongue-in-cheek reference to Marlo Thomas is rather ironic. Marlo Thomas is well known for her 1972 album *Free to Be . . . You and Me*, a product of second-wave feminist thought and activism; the album was released as part of a *Ms.* Foundation for Women initiative. The album's contributors included major recording artists of the time, including Carol Channing, Michael Jackson, and Diana Ross. The album's content circulated expressive, safe zone messages about gender while challenging dominant gender

stereotypes—encouraging children to embrace individualistic choices, as exemplified by the song "William Wants a Doll." However, a rigid heteronormative frame exists within this idyllic gender-neutral text: William only wants to play with a doll because he expects to marry a woman and become a father someday. Well before *Free to Be . . . You and Me,* Thomas was the star of the television sitcom, *That Girl* (1966–1971), and was only the second woman (after Lucille Ball) to carry a hit show. Steinem and Thomas are also notably heterosexual.

18. For an excellent discussion of rural queer stylistics and a critique of queer metronormativity, see Scott Herring's *Another Country: Queer Anti-Urbanism* (New York: New York University Press, 2010).

19. For more on the history and scope of the "It Gets Better Project," created by the nationally syndicated sex columnist Dan Savage, consult itgetsbetter.org.

Works Cited

Alwood, Edward. "The Gift of Gab: How Independent Broadcasters Gave Gay Rights Pioneers a Chance To Be Heard." *Media Queered: Visibility and Its Discontents.* Ed. Kevin G. Barnhurst. New York: Peter Lang Publishing, Inc., 2007. 25–47. Print.

Battaglia, Stephen. *David Susskind: A Televised Life.* New York: St. Martin's Press, 2010. Print.

Castle, Terry. *The Apparitional Lesbian.* New York: Columbia University Press, 1997. Print.

Chambers, Jane. *Last Summer at Bluefish Cove.* The JH Press Gay Play Script Series. New York: JH Press, 1982. Print.

———. *A Late Snow.* The JH Press Gay Play Script Series. New York: JH Press, 1970. Print.

———. *My Blue Heaven.* The JH Press Gay Play Script Series. New York: JH Press, 1982. Print.

Chenault, Wesley, and Stacey Braukman, eds. *Gay and Lesbian Atlanta.* Dover: Arcadia Publishing, 2008. Print.

Davy, Kate. "Constructing the Spectator: Reception, Context, and Address in Lesbian Performance." *Performing Arts Journal* 10.2 (1986): 43–52. *JSTOR.* Accessed 16 May 2014. Electronic.

de Lauretis, Teresa. "Sexual Indifference and Lesbian Representation." *Theatre Journal* 40.2 (1998): 155–177. *JSTOR.* Accessed 16 May 2014. Electronic.

Faderman, Lillian. *Odd Girls and Twilight Lovers: A History of Lesbian Life in Twentieth-Century America.* New York: Penguin, 1992. Print.

Flora, Joseph M., Lucinda Hardwick MacKethan, and Todd W. Taylor, eds. *The Companion to Southern Literature: Themes, Genres, Places, People.* Baton Rouge: Louisiana State UP, 2001. Print.

Haggerty, George E., John Beynon, and Douglas Eisner, eds. *Encyclopedia of Lesbian and Gay Histories and Cultures.* Vol. 2. New York: Routledge, 2000. Print.

Helbing, Terry. "Gay Plays, Gay Theatre, Gay Performance." *Drama Review* 25.1 (1981): 35–46. *JSTOR.* Accessed 19 May 2014. Electronic.

Hill, Holly. "How Do Playwrights Make a Living?" *Theatre Journal* 33.4 (1981): 517–526. *JSTOR*. Accessed 16 May 2014. Electronic.

Klein, Alvin. "Play's Theme: Lesbians With Out Apology." *New York Times* 8 Feb. 1981. http://www.nytimes.com/1981/02/08/nyregion/play-s-theme-lesbians-with-out-apology.html. Accessed 13 May 2014. Electronic.

Patton, Cindy. "Tremble, Hetero Swine!" *Fear of a Queer Planet: Queer Politics and Social Theory*. Minneapolis: U of Minnesota P, 1993. 143–177. Print.

Peterson, Jane, and Suzanne Bennet, eds. *Women Playwrights of Diversity: A Bio-bibliographical Sourcebook*. Atlanta: Greenwood, 1997. Print.

Sinfield, Alan. *Out on Stage: Lesbian and Gay Theatre in the Twentieth Century*. New Haven: Yale UP, 1999. Print.

Sisley, Emily L. "Notes on Lesbian Theatre." *Drama Review: Sex and Performance Issue* 25.1 (1981): 47–56. *JSTOR*. Accessed 16 May 2014. Electronic.

Steinem, Gloria. "What Would It Be Like If Women Win?" *Time* 31 Aug. 1970. http://content.time.com/time/magazine/article/0,9171,876786,00.html. Accessed 16 May 2014. Online.

Tobin, Kay, and Randy Wicker. *The Gay Crusaders*. New York: Paperback Library, 1972.

Warner, Michael. *Publics and Counterpublics*. New York: Zone Books, 2005. Print.

Williams, Albert. "My Blue Heaven" Footsteps Theatre Review. *ChicagoReader* 7 March 1991. *Theatre Reviews*. Accessed 18 May 2014. Electronic.

Zimmerman, Bonnie. "The Politics of Transliteration: Lesbian Personal Narratives." *Signs: The Lesbian Issue* 9.4 (1984): 663–682.

Chapter 9

Creating a Nonpatriarchal Lineage in Bertha Harris's *Lover*

Laura Christine Godfrey

Bertha Harris's 1976 novel *Lover* garnered critical attention for its postmodern style, its commentary on lesbian identity, its use of nonlinear time in narration, and its redefinition of familial relations. Yet, one stylistic choice that is most apparent in reading the novel is absent from most critical investigation. Throughout the novel, Harris prefaces each chapter with an epigraph about a female saint, usually consisting of a few sentences on her life and death, yet these prominent pieces have been overlooked by all but one critic in the small pantheon of *Lover* criticism. *Lover*'s experimental form shapes a new identity for the sexual subversives of the novel's narrative and of the reading audience, those who seek life beyond patriarchal community. In this chapter, I propose that Harris uses saints' narratives to provide alternative biological and familial connections in her creation of a nonpatriarchal lineage for women who seek to escape the confines of traditional gender roles.

As Harris's *Lover* leaps forward and backward in time to present stories about both familiar and unfamiliar characters, the main narrative defies simple summary. Samaria and Veronica, the novel's protagonists and matriarchal leaders, were both previously married to Theophilus and, after his death, met and became inseparable. Veronica occupies various roles throughout the novel: forger of art, meta-fictional author of *Lover* itself, and cross-dresser Harold Horoscope. Samaria maintains a steady role as biological mother to the other female characters: Flynn, who wants to live as a brain separate from the body, and formerly congenital twins Rose and Rose-lima, who create a screenplay of *Lover* including scenes of twenty-foot-tall women with "gallons of blood pouring from their bodies—out of you-know-where" (196). These women are, for Harris, the sexual-subversives of second-wave feminism for whom she created a new world, a "pleasure dome," and "Renaissance heaven . . . where there's sex" (xxi). The characters of the novel's main narrative, as well as the women saints of the epigraphs, fully enjoy the sexual and spiritual ecstasy that characterizes the new all-women community, though not until after experiencing the oppressive violence of the patriarchal society they aim to leave. The experiences of Veronica and her community exist "to assess similarities of the players and to find a common basis for a community of women," including the novel's reading audience (Stimpson 378). The epigraphs of female saints that precede all but three of the novel's forty-five chapters provide proof of an extant separatist community into which the novel's characters and audience can enter.

These forty-two epigraphs offer condensed biographies of forty-eight saints who were formerly or are still officially recognized by the Roman Catholic or Eastern Orthodox churches. In her introduction to the 1993 reprint, Harris explains that *Lover*'s characters and the saints of the epigraphs are modeled on the saints' cards Harris earned in school, among other things. These cards were "intended as aids in meditation and prayer," but Harris "deliberately mistook" them "as objects of art" (xxiii). Most of these saints are present in hagiographies like Ælfric's *Lives of the Saints*, Jacobus de Voragine's *Legenda Aurea* (*Golden Legend*), and Butler's *Lives of Saints*. I will refer to the women as saints, though a few women—such as Judith, Jane Patricia Rabutin, and those not present in hagiographic sources—are not officially canonized but rather recognized by the lay population as important religious women. The women of the epigraphs span various centuries and cultures. Ultimately, after spiritual trials and death or martyrdom, these women join a larger community, not in the biblical heaven but "into the 'heaven' of *Lover*" (xxi).

Of the forty-two saints' epilogues, I could not accurately identify seven for reasons of ambiguity or authorial invention. The following women and their respective epigraphs do not match extant hagiographic sources: Susanna (104), Zaraina (108), Hester (114), Cornelia (152), Mary (156), Placidia (173), and Romaine (188). These epigraphs of ambiguous or invented saints appear in the last half of the novel, yet most of the saints from the first half of the novel—Lucy, Agnes, Teresa of Avila—are well known and present in at least one hagiographic source. These more recognizable saints establish credibility for Harris's overall collection, and the latter half of the novel draws on them to inform tropes of suffering and to legitimate the lesser known or invented saints.

Whether officially canonized or fabricated by Harris, the women of *Lover's* epigraphs cannot be described under one rubric, but, because most of them are canonized by the church, I will refer to them as saints. Kendra Smith, the only critic to date who has commented on the epigraphs, calls the women "virgin martyrs" (198). On one hand, this term does accurately define many of the women, for most were killed for refusal to marry or died of old age or illness as celibate nuns. On the other hand, the term applies only to about twenty-four women who were actually martyred—out of the forty-eight women of the epigraphs. For instance, the rate of martyrdom declines in the second half of the novel as Harris presents more women who die of natural causes, like Gemma of Camigliano who died of tuberculosis (*Lover* 124) or Arabella who "*lived to a ripe and lively old age*" (122). By including nonmartyred saints and noncanonized spiritual women, Harris creates an inclusive identity regardless of adversities; therefore, the connection to the narrative's central characters need not be rooted in martyrdom, or violent oppression by patriarchal society, but should be defined rather as a general rejection of patriarchal society, values, and roles.

The second half of the novel presents more contemporary saints to whom the lesbian protagonists may feel a closer bond of community, particularly saints who are community-minded: Rhipseme of Rome, who dies with her society of virgins while fleeing the Diocletian persecutions (86); Jane Patricia Rabutin, who founds eighty Orders of the Visitation as an alternative female monastic lifestyle (143–144); and Bartolomea Capitanio and Vincentia Gerosa, who, according to Harris's epigraph, establish a community to serve "*women who had lived formerly in a state of neglect and ignorance*" (134).[1] The increasing modernity and community-mindedness of the saints' epigraphs both call on and construct an existing community of women who want to escape patriarchal society. This construction then serves as an example of the community available to *Lover's* audience.

The saints that Harris chooses to portray—whether martyrs or not, modern or classical, real or invented—live in opposition to patriarchal values and gender roles. As Harris notes in her introduction, these saints lived "to escape the destiny of their gender" by refusing to marry and by living chaste, holy lives devoted to their only lover, Christ (xxiii). The women of *Lover* do the same, as Flynn and twins Rose and Rose-lima "escape" the seeming inevitability of menstrual cycles, as Veronica "escapes" life as a woman by becoming Harold Horoscope, and as Samaria "escapes" biological motherhood for spiritual motherhood within the community. Harris is concerned that "lesbians have been unable to enact a complete lesbian reality—and therefore, a literature—because of such reliance on the sensational as proof of existence" ("*What We Mean To Say*" 6). By including a cast of characters not solely concerned with their sexual expression but also with community-building and familial relationships, Harris successfully models this reality for her activist audience. One review states "*Lover* is about art as a masterful forgery of life" (Rule 4), and indeed, Harris creates a novel full of "masterful" plots and characters that mirrors her desire and the desires of her audience to "enact a complete lesbian reality."

Absence of Epigraphs

Of the forty-five chapters of *Lover*, three are not prefaced with epigraphs. Each of these chapters reveals patriarchal oppression by narrating crude and violent acts against women: narrating Samaria's past, demonstrating the oppression of remaining within patriarchal gender roles, and presenting a violently oppressive male figure. In Harris's 1993 introduction, she asserts that her characters resemble saints "who single-mindedly pursued any extreme, the more implausible the better, to escape the destiny of their gender" (xxii–xxiii). The women of these three chapters in particular are canonized through their "extreme" and often "implausible" oppression, replacing the saint of the absent epigraph, in order "to escape the destiny of their gender." This connection upends patriarchal hierarchy by venerating modern women who suffer daily and by associating them with their officially canonized predecessors.

In discussing her own life in the novel's introduction, Harris writes that "it was, however, the 'common' woman who was being canonized by radical and lesbian feminism in those days: the more victimized by sexism or by patriarchal institutions, the more, so to speak, sainted" (l). The women who are "canonized" in these chapters experience violent physical and emotional oppression and seek, however unsuccessfully, to fight against the patriarchy. If these women are able to join the spiritual community of their saintly predecessors, then there is room for other oppressed women to advance beyond the oppression of patriarchal society.

The first chapter without an epigraph (26–33) begins with Samaria's speculation about her connection to the Samaritan woman at the well, a connection that is verified eight chapters later. Instead of prefacing with this story of another woman, Harris provides us with an entire chapter in which Samaria narrates parts of her life with all its mythos and tragedy, imitating a saint's life. The majority of the chapter is a conversation between Samaria and the head of the orphanage where she lived as a child. From the conversation, Samaria learns why she was taken from her mother and aunt, both prostitutes. Her unspoken realization that her mother permitted men to sexually abuse her as a child comes without comment or emotion. The lack of an epigraph forces the reader to "canonize" Samaria based on her oppression similar to the other saints.

The second unaccompanied chapter (55–56) presents a story of the loss of agency for women who continue living within socially constructed roles. The mother character in this chapter pursues societal normalcy and does not attempt to escape imposed gender roles, unlike most of Harris's characters. As she passively watches her husband cut her hydrangea bush to a stump, she says, "What can I do? . . . My bush is dead now and there's nothing I can do," before noting the retributive acts the husband will most likely perform if she asserts her own will (56). The fear of retaliation by the patriarchal figure drives this woman into submission and into an inability to fight against her societal role. Harris's characters are often unlike this woman, for they do what Harris's saints do: they fight against "the destiny of their gender." This woman, though, demonstrates the hardships of female oppression and the need for an all-female community in which she can experience freedom.

The penultimate chapter is the third and final chapter without an epigraph, containing two parts. The first is told from the perspective of a male rapist-murderer; the second is Samaria's boat journey across the lake and discovery of the rapist-murderer's buried victims. Though this is not the first instance of violence in the novel, it is the first instance in which the violence is contemporary to the novel's main action. The rapist-murderer's section narrates the stench of the half-buried bodies of his female victims and the nauseating effects the smell has on the man. He contemplates killing Veronica and her community, though he takes no action: "But if he smashed them down, a swatter against flies, then they would stink too. Would that be worse or better than watching them move like little colored spotlights there across the water?" (204). Though this portion of the chapter does not include active rape or murder of his victims, the narration of the powerful stench makes the man's character even more abominable, elevating his victims to the status of martyrs. He has spent days in a hot van with the corpses of his victims, and the chapter even ends with his attempted masturbation then self-harm: "So he shut it up again all in the dark, and he hit it and hit it because it was bad" (204).

Samaria does not encounter the man's victims until she has crossed the lake to reach the boathouse, yet she does not respond to the bodies as one would expect: "Her toes tangled in the hair of a human head. When she looked and saw what she saw, she praised the distraction as though it were miracle and she a saint discovering not roses but bread in her apron pocket. Gazing on a severed head was ease; it was rest" (206). When Samaria "praised the distraction," the novel acknowledges the inevitability of further patriarchal oppression and violence, for this "distraction" occurs during Samaria's internal struggle with her role in the lesbian community and her past as wife and mother of traditional patriarchal society. Samaria's journey to the boathouse is an escape from the reality of her love for Flynn, her biological granddaughter, and after seeing the reality of patriarchal violence and oppression wrapped around her toes, Samaria is brought to peace with her love for Flynn and her identity as "lover." For readers, this description of the severed heads as a miracle that eases her mind reemphasizes the reality of violence and the need for the type of community that Veronica and Samaria have established.

Lover: A Lesbian Separatist Community

Lover features two types of communes—the spiritual communes of the saints and the lesbian commune of the protagonists. The latter is a new inclusive community, a lesbian separatist community, into which *Lover*'s readers may also enter. While the fragmentary nature of Harris's narration of this developing community may alienate some, the emphasis Harris places on various types of women's communities furthers her goal for external action via the novel. The epigraphs are physically separated from the narrative, but they establish a community ready for Harris's central characters and readers to build on.

The women of the epigraphs often live in nunneries or convents, meant to separate women from the monastic life of men, but Harris's epigraphs demonstrate community-building as essential to her new community by including women such as Bartolomea Capitanio and Vincentia Gerosa (*Butler's Lives* 3:191–192; 2:476–477), who developed their own community for women, Sisters of Charity of Lovere, separate from the patriarchal invention of the convent: "Bartolomea Capitanio and Vincentia Gerosa met when they were, respectively, twenty-six and forty. Unabashed by the great age difference, they agreed to form a partnership whose chief aim was ministering to the spiritual and physical needs of a small community of women whom they drew around them; women who had lived formerly in a state of neglect and ignorance. Weeping crowds at their funeral (they died, in mysterious circumstances, together) testified to their great popularity and reputation for merriment" (*Lover* 134). The communities of Christian women of the novel's epigraphs are based on mutual love for Christ and a desire to bring other women into this same love—and out of the oppression and violence of non-Christians, generally violent men. The protagonists of the main narrative, though not joined by this same bond, are also bound by mutual love and the desire to bring women together into a nurturing community free of patriarchal oppression and violence.

The women of *Lover*'s main narrative create a similar community that, instead of being held together by the love of Christ, is held together by eroticism and mutual rejection of the patriarchy. This lesbian community is expanding, as seen on the family tree at the start of the novel, which includes more lovers than the original Samaria, Veronica, and their close blood kin. It also establishes itself in a physically separate place, secluded by woods and water, and in a spiritually separate space, free from patriarchy.

Lover's Family Tree

Harris reinvents familial relationships by prefacing *Lover* with a hand-drawn family tree that parodies patriarchal lineage and connects the novel's lesbian protagonists to three classical saints, eight cats, a dog named Sport, and a British bottle of vinegar, all of which are mentioned in passing throughout the novel. Though more of a vine or "genealogical kudzu," as Elizabeth Freeman terms it (37), the tree connects seemingly arbitrary people, animals, and things, subverting the biological notion of a patriarchal lineage. It links the twins, Rose and Rose-lima, both to "Virgin Mary Ten-Foot Women," a character in their film script of *Lover*, and to their biological mother Daisy (1). Like the novel itself, the generations of women are not organized linearly by time or by predictable genetic relationships. This lack of organization demonstrates the flexibility of relationships among and between women and the world. By parodying patriarchal lineage at the start of the novel, Harris sets her readers up for reinvention of the patriarchy, and the inclusion of saints in this family tree before their introduction in epigraphs establishes an extant familial community of all women regardless of genetic links.

Saintly women are bound spiritually, not biologically, through their mutual love of Christ and rejection of the world. The three iconic Christian martyrs included in the novel's opening family tree—Lucy, Agnes, and Catherine—serve as initial matriarchs of Harris's new community. Harris offers an epigraph for each saint describing each woman's life and death: Lucy, before her martyrdom, "*gouged out her own eyes*" to prevent her marriage to a pagan man (5); Agnes, after surviving various unsuccessful attempts on her life, "*died by a sword through her throat*" rather than marry and compromise her vow of chastity (36–37); and Catherine was tortured on a wheel, afterward called the Catherine Wheel, and eventually beheaded for refusing to renounce her faith. Unlike Lucy and Agnes, Catherine is not present in the novel's epigraphs, though she is not entirely absent from the main narrative. The wheel is mentioned as a prop that Loretta (Lydia off-stage) Somerleyton uses in her magic show, but the prop is renamed the Loretta Wheel and used for erotic acts instead of torture and death (171–172). These three Christian martyrs establish a community of women that the characters and readers of the novel may join. Furthermore, the nonlinear, nonchronological organization of the "genealogical kudzu" establishes a more fluid, abstract version of matriarchal family that rejects the necessity of patriarchal relationships.

Redefining Motherhood

The novel's family tree presents Harris's creation of lineage that redefines motherhood as essential for community-building as well as for population growth. The saints Bartolomea Capitanio and Vincentia Gerosa demonstrate motherhood as community-building, for they create a place for women to be nurtured and cared for by other women. This function of motherhood is most important in the novel's main narrative, yet Harris does not abandon its biologically procreative function. Harris incorporates epigraphs of women like Julitta, whose daughter Cyrica is killed by Governor Alexander (139); Cornelia, who devotes her widowhood to raising her daughters (152); Jane Patricia Rabutin, who "took charge of an unusually large number of her son's petite amies and organized them into a community which she called the Order of the Visitation" (143–144); and even Marina, who "lived disguised as a monk" and "was accused of fathering a child of an innkeeper's daughter" (83). Their inclusion shows the community's acceptance of all women, neither condemning nor praising biological motherhood; yet, the main narrative of the novel emphasizes community-building as the more important aspect of motherhood.

Harris explains her intentions in highlighting motherhood in the novel: "The mothers in *Lover* must make themselves reproductively useful before they may enjoy ecstacy [*sic*]. Motherhood in *Lover* is the real worm in the bowl of wax fruit: which is *Lover*. Every biological reality in *Lover*, but especially motherhood, contaminates the aesthetic surround" (xxvi). For Harris, motherhood in a patriarchal society means making oneself "reproductively useful." This particular definition of motherhood is antithetical to the lesbian community, so *Lover*'s mothers extend the definition to include nurturing rather than strictly reproducing. Within the novel's community, the *reproductive* role alone truly "contaminates the aesthetic surround" by its reliance on men, as seen when Daisy continuously leaves the community to marry. Yet the *nurturing* role of motherhood is essential for this "aesthetic surround" to thrive.

Harris's preoccupation with motherhood fights the notions that "mothers cannot be lovers, and lesbians/'lovers' cannot be mothers" (Allen 8). Defining motherhood as reproductive is initially necessary for the lesbian community. At first, the community is populated almost solely by Samaria, Veronica, and their respective daughters and granddaughters; reproduction becomes essential for its continued thriving. But by also defining motherhood as nurturing, both the lesbian and saint communities can grow and thrive through the inclusion, raising, and teaching, of all women. A mother in the lesbian community, who is now defined by her nurturing and not simply reproductive role, creates new, alternative lineages and familial relationships.

Elizabeth Freeman discusses how the mothers in *Lover* redefine the cultural definitions of motherhood to establish alternative relationships: "Thus *Lover* certainly privileges 'unnatural' reproduction, at once denaturalizing motherhood, linking it to women's other creative, culture-making activities, and suggesting webs of caretaking and exchange for which the normative kinship diagram and generational logic seem entirely inadequate" (57). The role of mother, then, transforms as its procreative qualities shift to allow the mothers to create and raise the community of women through "culture-making activities" such as writing and art, as Veronica does, or prayer and charity, as the saints do. These activities also solidify and legitimate the existence of the community by providing physical evidence of community-making, much like relics of a saint's bones or clothing legitimate a woman's existence in the spiritual community.

Flynn, who has witnessed her mother Daisy's various relationships with both men and women, states, "There is no intimacy between woman and woman which is not preceded by a long narrative of the mother" (173). Flynn notes that her sexuality is learned from Daisy, since Daisy has acted not only as a biological mother but also as a nurturing mother who has taught her the intricacies of relationships. This, too, is reflected in spiritual communities such as nunneries, where women learn from other women about how to serve God through prayer, community-building, and even martyrdom. Motherhood, for these saints and the lesbians of the main narrative, becomes a role of nurturing, not necessarily based on biological reproduction. They, instead, reproduce culturally by nurturing and teaching younger women to follow their example.

Whether referring to the biological reality of motherhood or its nurturing, community-building role, Harris asserts that motherhood must occur *before* a woman may enjoy ecstasy. In the role of reproduction, it is clear that *Lover*'s lesbian characters must leave the patriarchal oppression of reproduction before enjoying sexual ecstasy in the lesbian community, yet the nurturing role of motherhood must also begin before ecstasy. Once a community has been established and begins to grow, the members can then enjoy the products of the kinship. For the saints, their religious and spiritual ecstasy, their full devotion to Christ, may begin after establishing or joining a community, whether on Earth or in heaven. For *Lover*'s lovers, before enjoying true ecstasy, they must separate from patriarchal society and its oppressively defined roles of motherhood and of *woman*.

Blood, Suffering, and Eroticism

The stigmata of Gemma of Camigliano (known as Maria Gemma Umberta Pia Galgani), though painful, is a grace from God. ("Gemma of Camigliano desired, from the age of sixteen, nothing more than to spend her life as a Passionist, but was prevented from fully realizing her vocation because of a withered hand. Nevertheless, her fervency was continually remarked upon and many extraordinary ecstacies [*sic*] are attributed to her. At her death, it was discovered that her body bore several visible traces of her passion" [124].) She describes her experience of receiving the five wounds of Christ: "The pains, the suffering, instead of afflicting me, gave me perfect peace" (Bell and Mazzoni 55). The bloody suffering of Gemma's stigmata led her to a fuller realization of Christ's importance in her daily devotion. Women suffering stigmata surmount physical suffering and enter spiritual ecstasy in the sharing in Christ's passion. This is the ecstasy that the saints strive to achieve, and like the saints, *Lover*'s lesbian characters must also bleed and suffer to reach their ecstasy.

Blood, suffering, and eroticism, along with maternal community-building, advance the novel's agenda of creating an alternative nonpatriarchal lineage. Rather than being governed by genetic blood lines, the alternative lineage of the saints and lesbians of the novel is based on rejection of the patriarchy and is held together by the common experience and rejection of menstruation, the pain of suffering under the hands of the patriarchy, and the shared eroticism that is a result and reward of all these things. The community of saints is bound by mutual love of God, rejection of patriarchal marriage, and spiritual ecstasy. Harris's epigraph collection of bleeding, suffering, but rejoicing saints demonstrates a community of women who suffer under the patriarchy and ultimately transform their suffering and oppression into an enjoyment of spiritual ecstasy. The novel's lesbian commune joins this established community by rejecting the blood and suffering of patriarchal society in order to enjoy ecstasy together.

Patriarchal lineage is established through bloodlines, and the preoccupation with blood and bodily fluids in the novel provides an alternative, strictly matriarchal, bloodline. Although pregnancy is an instrument of patriarchal lineage, birthing is solely matriarchal. As the novel opens, the protagonists meet in a birthing scene, a purely female space:

> This one was lying strapped to a table. Covered in her juices, Samaria was being pulled through the lips of her vulva. That is how Samaria met her.
>
> She was being pulled, yelling already, through the lips of Daisy's vulva. That is how Flynn met Daisy.
>
> Veronica, however, came out of nowhere, and so she used to go exclusively with Veronica. (5)

Birth is the first meeting of the novel's major characters, as Samaria meets her daughter, Daisy, who then meets her daughter, Flynn. While these characters are related genetically, the novel's opening scene destroys the relational boundaries by leaving the relation of Flynn to Samaria unspecified. This birthing scene "sets the tone for a narrative in which characters fade into one another, shift shape and occasionally gender, perform as actors, as forgers, as rope-walkers on beams of light" (Allen 8). Since they are allowed to "fade into one another," the notion of direct, patriarchal lineage is undermined as the women do not exist in traditional relational spaces.

Blood creates women, as Samaria asserts in recounting her first menstruation, yet the idea of woman is rejected by most of the characters in the novel. As blood drips down her legs, squishes inside her shoes, and leaves a trail behind her down the school hall, she notes that she was told, "Now you are a woman," then sadly comments, "*I* had been exchanged for a *woman*" (102). When she stops the menstrual bleeding that socially defines a woman, she fully rejects *woman* and embraces the novel's lesbian community and her new identity as *lover*: "I could become a lover and could stop being a woman. What they said, *a woman*. That's why I am here, in spite of it, and not in a cage, like the rest of them, in a freak show. I am a lover, not a woman" (102–103). By rejecting menstruation and the patriarchal definition of womanhood, the lovers redefine blood lineage in a lesbian commune that lacks blood altogether.

Shedding blood through menstruation or through wounds obtained in suffering leads to an eroticism that further unifies the nonpatriarchal community. For the lesbian characters, this happens through the rejection of menstruation that defines *woman*. For religious women, Christ's bleeding on the cross becomes a devotional image that not only describes the passion and death of Christ, but that also inspires many of these women to pray to share in the suffering. These experiences are often described as erotic. Karma Lochrie famously discusses the erotics of Christ's wound specifically with the Latin puns on *vulva/vagina* and *vulnus* meaning *wound*: "This transitivity of wound to vulva/vagina, of masculine to feminine bodies, and of sexualities is most vividly rendered in late medieval devotional imagery. . . . Such inscription [providing the exact size of the wound] is a fairly common invocation to devotional practice among wound images by providing a vivid, quantifiable measure of Christ's suffering and hence his love. At the same time, the sexual connotation of this image is unmistakable. . . . There is evidence in devotional texts for and by women that the wound was a locus for sexual experiences of mystical union. Religious instruction and devotional texts for women explicitly invite them to touch, kiss, suck, and enter the wound of Christ" (190). The visual association and linguistic pun comparing the wound of Christ with a vagina eroticizes devotion. While the image of a wound in *Lover* is not eroticized in the same manner, this connection between suffering and eroticism suggests that the violent experiences of the lovers' pasts should not hinder their full enjoyment of ecstasy within *Lover*'s lesbian commune.

Kendra Smith notes that the saints participate in erotic experiences "insofar as their martyrdom affects the body and limns the contours of community solidarity (both pagan and Christian)" (205). As long as these experiences of eroticism are contained within the spiritual realm, the saints may enjoy them, yet enjoyment is mostly an acceptance of an experience that will lead to heavenly pleasure after death or martyrdom. Even those saints who are not martyred still experience corporal erotics through spiritual experiences, such as the stigmata of Gemma of Camigliano. In suffering the same wounds as Christ, Gemma develops a closer relationship with Him, enhancing her place in the community of worshipers. Physical suffering establishes a closer connection to Christ, the heavenly "lover" for the saints of the epigraphs.

Lover begins and ends with saints experiencing, personally or not, bloody suffering: the first epigraph narrates Lucy gouging out her own eyes; the last epigraph tells of Saint Veronica, possibly the woman healed from a hemorrhage, wiping Christ's sweaty, bloody face with her veil. For the women of the novel's main narrative, shared experience and rejection of menstruation creates a new blood lineage distinct from that of patriarchal society. Together, all of these women must participate in a bloody suffering of some sort before joining a larger community that eschews the patriarchal definition of *woman*. Once the women establish this new blood lineage, they may finally experience their promised ecstasy within a community led by their matriarchal leaders Samaria and Veronica.

Samaria as the Samaritan Woman

The epigraph about Samaria and its corresponding chapter are unique in that the epigraph merges into the narrative itself.

> "My name is Samaria, Ma'am.
>
> "*The Woman of Samaria was asked to draw water from the well. And she said, 'How is that, being a Jew, you ask me, a woman of Samaria, to draw you water?' And was answered, 'If you had asked it of me, I would have given you living water and you would never thirst again.'*"
>
> "I don't understand."
>
> "I don't either. But I was named Samaria and told the story." (58)

Take note of the punctuation: instead of beginning immediately with the epigraph, the novel's Samaria begins, "'My name is Samaria, Ma'am," which includes opening quotation marks but excludes closing quotation marks (58). After a paragraph break and another set of opening quotation marks, the epigraph itself begins. This signals Samaria's continued speech. The epigraph itself, which narrates the biblical story of the Samaritan woman at the well, ends in closing quotation marks. This marks the end of the speech begun "'My name is Samaria, Ma'am" (58). Following this is Veronica's response, "'I don't understand.'" Samaria shares in Veronica's confusion by saying, "'I don't either. But I was named Samaria and told the story,'" essentially clarifying the inclusion of the epigraph in her speech (58). Samaria's acknowledgment of her connection to the Samaritan woman allows for a comparison between the role of the biblical Samaritan woman and Samaria's role in *Lover*'s community.

The Samaritan woman, known as Saint Photina in the Eastern Orthodox tradition (*Butler's Lives* 1:636), is described by Samaria earlier in the novel as "a person of Hellenistic background whom a prominent young Hebrew of her day used as an example to show that it is the spirit of worship that counts rather than inheritance or culture" (26). This rejection of "inheritance or culture" corresponds with the overall rejection of patriarchal society and lineage in *Lover* and with the characterization of Samaria as one of the two lesbian matriarchs. The epigraph of the Samaritan woman closely resembles the well-known parable in the Gospel of John in which Jesus asks a woman to draw water from a well. The epigraph narrates the man's description of "living water" to the woman. Had she asked him for water, he would have given her "living water" so that she "would never thirst again" (58). In the biblical account, Jesus is offering the woman a symbolic cleansing of her sins, yet the novel's epigraph functions as an explanation of Samaria's character. As one of the matriarchs, it is Samaria who offers the "living water" of the lesbian commune, a life outside established gender roles, to her descendants Daisy, Flynn, Rose and Rose-lima.

Veronica as Saint Veronica

Following Samaria's narration of her own epigraph, Veronica, the community's second matriarch, offers her name, to which Samaria responds, "Like the veil. Veronica's veil took the face on itself and afterwards no one could tell which was the real face and which was the face of the veil" (58). Even though Veronica exclaims that she is "certainly not" the Veronica of this story, Harris confirms this connection in the novel's final epigraph: "*The story of Veronica goes: inspired by a suffering face, she held a cloth to it; and on the cloth was left an image of the face she had wiped. No one knows for sure, however. Some imagine her to be that woman who had 'an issue of blood.' Others point out that the English word 'vernicle' means* true image" (207). The layers of connection and definition of these two Veronicas are asserted throughout the novel, and they are worthy of more investigation than this essay allows, but the possibilities of Saint Veronica's identity in the epigraph provide evidence for the identity of the novel's Veronica and her function in the new nonpatriarchal community.

The matriarch Veronica's dynamic character allows her to exist in various patriarchal and matriarchal communities. Her connection to Saint Veronica creates a vivid picture of Harris's notion of lesbian identity, drawing specifically on blood as a uniting factor of matriarchal society. Present in the canonical Gospels, the apocryphal Gospel of Nicodemus, and Harris's epigraph, Saint Veronica is often identified as a woman with an "issue of blood," an unspecified hemorrhage often defined as perpetual menstrual bleeding that stopped when she touched the hem of Christ's robe. In the Gospels, this is evidence of Christ's miracles and his compassion for those cast out from society. Its place in the novel suggests that the original Veronica transcended *woman* to become *lover* with the help of Christ. The novel's Veronica and her newly established community may also transcend *woman* by striving for a fully separate all-women's community.

The Veil of Veronica, as legend has it, was held to the face of Jesus during his passion, producing an image on the cloth by Christ's sweat and blood. The veil shows only the impression of Christ's face, not his whole body as is shown on the shroud of Turin (the two are commonly confused) (Kuryluk 1). Many European churches display what they believe is the true Veil of Veronica, but these are simply painted pieces of canvas. Due to the number of veils claimed as the true Veil of Veronica, the question of its legitimacy cannot be answered

(3). For centuries, popular likenesses of Veronica holding the veil perpetuated the myth of the original's existence, and of the existence of Saint Veronica. Many scholars, including *Lover* critic Victoria Smith, believe the name *Veronica* simply means "true image," a combination of *vera* (true) and *icon* (image) (Kuryluk 5; V. Smith 91n7). Regardless, Harris makes the connection between the two Veronicas explicit. If Saint Veronica is the woman with permanent menstruation that stops after Christ heals her, then she has shifted from woman to lover and is one of the founding mothers of this new community.

Lesbian Heaven

Through all their sufferings, the women of *Lover*, lesbians and saints alike, end up in a type of erotic heaven, canonized and living forever as icons of female communities. Like Tibia Perpetua and Felicity, Harris's protagonists have suffered in the arena of patriarchal oppression and, upon entering into a purely female community, can "go and play." ("At their trial, Tibia Perpetua and Felicity were condemned to death by wild beasts. . . . On the day of their death, they entered the arena 'with gay and gallant looks' and proclaimed themselves, in loud tones, 'the darlings of God.' After encountering a leopard, a bear, and a cow, they were each killed by a sword through the throat but only after they had kissed each other so that their death 'might be perfected.' Upon their arrival in Heaven, they were told to 'Go and play'" [192–193].) Harris envisions the novel as a perfect place for the sexually subversive, placing them "into the 'heaven' of *Lover*": "I wanted them to have a good time, unmolested by women who were afraid of pleasure" (xxi). Harris's protagonists clearly enjoy their sexual relationships, and by creating a separate community for them to experience pleasure, Harris creates a lesbian heaven that is prefaced by the saints' enjoyment of spiritual ecstasy in heaven with their beloved Christ. Thus, Harris creates a community of saints and lesbians who coexist and share the erotic pleasure of a nonpatriarchal lineage and no longer need to escape their gender roles.

The novel's protagonists, Samaria and Veronica, are connected most closely to the saints of the novel's epigraphs, but by redefining lineage, these women may live within a nonpatriarchal community that is focused on true ecstasy, whether spiritual, sexual, or both. Criticism of Bertha Harris's *Lover* has overlooked these epigraphs and how essential they are to Harris's broader goal of creating an all-female community extending across time and space. The family tree at the start of the novel is the initial gesture, and the novel's preoccupation with shared experience and with recreating a new lineage then allows the family tree to become fully realized. Blood no longer functions as a defining connection as in patriarchal lineage. Instead, the blood of birth, menstruation, and suffering connects women across time through shared experience. Blood also defines the difference between woman and lover that must be transcended for inclusion in the novel's lesbian community.

Harris's attempt at recreating lineage in *Lover* deserves more critical attention, specifically in further investigating her selection of saints—the exclusion of Catherine from the epigraphs and the inclusion of unknown or invented saints, for example. Future critical work should not ignore these epigraphs or merely gloss over them as a stylistic choice. Harris's intentional use of classical, medieval, and modern saints allows for a more imaginatively realized community of women who successfully live outside the confines of patriarchal society, creating for themselves a new heaven on Earth.

Notes

1. In all of the quotes from Harris, the emphasis is Harris's.

Works Cited

Allen, Carolyn. "Djuna Barnes and Bertha Harris: Reading Erotics/Following Djuna." Introduction. *Following Djuna: Women Lovers and the Erotics of Loss*. Bloomington: Indiana UP, 1996. 1–20. Print.

Bell, Rudolph M., and Cristina Mazzoni. *The Voices of Gemma Galgani: The Life and Afterlife of a Modern Saint.* Chicago: U of Chicago P, 2003. Print.

Butler's Lives of Saints. Ed. Herbert Thurston and Donald Attwater. 3 vols. New York: P. J. Kennedy, 1956. Print.

Clayton, Mary, and Hugh Magennis. *The Old English Lives of St Margaret.* Cambridge: Cambridge UP, 1994. Print.

de Voragine, Jacobus. *The Golden Legend of Jacobus de Voragine*. Trans. Granger Ryan and Helmut Ripperger. New York: Longmans, Green, 1948. Print.

Freeman, Elizabeth. "Junk Inheritances, Bad Timing: Familial Arrhythmia in Three Working-Class Dyke Narratives." *Time Binds: Queer Temporalities, Queer Histories*. Durham, NC: Duke UP, 2010. 21–58. Print.

Harris, Bertha. *Lover*. 1976. New York: NYU P, 1993. Print.

———. "*What We Mean To Say*: Notes Toward Defining the Nature of Lesbian Literature." *Heresies* 1.3 (1977): 5–8. Print.

Kuryluk, Ewa. *Veronica and Her Cloth: History, Symbolism, and Structure of a "True Image."* Cambridge: Blackwell, 1991. Print.

Lochrie, Karma. "Mystical Acts, Queer Tendencies." *Constructing Medieval Sexuality*. Ed. Karma Lochrie, Peggy McCracken, and James A. Schultz. Minneapolis: University of Minnesota Press, 1997. 180–200. Print.

Rule, Jane. Rev. of *Lover*, by Bertha Harris. *Body Politic* 31 (1977): 4. Print.

Smith, Kendra. "Queer Relics: Martyrological Time and the Eroto-Aesthetics of Suffering in Bertha Harris' *Lover*." *Postmedieval: A Journal of Medieval Cultural Studies* 3 (2012): 195–211. Print.

Smith, Victoria. "Starting from Snatch: The Seduction of Performance in Bertha Harris's *Lover*." *Sex Positives?: The Cultural Politics of Dissident Sexualities*. New York: NYU P, 1997. 68–94. Print.

Stimpson, Catharine R. "Zero Degree Deviancy: The Lesbian Novel in English." *Critical Inquiry* 8.2 (1981): 363–379. *JSTOR*. Accessed 21 Oct. 2012. Web.

Chapter 10

The Color Purple and the Wine-Dark Kiss of Death

How a Second-Wave Feminist Wrote the First American AIDS Narrative

Phillip Gordon

Alice Walker's 1982 *The Color Purple* is arguably the most commercially successful and universally embraced literary product of second-wave feminism. The novel about a poor, abused African American woman living in the rural South in the first half of the twentieth century would win the Pulitzer Prize and the National Book Award before going on to become an Oscar-winning movie. Grammy-winning artist Erykah Badu signified on the movie (and the original book) in her music video for her single "On and On," confident that her audience would easily understand the popular imagery on which her video relies. Most recently, the novel has been adapted to a Tony-award-winning musical. Despite appearing on banned book lists, *The Color Purple* still enjoys an immense readership, in addition to its popular viewership, and has clearly emerged as one of the major works of American literature from the second half of the twentieth century.

Unfortunately, the celebrity of the novel has precluded a specific and contextual understanding of some of the key elements of the text. The movie all but cuts the lesbian material, for example, as does the musical, to a degree, despite the importance of the relationship between Shug and Celie as a depiction of women-centric relationships ranging from familial to sexual on a broad and all-encompassing spectrum.[1] Additionally, much of the African material in Nettie's letters is excessively summarized in both the movie and the musical and ultimately subsumed by Celie's bondage-to-freedom narrative, though that material is vital to the book and points to the larger post-colonial discourse at its heart.

Broadly speaking, the universal appeal of the novel rests on the elision of the African American elements of its narrative structure into the central story of a woman struggling to express herself. The universality of Celie's story relies on forgoing Celie's race to focus on her plight as representative of the struggles faced by women of all class and racial backgrounds in any part of the world, not just the specific challenges faced by a poor black woman in a particular sexual economy in the rural South between World War I and the civil rights era. Though this forgoing of race for concerns of gender and Women's Liberation may serve to further the goals of second-wave feminism—and Walker's novel is a vital addition to the canon of that movement and of immeasurable importance to the subsequent generation of American women writers of all backgrounds—the context of the novel, considered in full, points to a much more specific vision of Celie's life, grounded in its place and time but with vital connections to the places and time in which Walker wrote and relevant to our time for the telltale signs visible in the novel when we turn our eye to them and dare to see them for what they are.

Walker's 1982 novel appeared in the early months of the AIDS crisis, as the disease was first "discovered" and its presence in the world at large was just barely visible. In this paper, I read *The Color Purple* as an AIDS narrative by reading into the surrounding details of its publication to uncover what may have been an accidental narrative for Walker as she wrote her masterpiece but that proves nonetheless as important for our current moment as the novel was, in the moment of its publication, for second-wave feminism.

A close consideration of the details of the novel reveals a subnarrative with devastating relevance to the lives of black women living in the Southeastern United States in the opening decades of the twenty-first century. By considering the sexual economy, the emphasis on illness and sexual contact, the post-colonial interests (which is to say, considering Africa), and the time and place of its writing, I argue that *The Color Purple* should be read as the first AIDS narrative in American literature. Such a reading is a profound revision of our current model of AIDS literature and bears implications for our current political understanding of HIV/AIDS, a disease long associated with forgotten and unwanted populations. Such a reading does, however, stay true to the original impetus of the novel, for to acknowledge that *The Color Purple* is the first AIDS narrative and a prescient model for the spread and impact of the disease is to revise a political history that has led to the current AIDS crisis among black women. Such an acknowledgment tells a story of a marginalized group and may help us combat the crisis that group now faces as well.

A Brief History of AIDS Narratives

The first step to understanding *The Color Purple* as an AIDS narrative is understanding why it has not so far been placed in a canon of AIDS literature. This omission is not for as simple a fact as that the novel makes no ostensible mention of HIV/AIDS. The reason for this oversight is that AIDS literature is traditionally bound, first and foremost, to gay male literary/theatrical output.

In the more than thirty years since scientists first identified HIV/AIDS, numerous authors have contributed to the genre of AIDS literature, including Sapphire's *Push* and its sequel *The Kid*, the former arguably a retelling of *The Color Purple* as a contemporary AIDS narrative set in 1980s' Harlem. The list of *firsts* in the genre, however, is distinctly a gay male list. The first mention of HIV/AIDS in medical discourse appeared in the *Morbidity and Mortality Weekly Report* (*MMWR*) on July 4, 1981, in a report titled "Kaposi's Sarcoma and *Pneumocystis* Pneumonia among Homosexual Men—New York and San Francisco."[2] The appearance of these rare diseases among a population of gay men in urban environments would shadow the subsequent understanding of the disease in popular culture. The first political action groups devoted to the AIDS crisis, though often run by women such as Sarah Schulman, focused on the crisis as a gay male disease. The first AIDS-prevention sex education literature was pioneered by gay men for gay male sexual encounters.[3] The first significant work of AIDS-themed literature was Larry Kramer's gay-themed play *The Normal Heart* (1985). The first film to depict an AIDS patient was the gay-themed *Parting Glances* (1986). The first significant history of AIDS was Randy Shilts's *And the Band Played On* (1987), about the AIDS crisis in the gay communities in New York, Los Angeles, and San Francisco.

From these original works sprung fiction in the 1990s and early 2000s that would win the first major awards for AIDS literature. In the first AIDS-themed play to win a Pulitzer Prize (1993), Tony Kushner relies on a series of associations surrounding AIDS to introduce his main characters. In act 1 of *Angels in America: A Gay Fantasia on National Themes,* part 1, "Millennium Approaches," Prior Walter sits his lover, Louis, down on a bench while they wait for a bus and proceeds to break the news to him: Prior has AIDS. Rather than say these exacts words, though, he pulls back his sleeve and shows Louis "K. S., baby. Lesion number one. Lookit. The wine-dark kiss of the angel of death" (27). The purple lesion that Prior shows Louis, K. S., or Kaposi's sarcoma, was so associated with HIV/AIDS that Prior need say nothing more to Louis to confirm the diagnosis. Furthermore, HIV/AIDS was so associated with male homosexuality that Kaposi's sarcoma came to be called "the gay cancer," the telltale sign of the disease first named GRID, or gay-related immune deficiency, before scientists, realizing the syndrome was not only gay-related, renamed it. In the 1993 movie *Philadelphia*, Andrew Beckett (Tom Hanks) is fired from his law firm when a visible K. S. lesion appears on his face, revealing to his legal partners both that he is gay and that he has AIDS. Michael Cunningham repeated this motif in *A Home at the End of the World* to introduce the disease that would kill Jonathan Glover, who is depicted throughout the novel as a promiscuous gay man. Cunningham's *The Hours*, with its portrayal of a gay AIDS victim suffering from dementia, would be the first ostensibly AIDS-themed novel to win the Pulitzer Prize.

The reason gay men figure so prominently in the history of AIDS literature is that gay men were the first and most visible population struck by the AIDS crisis when the world first began to realize there was a crisis. AIDS narratives developed in the 1980s largely as a creative response by members of the gay community, which most publicly responded to HIV/AIDS in the early years after its discovery and was most publicly stigmatized for it. AIDS narratives, Kushner's included, follow a basic pattern, explained by Susan Sontag in her brief philosophical treatise *AIDS and Its Metaphors*. Sontag claims that the definition of AIDS "depends on constructing a temporal sequence of events," or, to state her meaning more plainly, to craft a narrative in which "telltale symptoms" become a "clinical construction, an inference" that revises the story of one's life to account for how this could happen, how one could have contracted AIDS (22, 20). AIDS narratives are revisions of history made more meaningful by the abundance of signs pointing to the climax, the diagnosis, signs that only in retrospect chart the story of a life now redefined by HIV/AIDS. Sontag implies that all AIDS narratives are revisionary retellings. They appear later, the wine-dark kiss of death that reveals the hidden condition, and only by reading backward can we deduce the meaning they carried all along.

The fundamental flaw in AIDS literature, though, is how wed it has been to genres of gay literature when the worldwide profile of AIDS is one in which homosexuality plays very little part. Indeed, Sontag admonishes her readers to think beyond the stigma of AIDS infection and assumptions about homosexuality, assumptions that, she explains, could only hold true "if Africa did not exist" (26). Only when AIDS entered the American population did virologists and epidemiologists scrambled to counter it. When their search for its origins took them to Africa, they were stunned to realize that sick and dying people had been right there in front of them for decades. Yet, AIDS narratives are still largely gay narratives, and AIDS is still largely assumed to be a gay disease. The heterosexual and nonsexually transmitted prevalence of the disease vastly outweighs the homosexual coincidence of its discovery, but then, how difficult to admit that when thousands of Africans die, no one notices, but when five Americans die, even gay ones, the world shakes. Beyond the supposed moment of discovery of the disease and the visibility of the community that first recognized its effects, a very different AIDS history has disappeared from the consciousness of mainstream culture.

The True History of AIDS

The actual history of AIDS in human populations begins in Africa at or near the time when Walker has Nettie and the Rev. Samuels family arrive there for their mission work—including medical mission work—that becomes a counterpoint to Celie's enslaved life in rural Georgia.[4] HIV/AIDS entered human populations somewhere in central Africa, most likely in the limited range inhabited by the species of chimpanzee *Pan troglodytes troglodytes*, sometime in the latter nineteenth or early twentieth century. In his recent study *The Origin of AIDS*, Jacques Pepin uses advanced genetic and biomolecular analysis to trace and date the initial cross-species spread of the virus along a very specific corridor of the central African rainforest.[5] The original population exposed to the virus, largely hunting-based populations living in isolated villages in and around the Congo River basin, may have contracted various mutations of the disease for many years prior to the emergence of the currently identifiable "patient zero" who would spread the disease to other populations beyond its original range.

Pepin dates the so-called patient zero to 1921. How this patient was infected remains conjectural, but genetic analysis can trace the disease back to a common source, most likely in one of the major colonial cities on the Congo River, in or around this date. Basically, around 1921, a person emerged from the bush and entered a colonial city—probably Brazzaville on the French side of Stanley Pool—with a large and diverse population. That person was infected with the virus. Through numerous means, which Pepin links to the broad categories of "colonisation, urbanisation, and probably well-intentioned public health campaigns" (5), the virus in that one patient would eventually spread to the rest of the world. As Pepin summarizes, "There is compelling evidence that the common ancestor of HIV-1 existed in a human being sometime in the first three decades of the twentieth century, and that the whole group M pandemic was started by a single cross-species transmission" (42). This original patient would introduce the virus to the larger world, where it would fester, seemingly undetected, for sixty years before its "discovery" in a gay male population in California.

Pepin links his patient zero with a specific colonial event, the construction of a railroad to link Brazzaville on Stanley Pool on the Congo River to the sea, an event that led to large migrations—forced and voluntary—of native Africans from rural villages to the large colonial boomtowns on the river.[6] Pepin employs a vast sociological framework to debunk the notion that the original patient spread the disease entirely through sexual contact or that sexual contact alone could have led to the pandemic explosion of HIV/AIDS in human populations that followed this colonial path.[7] While sex does, in fact, lead to the spread of any sexually transmitted disease (STD), that spread occurs at a glacial rate relative to the exponential dissemination of HIV that led one patient in 1921 to become sixty million in 2013. Rather, colonial health care practices took a slow spreading, latent disease and exposed almost the entire population of the African colonies to it in a matter of years. Then, through the increasing globalization of the twentieth century, HIV spread to the entire world.

Pepin focuses much of his attention on Leon Pales, a colonial doctor who arrived in Brazzaville in 1931 to oversee the health care of the native population constructing the railroad. Pales recorded a condition among the adult male population that he termed "Cachexie du Mayombe" (37), a wasting-away condition that fit no known pathology and came back negative for all known screenings. Pepin argues that this condition fits the profile of AIDS, and that Pales's notes may be the first significant documentation of the syndrome. The deplorable conditions Pales encountered on the railroad had already led several journalists (including Andre Gide, traveling on the continent at the time) to visit the Congo region and report on the inhumane treatment of workers and the variety of illnesses from which they suffered (arguably, the work of these journalists represent the world's first AIDS narratives). French colonial administrators responded to the health crisis along the Congo River by creating a systematic, almost industrial approach to health care. Caring little for the health of any individual African but concerned instead for the overall health of the population, health officials instituted a public health program of vaccinations and mobile bush hospitals.

Relative to the known pathogens of the period, their model was stunningly successful. Unfortunately, at the time, the limited supply of medical equipment and the reuse of syringes for multiple patients, along with working conditions that were not conducive to proper sterilization, expanded the spread of the virus exponentially. Public health practices inadvertently created the perfect conditions for a mass dissemination of an unidentified blood-borne virus. The reiteration of similar public health models in other African colonies and countries through the twentieth century coincide with spikes in AIDS prevalence (campaigns for polio vaccination in particular had a devastating unintended effect of greatly increasing the spread of the disease). Thus, through well-intended health care practices, HIV/AIDS as we know it was born.

The significance of Pepin's epidemiological study is that it points to a "true" pathology for the spread of HIV/AIDS as driven mainly by public health practices rather than sexual transmission. In communities where sexual expression is broadened to embrace a multitude of partners, the disease can spread more quickly and with more ostensible effects.[8] The intense focus on homosexuality, however, to the preclusion of consideration of heterosexual contact and colonial medical practices (not to mention blood banking)[9] has had a devastating effect on nongay populations. Even to this day in the United States, we tend to overlook the disturbing trends of the disease unless our interest is piqued by Rock Hudson or Magic Johnson or by shocking accounts about men on the "Down Low" or a fuming explosion by Terry McMillan about her down-low husband exposing her to AIDS. In *The Color Purple*, the heterosexual and medical transmission of the disease, linked to colonial practices, prove to be the "true" legacy of AIDS. Walker's novel traces both, if only inadvertently.

AIDS in America Today

The emphasis in *The Color Purple* on rural Southern African American lives makes it an important work to consider in relation to the current demographics of HIV/AIDS. According to the Centers for Disease Control and Prevention (CDC), of the nearly 1.2 million HIV-infected individuals living in the United States, 40 percent of them live in the South.[10] Also, the CDC stresses, "the South is currently the region with the largest proportion of AIDS cases from less urban and nonurban areas," though the five cities with the highest HIV infections rates all fall inside the region the CDC identifies as the South. This data suggests that the profile of HIV/AIDS in the South is as rural as it is urban, a profile explored most recently in Andrew J. Skerritt's 2011 study *Ashamed to Die: Silence, Denial, and the AIDS Epidemic in the South* and by a series of reports from CNN about the AIDS crisis in the South that commemorated

World AIDS day in 2011. Skerritt focuses his work on a small town in rural South Carolina. The CNN series for World AIDS day emphasized AIDS prevalence in Jacksonville, Florida. These two poles represent the ubiquity of the disease throughout Southern populations. More geographically and metaphorically pertinent, the space between these two locations is the rural southern Georgia of Walker's youth, where she set her most famous novel.

Demographically, the South has the largest percentage of African Americans in the nation. The large numbers of African Americans in the South suffer unduly from the disease, far in excess of their statistical presence. Nationwide, 466,000 African Americans are living with HIV, representing 38 percent of the HIV-infected U.S. population, though African Americans make up only 13 percent of the U.S. population as a whole. In the South, 61 percent of HIV-infected individuals are African Americans. Nationally, this means 24 percent of HIV-infected Americans are African Americans living in the U.S. South. The CDC links such statistics concerning the current African American AIDS crisis nationwide to poverty, lack of access to high-quality health care, and lack of awareness of one's HIV status. In the U.S. South, these conditions have exacerbated the crisis to its present proportions.

Nonetheless, it is tempting to look at other AIDS demographics to explain these numbers, particularly to turn to another demographic with a staggeringly disproportionate incidence rate, whom the CDC terms "men who have sex with men." While there is no doubt that certain sexual practices carry a greater risk of exposure and transmission of HIV/AIDS, to seek male same-sex activity as the source of the AIDS crisis in the African American community as a whole is a red herring, and possibly helps explain why *The Color Purple*, with its lesbian and womanist themes, falls under the radar of AIDS narratives. However, while the rhetoric of homosexuality has entered our collective consciousness about HIV/AIDS, it distracts from the ultimate cause of homosexual transmission: not the "homo" but the "sexual." The pandemic of AIDS in 1981 that caught the attention of epidemiologists was a result of prolific sexual encounters among gay men in the wake of gay liberation movements from the mid-1970s. Because this crisis marks the "discovery" of the disease, activists from Randy Shilts to J. L. King have tried to find a gay man at the source of all subsequent AIDS diagnoses. Even in less prolifically multipartner sexual communities, however, HIV will still spread, only more slowly and with less chance of detection until it acquires a critical mass that can no longer be ignored, as was the case with HIV/AIDS in colonial and postcolonial Africa for most of the twentieth century—until five gay men in large American cities developed a rare cancer and signaled to the world that something was wrong.

Tracing (Hetero)Sexual Transmission, Latent and Overt

The Color Purple lacks any explicit male-male same-sex sexual contact. There is no male homosexuality in the novel to speak of. There is, though, a pervasive sexual economy in the black community in the novel that links nearly every member of that community to each other in ways far more closely than a surface glance would reveal. Though not all of these sexual encounters are "equal"—some are blatantly rape, most are coercive, and only a few are predicated on joint consent and love—any sexual encounter can lead to the spread of an STD. Therefore, I will describe all the encounters simply as "sex." Also, Shug functions as the central node on a chart of sexual partners that links the multiple encounters of everyone else to one other. I will, however, begin on the margin and work inward to help make the sexual connections clear.

First, Celie's real father has sex with Celie's Ma, who in turn has sex with the man Celie thinks is her "Pa." Celie's "Pa" has sex with Celie and with his next wife, May Ellen, and eventually with his final wife, Daisy. Celie has sex with Mr. ____, who has previously had sex with (and children by) his first wife Annie Julie. Annie Julie has a boyfriend with whom she has sex even after she is married to Mr. __ and who eventually kills her. Mr. __ has his own "other" girlfriend, Shug. Shug and Mr. __ have sex, but then Shug also has sex with Celie. Shug eventually marries Grady, who cheats on Shug and has sex with Squeak. Squeak was married to Harpo and had sex with him. Harpo also had sex with (and children by) Sophia when he was married to her, though she subsequently began a sexual relationship with Buster before returning to Harpo after she gets out of jail. Shug also has sex with Germaine, a young man she meets after she and Celie have started living together, and after Squeak and Grady have begun their sexual affair (though Shug continues having sex with Celie, and her sexual encounters with Grady seem to continue past his beginning his sexual encounters with Squeak). Most notably, this sexual network is not hermetically sealed to just the African American community in the town (and in Memphis, where Shug meets Germaine). Squeak is raped by her uncle, the white warden in charge of Sophia. As a type of sexual encounter, rape can pass STDs between the two people, rapist and victim, just as rape can result in pregnancy despite the objections of certain politicians who believe pure will can prevent the occurrence of basic biological probabilities.

To trace the far-reaching edges of the sexual economy in the novel is to discover that quite literally every adult has sex with someone who links them to every other adult. (Children are not necessarily immune to this economy, but a child born to an HIV-infected mother is not necessarily infected with HIV. Also, with the exception of the chain that links Harpo to Squeak to Grady to Shug to Mr. __, Harpo's father, no other children have a direct connection to the larger sexual network as sexual participants.) Obviously, *when* these sexual encounters occur matters, as STDs do not retroactively infect previous sexual partners, only current and subsequent ones. Unfortunately, even from her earliest rhetorical gestures about sex and its outcomes, Celie suggests that illness has an a priori place in the sexual economy; thus, it must affect all subsequent sexual encounters and taint them with the possibility of its spread.

Celie's common rhetorical strategy is to describe a woman after she first enters this sexual community by using one of two words: she gets "big," meaning pregnant, or she gets "sick." After having sex with Celie's Pa, Celie's Ma gets sick and eventually dies. Pa turns his sexual attention to Celie at first, who gets "big" and has two children by him, before he remarries a young girl named May Ellen. This new wife proves unsatisfactory. Pa describes her to Mr. __ as "fresh," meaning she's had no children, but he also explains "she sick all the time" after her arrival (7). The chain in this instance is powerful and foreboding: if Ma was sick, then all Pa's subsequent sexual encounters could spread whatever sickness she had to Celie and to May Ellen. Pa is likely the carrier who infected Celie's Ma in the first place (more on this later), and then Celie (a latent carrier) and May Ellen, who gets sick almost immediately after she marries Pa. In a supreme act of love for Nettie, Celie offers herself to Pa as a sexual partner in Nettie's place: "I ast him to take me instead of Nettie while our new mammy sick" (7). This action may have been less a result of Celie's fear of Nettie becoming pregnant, and more a fear of Nettie also becoming "sick." Instead, Pa offers her to Mr. __ in Nettie's place when Mr. __ comes calling to get a wife to replace the one who just died at the hands of her other boyfriend. When Nettie can no longer rebuff Pa's advances, she flees to stay with Celie. She stays there until she can no longer rebuff Mr. __'s advances. Up to this point, Nettie remains outside the sexual economy and does not get "sick."

Meanwhile, Mr. __'s first wife has been killed by her other lover. Mr. __ has long had his own affair with Shug Avery, by whom he has fathered three children. When Mr. __ marries Celie, they begin having sex, but Mr. __ also continues having sex with Shug. Later, when Shug arrives at Mr. __'s house for the first time after he marries Celie, she has "maybe two berkulosis or some kind of nasty woman disease" (43). While Mr. __ could be exposed to an STD through Celie (from Pa), that Shug is sick when she first arrives (before Mr. __, who is now having sex with Celie, has a chance to pass on any disease from Celie to Shug) is also foreboding. There are multiple vectors through which an

STD seems to be spreading in this community if Celie's descriptions of sickness are to be followed to find a source. Also, as with all STDs, including AIDS, the community responds with reproach: "even the preacher got his mouth on Shug Avery now she down. He take her condition for his text" and calls her "a strumpet . . . slut, hussy, heifer and streetcleaner" (43–44). Despite her illness, Mr. __ carries on a sexual relationship with her. When she leaves, he continues having sex with Celie. Celie eventually begins a relationship with Shug and will continue that relationship after Shug marries Grady and after Grady begins flirting with (and probably sleeping with) Squeak, previously Harpo's lover and father of a child, Suzie Q, by him.

That Nettie seems to escape this economy is misleading. The most damning endorsement of its ubiquity is that she actually marries a man who was a member of it, long before the action of the novel; thus, the timing of his appearance in it reaffirms the a priori presence of illness in its matrix and the spread of that disease through it over time. It is easy to assume that Nettie escapes with her virginity to Africa after Celie works so hard to protect her from Pa and Mr. __, but she eventually marries Rev. Samuels, who used to "run with [Pa] long before he found Christ" (177), as he explains to Nettie when he explains why he and his wife Corrine took her in to begin with. This connection provides the basis to believe that Rev. Samuels had his share of sexual encounters in the community in the past (and also implicates Pa in sexual activities prior to his marriage that could have exposed him to an STD to bring to his eventual marriage to Celie's Ma). If Rev. Samuels "ran with" Pa and had not yet "found Christ," it is not much of a leap to assume that he was less than chaste in those former years as well. Corrine's death, which Nettie explains as a result of "African fever" (172), could as easily have occurred as a result of an infection with a long latency period acquired from her husband in Georgia before the family left for African as from exposure to an infection in Africa.[11] Nettie goes on to describe—with Victorian delicacy—her first sexual encounter with Rev. Samuels after Corrine's death (241–242), thus linking her with the same chain of sexual encounters so detrimental to the health of women in the Georgia landscape that she had left behind.

The other notable absences in this sexual economy are the children Adam, Olivia, Tashi, Henrietta, and Suzie Q. Though Adam and Olivia are the result of the "union" between Pa and Celie, they would not necessarily have gotten "sick" from their parents, as children can be born to HIV-infected mothers and not contract the disease. That Pa takes them away so quickly prevents Celie from breast-feeding them. Celie describes her "breast full of milk running down [her]self" (3), as if wasted, after Pa takes the children away. Breast-feeding carries a high risk of exposure to HIV/AIDS, so Celie's not breastfeeding her children may have saved them, in a cruel irony. Henrietta, the child of Sofia and Buster, on the other hand, does inherit a disease from her parents. Her unnamed blood disease makes it where "she look fine" when in reality "she got some sort of blood disease. Blood sort of clot up in her veins every once in a while, make her sick as a dog" (226). Her condition is likely sickle-cell anemia or a related disease, but that the members of the community explain that she looks fine except for this blood disease that just crops up every once in a while and makes her sick is a bitterly prescient folk description of AIDS. Thankfully, Nettie has explained in a letter that Africans have a long history of dealing with blood diseases and have developed treatments for them. Yams, which help Henrietta, do not cure AIDS. That African populations had long been dealing with AIDS when it arrived in the United States, however, allows that this exchange of medical treatments be read for its metaphoric relationship to AIDS and speaks to the wisdom we gain by confronting the 22.9 million HIV-infected individuals living in sub-Saharan Africa, where the disease has been spreading (with little or no homosexual impetus) since the 1920s.

Colonization and Health Care Practices—AIDS in Africa

Sontag's admonishment in *AIDS and Its Metaphors* to remember that Africa exists and must be considered in our understanding of AIDS could not be more significant to this reading of *The Color Purple*. Nettie's removal to Africa for the majority of the novel and the details she shares with her sister in her steady stream of letters from the Olinka village are no mere Marcus Garvey-esque apparitions of a lost homeland with the promise of return (in the movie, the screenwriters give Celie an idealized dream-vision of her children playing and growing up healthy in Africa, though the novel never makes such an explicit gesture to the romance of Celie's imaginary). By placing Nettie in Africa during a moment of great colonial upheaval, Walker actually implicates the larger postcolonial condition of women in both Africa and the Southern United States. The parallel lives of the two sisters, despite being separated by an ocean, only apparently diverge. The reunion at the end of the novel—complete with barbeque, a cultural element of both African and Southern American populations—suggests that their separate experiences bring both sisters to the same ultimate place, together, as if they had been holding hands all along despite removals and distance. Africa and Georgia are equally significant locations in the story. Placing Nettie in Africa to witness the uprooting of the Olinka village so a new colonial road can be built, however, takes on added meaning when viewed through the lens of the true history of HIV/AIDS, another colonial legacy with profound implications for the latter twentieth century.

The emphasis on sexual encounters causing women to get "sick" in a community wherein sexual contacts link almost all members to each other strikes an ominous note for a novel published in 1982, but written throughout 1981, as AIDS first appeared in population centers and among sexual communities in San Francisco, New York, and Los Angeles. Yet, that appearance of the disease only pointed to the larger and longer-term circulation of it in African populations. In *The Color Purple,* Walker's sexual economy in rural Georgia hints at a narrative of infection that, in retrospect, eerily parallels the spread of a disease like HIV/AIDS. The more devastating details of Walker's novel in relation to HIV/AIDS come from Nettie's letters from Africa. Her life in Africa as a missionary, and the attendant role she and the Rev. Samuels's family play as medical caregivers in their mission work, point directly to the conditions that existed there long before Walker published her novel. Only later would the world recognize those conditions as those giving rise to AIDS.

Nettie's life among the Olinka roughly parallels the great colonial upheavals that led to the mass migrations that Pepin characterizes in his study. Nettie arrives in Africa in the early 1920s, just on the verge of the colonial mandate that a road be built through the Olinka village. She details her time among the Olinka from their final years in their home territory to their contact with white colonialists and the subsequent effects of that contact. When Nettie first arrives in Africa, she describes "twenty miles through the jungle is a very long trip" (151), and even though the Olinka are within a few days journey of the coast, few have seen any white "missionaries" or other colonists. The Olinka are effectively an isolated population when they first encounter Nettie and the Samuels family. Their isolation and the patterns of their lives change, though, when "the road approaches! The road approaches!" (164) and the Olinka village is destroyed by the new road built to connect inland trade centers to the sea and improve economic development in the dense jungle of West Africa.

Pepin's study traces the first true spike in HIV-infection from a similar incident: the construction of a road to link Brazzaville to the sea. In the early 1930s, when Leon Pales arrived as the medical supervisor for the work crews, he found widespread illness, and, again, he concluded that an unknown pathogen was spreading through the population of native workers. In Walker's novel, the Olinka make a similar connection between the road and an increase in disease among their population, though they base their inferences not on medical procedures but on their belief system. They interpret the tragedy of illness and death that stems from their dislocation as punishment for their loss of connection to the land and specifically to the roofleaf that provides them shelter. When the road comes through their village, the Olinka are removed from access to their sacred roofleaf. Without their roofleaf, the Olinka begin to suffer, and sickness spreads through the population. In place of their older way of life, they are moved onto new farmland and made to pay rent to colonial masters as new cities and a new economy takes hold in the land.

Also, the Olinka do not seem to take part in building the road, but they do interact with the road builders, often other Africans from other villages who now work for the colonial government charged with building the road. Though the origins of these other Africans is not made clear in the novel, they represent movement and contact between previously relatively confined communities which are now finding an increased incidence of contact with outside people (and any pathogens those people may carry with them). From the perspective of epidemiology, such contact provides the impetus for the spread of diseases into new populations, even if these workers and the Olinka are primarily West African, from areas outside the original zone of the cross-species transmission of HIV.

The result of this upheaval is distinctly significant for understanding *The Color Purple* as an AIDS narrative. Indeed, the Olinka seem to be constructed as a West African people, possibly living in or around Nigeria. Pepin's study traces the origins of AIDS to a specific area in Africa to the east of Nigeria, in central Africa near the Congo River basin. When their village is destroyed, many Olinka, including Tashi and Adam, run away to join the *mbeles* in the east. Nettie describes, "there is a 'small' rift on our side [of Africa], several thousand acres large . . . in this overgrown canyon there are thousands of people from dozens of African tribes, and even one colored man—Adam swears—from Alabama" (282). The rift valley in the east—as opposed to the Great Rift Valley in Kenya—lies in the crook of Africa, where the coastline of West Africa turns south, or roughly midway between the Niger and Congo River basins. The migration that Nettie refers to both moves the Olinka into a closer geographic proximity to the original populations infected with HIV and puts the Olinka in direct contact with those populations, since the rift is home to "dozens of African tribes," not just runaways from West Africa. Of the thousands of people in the canyon, some could easily be refugees from the Congo River basin who have moved north and west to escape colonial oppression as the Olinka have moved east and south to the same area. To put the full scale of this upheaval into epidemiological terms, an isolated population first encounter an influx of workers on the road, for whom the Olinka often prepared food and treated as guests, according to Nettie, even as they destroyed the village. In response to displacement, many Olinka retreated deeper inland to a valley with numerous other previously isolated peoples. Such conditions are conducive to the spread of any virus; in particular, the widespread dissemination of HIV/AIDS has been linked to precisely these types of colonial displacements.

Contacts among previously disparate peoples does not alone explain the explosive increase in AIDS infection rates after 1921. The key to Pepin's history of AIDS rests on colonial medical practices, where even in large population centers, proper sterilization of needles was difficult given the miniscule resources devoted to native health and the huge demand natives, particularly workers on colonial construction projects, had for health care services. Even with the best of intentions, colonial doctors in remote villages often found themselves using needles and medicines contaminated by a virus that they did not even know existed on hundreds, sometimes thousands, of patients. Thus, via vaccinations or intravenous treatments, HIV broke the confines of purely sexual transmission, one partner to one partner, slowly spreading through the population. With colonial medical practices, the needle used on an infected patient in the morning might be used tens of times throughout the day, geometrically spreading HIV to countless new hosts. So it is no minor detail that Nettie describes the supplies that accompany her and Rev. Samuels to Africa: "With all of our belongings we filled three [dugout canoes], and a fourth one carried our medical and teaching supplies" (149). Given that they stay in Africa for such a long period of time, the reuse of those meager resources, filling one canoe, seems highly likely. From her entrance in Africa in the early 1920s until her leaving in or around the start of World War II, Nettie's tenure as a missionary coincides with the large-scale dissemination of the virus so that, by the 1950s and 1960s, a large enough population was infected that a global pandemic was all but inevitable. Unbeknownst to Nettie and the Rev. Samuels, their desire to help the native population with medical care may very well have contributed to the spread of an unknown blood-borne disease among that population.

The Last Detail

I would not claim that Alice Walker intentionally meant to write an AIDS narrative. She did, however, succeed in laying the breadcrumbs to a larger global catastrophe than she may have ever imagined. Her detailing what appears to be a sexually transmitted illness in a rural Southern population, her narrative of colonial dispossession and diaspora, and her inclusion of material relevant to colonial (in her case missionary) medical practices all accord with the most current data concerning AIDS in America and AIDS history in Africa as the disease began its spread to its current global proportions. One other detail about the novel also stands out, though, a detail of time and *place* that may be purely coincidental but, given the myth of AIDS in the early 1980s, is nonetheless critical.

Walker describes the process of writing *The Color Purple* in a short essay in her collection *In Search of Our Mothers' Gardens.* There she details that when she began work on the novel, she was living in New York. That environment did not suit her characters—Walker has long referred to her characters as figurative beings who come to her and speak through her. So she "disposed of [her] house, stored [her] furniture, packed [her] suitcases, and flew alone to San Francisco . . . where all the people in the novel promptly fell silent—I think, in awe" (356). Walker eventually moved from San Francisco, her characters having complained that their sufferings were not prone to earthquakes. She found a more rural residence in northern California and took trips to Georgia for inspiration to complete her novel. While too much stock has been invested in the American myth of AIDS as having "occurred" in the cities of New York and, particularly, San Francisco, Walker's presence in both cities as she wrote her novel—in the final months before a virus that had long circulated among the gay communities there drew enough attention to be discovered—brings an understanding of *The Color Purple* as an AIDS narrative full circle. Indeed, Randy Shilts may fail to mention Walker in his historical study of AIDS and American politics, but Walker was, in fact, *there* at the beginning. As she composed her book, she was in the very cities with which AIDS would be so associated. She was also in Georgia, where she travelled for further inspiration, according to her essay. Though that location may seem insignificant to the early years of the AIDS crisis, the Southeastern United States has since become ground zero of the pandemic over the slow course of the last thirty years.

Conclusion

Generally speaking, lesbian sexual practices carry a far lower incidence of communication of HIV/AIDS between the two sexual partners, certainly far less an incidence than certain sexual practices among men who have sex with other men and even less than many heterosexual practices. Perhaps Walker's lesbian-themed novel simply did not register as a catalog of AIDS for a reason as simple as its apparent focus. The true history of AIDS, however, is not a simple network of communication through sexual contact. AIDS history is a history of colonialism and public health initiatives. It is a history of people, uneducated to the true nature of the disease, continuing to live their lives unaware of the danger surrounding them (or, if aware of anything, aware that a disease is affecting someone else somewhere else even if the signs point to a very different reality from the one most people accept as "true"). Walker claims that her novel was her attempt to write an historical novel, though she also claims that "in an interview, discussing my work, a black male critic said he'd heard I might write a historical novel someday, and went on to say, in effect: Heaven protect us" (*In Search* 355–356).

A better response would have been, "Thank Heavens, you've shown us the way!" Walker's history is more accurate than the history we currently ascribe to concerning HIV/AIDS and the populations most acutely suffering from it in our contemporary society. Viewed through the lens of what we now know about AIDS, how it spreads, and the lives it is impacting, we can finally see the signs that have been apparent all along and understand AIDS history better thanks to Walker's efforts, however inadvertent.

In a way, Walker even warned us to pay attention to what her novel has to say and not miss the details that animate it. Whether or not she consciously constructed an AIDS narrative, she gave Shug Avery a memorable line to explain the title: "I think it pisses God off if you walk by the color purple in a field somewhere and don't notice it" (197). In relation to the AIDS crisis and worldwide effects of the disease, the metaphoric value of this statement rings ominously true. If we are to understand AIDS and properly attempt to prevent it, we must recognize its full history and impact, and not merely see it as something that happened to gay communities in big cities, with no bearing on the larger world. For all its significance to second-wave feminism, *The Color Purple* is also the outward sign—the mark, K. S., lesion number one—that points to a deeper pathogen rampant in the patient if we pay attention to it and allow it to let us detect the underlying problem that we need to address. From this detection—or more accurately, this recognition—we may begin the process of reeducation so vital to curbing the terrifying prevalence of AIDS in the rural South, in America, and in the rest of the world.

Notes

1. For more on Walker's views of "womanism" and the relationships between women, see her collection *In Search of Our Mother's Gardens*. In the opening pages, she defines "womanism" (xi–xii) and the subsequent essays speak to her general interests as a writer.

2. For details on the medical and political history of the disease, see Randy Shilts, *And the Band Played On*. While I will work to counter the narrative that HIV/AIDS is a gay, urban disease, there is no better source for the actual playing out of political and cultural reactions to the disease in the early years after its discovery.

3. In addition to Shilts's study, two other significant histories of the disease in the United States, from its detection to its political consequences, are the documentary *The Age of AIDS* and *My American History*, a collection of political writings by activist Sarah Schulman. This list of *firsts* is largely compiled by cross-referencing these three sources then adding other references.

4. The prevalence of references to Africa in AIDS narratives is not limited to *The Color Purple*, as I discuss in a later section of this paper. Rather, Africa appears in other early AIDS literature as well. Most notably, in *Parting Glances*, Robert is preparing for a two-year trip to Africa. His eminent departure becomes the impetus for the ensuing action of the film, which includes the AIDS patient Nick stopping by Robert's apartment to make his good-byes. Also, though Randy Shilts spends the vast majority of *And the Band Played On* focusing on Washington, D.C., Los Angeles, San Francisco, and New York, he begins his study with a brief description of the final months of the life of Dr. Grethe Rask, a Danish physician (and lesbian) who contracted AIDS while doing medical work in Kinshasa, Zaire, in the mid-1970s. Her death in 1977 is the first death Shilts records, his proverbial patient zero.

5. Pepin actually traces what he identifies as HIV-1 and "group M" of the pandemic because these forms are the ones most pervasive today, though genetic analysis can also trace other groupings and mutations that have proven less potent and communicable. His history is a medical/epidemiological history that relies heavily on advanced biochemical and genetic scientific breakthroughs. As such, his study may be the most accurate history of AIDS on a biological level so far written. There is more to the story of AIDS than just the genetic history of a virus. Pepin cites other histories for a fuller account of the virus and its spread in populations. Among these he includes Shilts's *And the Band Played On* and Laurie Garrett's *The Coming Plague*, as "contain[ing] captivating descriptions of the early years of the pandemic in the US and Europe" (1). Additionally, he names John Illiffe's *The African AIDS Epidemic: A History* as the best source for a history of AIDS in Africa post-1981. For a pre-1981 history, he names Edward Hooper's *The River: A Journey Back to the Source of HIV and AIDS*, though to explain that Hooper's claims have been largely disproven (2). I would add to Pepin's list the 2012 study by Craig Timberg and Daniel Halperin, *Tinderbox: How the West Sparked the AIDS Epidemic and the World Can Finally Overcome It*, devoted to understanding the role of colonial policies in fostering the spread of HIV/AIDS. Pepin's study ranks as the authoritative medical/epidemiological study, though these other studies are worth pursuing for their insights. Pepin admits at times in his study that there are still holes in the history of the spread of the disease and he has to conjecture certain scenarios to try to fill those gaps. As of now, AIDS researchers are still working to piece the full history together. The one, great, all-encompassing history of HIV/AIDS has yet to be written.

6. Brazzaville remains the name of the city on Stanley Pool, but the pool has since been renamed Lake Malebo. Across that lake, the Belgian city Leopoldville has been renamed Kinshasa and has grown to become the largest city in Central Africa. I feel it important to explain that I am greatly summarizing Pepin's intricate, thoughtful, and extremely detailed

analysis. He considers colonial medical practices and economic/construction policies on both sides of the Congo River, where the differing colonial practices of the French and Belgian colonial systems produced vastly different outcomes in regard to HIV/AIDS. Pepin traces the original outbreak to Brazzaville. He also explores how policies across the lake in Leopoldville actually had more to do with the widespread dissemination of the disease through the 1940s–1960s.

7. Pepin bases his claim that sexual contact alone could not account for the increased incidence of AIDS in the 1920s and until the present time on two limitations to the process of sexual transmission. First, the latency period of the disease actually makes sexual transmission a relatively slow means by which to circulate the virus to new carriers. Second, actual analysis of the sexual practices of people in the cities on Stanley Pool suggests that even among sex workers, the overall sexual networks were both small and contained (one woman might share several men, but those men remained relatively faithful to that one woman and vice versa, for example).

8. The exception to this model of the spread of a blood-borne, sexually transmitted disease, was, in fact, the sexual freedoms of the urban gay communities in Los Angeles, San Francisco, and New York. The so-called bathhouse culture and sexual practices of gay men in these cities—practices that included multiple partners, anonymous sexual encounters, and a lack of safe sex practices such as the use of condoms—led to a spike in the incidence rate of AIDS. That spike occurred at a critical time in a first world country with a massive and advanced medical establishment. The medical establishment—medical researchers at research-focused hospitals, the CDC and National Institutes of Health, medical record-keepers, etc.—identified a pattern in a handful of individuals that had gone undetected for decades in large third world populations with less meticulous individual data (Pepin's study suggests that colonial health care practices were devoted to statistical analyses of populations rather than isolated care for individuals).

9. Both Shilts and the documentary *The Age of AIDS* detail the resistance of blood banks to acknowledge that their blood supply was infected, possibly as early as 1975. Pepin verifies these claims and expands on their implications to consider infection rates in third world countries, especially Haiti.

10. The data included in this study comes from information available on the CDC webpage in March and April 2012. Subsequent to that data being posted in a nicely prepared series of graphs and tables, the CDC has updated their data as of February 2013. The numbers are still fundamentally consistent and certainly do not show a decline in infection rates. Furthermore, the general census data that I use to crunch numbers and produce the 24 percent of AIDS-infected Americans are African Americans living in the South was computed using data from the 2010 U.S. Census (for the estimates on total population and percentages of minorities in different regions). The CDC data available in 2012 was compiled from statistical analysis from 2009 to 2011, so it is consistent with the demographics of the 2010 census. Therefore, I have kept this data as it appeared when I originally compiled it, though the numbers have slightly altered since I first wrote this paper.

11. "African fever" sounds an ominous warning as well. We can, though, reasonably assume that Corrine did not have sex with another man in Africa, which, if African fever were a reference to the "Cachexie du Mayombe," would beg the question of how she was exposed to it. If Corrine used medical supplies on herself (to administer a shot or run an IV) that she had previously used on an Olinka, she could conceivably have contracted the fever from that reuse, especially if the supplies were not properly sterilized. Thus, any subsequent sexual activity she has with her husband would expose him, who would later expose Nettie. Therefore, the reference to African fever could expose yet another vector through which Nettie could eventually be infected. Such a reading is hypothetical, and timing matters, since West African populations were not prone to HIV/AIDS infection until long after the 1930s, when migratory practices (usually among the labor force) might have brought them into contact with the disease. Whatever "sickness" is spreading in the sexual network of Southern Georgia (and all the way to Africa following this theoretical vector) is not HIV/AIDS in actuality. I am trying to demonstrate how the sexual economy of the novel presents pathways for the spread of the disease and how Walker even codes the language of that sexual economy with the rhetoric of sickness. Thus, she prefigures HIV/AIDS.

Works Cited

The Age of AIDS. Dirs. William Cran and Greg Barker. *Frontline*. Series Prod. Renata Simone. Narr. Will Lyman. PBS. 30–31 March 2006. Television.

Cunningham, Michael. *A Home at the End of the World*. New York: Picador: Farrar Straus, Giroux, 1990. Print.

———. *The Hours*. New York: Picador: Farrar, Straus, Giroux, 1998. Print.

Garrett, Laurie. *The Coming Plague: Newly Emerging Diseases in a World Out of Balance*. New York: Penguin, 1994. Print.

"HIV/AIDS." *The Center for Disease Control and Prevention*. http://www.cdc.gov/hiv/. Accessed 25 March 2012. Web.

Hooper, Edward. *The River: A Journey Back to the Source of HIV and AIDS*. London: Little Brown and Company, 1999. Print.

Illiffe, John. *The African AIDS Epidemic: A History*. Athens: Ohio UP, 2006. Print.

King, J. L. *On the Down Low: A Journey into the Lives of "Straight" Black Men Who Sleep with Men*. New York: Harlem Moon: Broadway Books, 2004. Print.

Kramer, Larry. *The Normal Heart*. New York: Samuel French, 1985. Print.

Kushner, Tony. *Angels in America: A Gay Fantasia on National Themes*. New York: Theatre Communication Group, 1995. Print.

Parting Glances. 1986. Dir. Bill Sherwood. First Run Features. 2000. DVD.

Pepin, Jacques. *The Origins of AIDS*. New York: Cambridge UP, 2011. Print.

Philadelphia. Dir. Jonathan Demme. Perf. Tom Hanks, Denzel Washington. Sony Pictures, 2002. DVD.

Sapphire. *The Kid*. New York: Penguin, 2012. Print.

———. *Push*. New York: Vintage: Random House, 1996. Print.

Schulman, Sarah. *My American History: Lesbian and Gay Life during the Reagan/Bush Years*. New York: Routledge, 1994. Print.

Shilts, Randy. *And the Band Played On: Politics, People, and the AIDS Epidemic*. New York: St. Martin's, 1987. Print.

Skerritt, Andrew J. *Ashamed To Die: Silence, Denial, and the AIDS Epidemic in the South*. Chicago: Lawrence Hill, 2011. Print.

Sontag, Susan. *AIDS and Its Metaphors*. New York: Farrar, Straus, Giroux, 1988. Print.

Timberg, Craig, and Daniel Halperin. *Tinderbox: How the West Sparked the AIDS Epidemic and How the World Can Finally Overcome It*. New York: Penguin, 2012. Print.

United States Census 2010. U.S. Census Bureau. Accessed 25 March 2012. Web.

Walker, Alice. *The Color Purple*. 1982. New York: Harvest: Harcourt, 1992. Print.

———. *In Search of Our Mother's Gardens*. New York: Harvest: Harcourt, 1983. Print.

Chapter 11

"This Really Isn't a Job for a Girl to Take on Alone"

Reappraising Feminism and Genre Fiction in Sara Paretsky's Crime Novel *Indemnity Only*

Charlotte Beyer

This chapter undertakes a reappraisal of Sara Paretsky's 1982 crime novel *Indemnity Only*, examining its critical engagement with genre and the diverse landscape of feminist criticism during the period of its publication, and discussing Paretsky's articulation of an evolving feminist position in genre fiction.[1] As we enter the fourth wave of feminism and new feminist initiatives and campaigns take off (Cochrane), an assessment of the importance of second-wave feminist literature in the light of those developments is timely.[2] A number of critics have discussed Paretsky's novel as an example of feminist appropriation of genre fiction.[3] This chapter extends these readings by arguing for its centrality to second-wave feminist fiction, focusing on specific areas and thematic concerns that highlight the complex relationship between Paretsky's text and feminist criticism and illustrate the ongoing dialogue between activism and fiction.[4]

These concerns form part of my overall argument that Paretsky's *Indemnity Only* portrays feminism and its successes realistically, as an evolving and ongoing project rather than an idealized state that has been achieved. My reading of *Indemnity Only* centers on the lasting importance of second-wave feminist ideas and continued feminist struggle, but it also surfaces some of the problems feminists face in reimagining strategies. I recognize that my discussion of second-wave feminism will inevitably present a subjective reading of a complex movement. This complexity extends to literature, and here I want to focus on feminist attempts to revision genre fiction to include feminist tactics and textual strategies. I argue that Paretsky's novel constitutes an example of how second-wave feminist ideals and ideas have been employed effectively in mainstream culture, without compromising radical political agendas.

The process of reappraising feminism in genre writing was initiated by second-wave feminist literary fiction and its gender-political priorities, during a phase Nicole Décuré describes as "the Golden Age of the American feminist novel" (227). *Indemnity Only* quickly became one of the leading models of the new female detective novel, paving the way for a new generation of female detective figures who also engaged with feminist debates. It also heralded a new literary development—a phenomenon that the critic and crime fiction author Carolyn Heilbrun calls a "revolution" (419).[5] Indeed, feminist crime writer Val McDermid singled this novel out as her "Book of a Lifetime" in a recent article. She says, "If I had to point to one book that had irrevocably changed my future, I would have to settle on Sara Paretsky's *Indemnity Only*."

One of the themes explored in *Indemnity Only* is women stepping out of the shadows of patriarchal authority and embracing independence and self-sufficiency. In narrative terms, this strategy forges a new thematic focus and constructs a female lead character by revising previous male-identified conventions. A sense of female agency had been largely absent from crime fiction until feminist second-wave authors took these dramatic steps (Heilbrun 427). However, this process has by no means been straightforward or uncomplicated, and Paretsky's novel acknowledges the work still to be done on unresolved issues, both in its examination of feminist politics and in its reimagining of the crime genre.

Genre Fiction and Feminist Politics: Reimagining the Tradition

Indemnity Only is part of the second-wave feminist literary and cultural developments of the 1960s to the mid-1980s. As this book argues, second-wave feminist fiction has been immensely influential and has had a long-term effect on the literary landscape. Nikki Gerrard states, "Since the 1960s, many of the novels of stature have been written by women; of these, most have been either explicitly feminist or clearly informed by feminism" (170). Margaret Kinsman describes the impact of second-wave feminism on women individually and collectively: "For many women, second-wave feminism provided a new way of seeing and understanding the world, overturning all the old certainties" ("Feminist" 159).

This "new way of seeing" resulted in a reassessment of literary conventions that had previously placed male identity at the center, and the process of "overturning" impacted not just literary fiction and its representations but also genre fiction, such as science fiction, espionage, romance, and crime.[6] Thus, the growth of feminist crime writing demonstrates how the second wave influenced crime fiction and popular culture through experimentation with and recasting of the genre's thematic conventions.[7] However, as Heilbrun points out, despite the growth of women's crime fiction, the female detective figure has been relatively overlooked and "rarely commented upon" (419). Crime fiction has been predominantly male-dominated (Reddy 191), and the hard-boiled genre in particular has traditionally been associated with a male private eye. Its female characters are portrayed as "either dangerous, seductive villains or nurturing" (Reddy 193), thereby reinforcing existing stereotypes about the gendering of crime and its portrayal.

Paretsky's *Indemnity Only* makes this point through intertextual allusions to iconic male sleuths from the crime fiction canon, foregrounding the gender-political dimension of detective characters and their depiction. Through phrases such as "Peter Wimsey would have gone in and charmed all those uncouth radicals into slobbering all over him" (213) and "'It's me. Sherlock Holmes,' I said" (218), the novel humorously subverts these male characters—as well as Raymond Chandler's iconic male private investigator, Philip Marlowe (59). Such references expose canonical figures and stereotyped representations, but also highlight the lack of comparable female reference points within the crime fiction canon.

By introducing a new kind of female detective, feminist revisions of the canon and its "from man to man" pattern (Reddy 191) have been significant (Kinsman "Feminist" 152). Subverting a hitherto male-dominated genre through a charismatic, politicized, and outspoken female private detective character, *Indemnity Only* examines a range of themes and ideas that are frequently marginalized in conventional crime fiction and in patriarchal society more broadly. Maureen Reddy and Margaret Kinsman have discussed this feminist countertradition in the crime and mystery genre. Kinsman observes, "The late 1970s and early 1980s saw American writers Marcia Mueller, Sue Grafton and Sara Paretsky . . . each creating a female private eye/investigator character; all three novelists subsequently developed commercially successful and popular series based on their mold-breaking female private eye creations" ("Feminist" 148).

The 1980s also saw the emergence of lesbian crime fiction, with lesbian characters at the center of works by Val McDermid, Claire McNab, Barbara Wilson, and others,[8] published by Naiad Press as well as Seal and Firebrand (Reddy

200–201). Lesbian crime fiction amplifies the challenge of revising hard-boiled crime fiction's conventional depictions of female dependency on males. As Reddy notes, "women's real danger lies in the radical threat lesbians pose to the status quo through rejecting the assumption that patriarchal order is desirable and insisting on the value of women's relationships with other women" (201). Lesbian crime novels further challenged the conventional gender coding and representation of sexuality in crime fiction and demonstrated how genre fiction can provide a platform for cultural and political interventions. Although its protagonist is a heterosexual woman and the novel has a mainstream readership (Gerrard 129), Paretsky's *Indemnity Only* can be placed alongside the novels published by these smaller presses as an illustration of second-wave feminist fiction because of its portrayals of sisterhood and its explicitly feminist themes.

Feminist revision such as these opened new debates about the role of the female detective, as Heilbrun explains: "Female detectives inherit the detective novel's traditions, but combine their elements into a *new form*" (420, my emphasis). The complexity of Paretsky's female detective character, V. I. Warshawski, is crucial to *Indemnity Only*. She embodies its articulation of a complex, evolving feminist position and personalizes the exploration of the gender-political dimensions of genre revision. Breaking away from stereotypical portrayal of female characters in crime fiction has shaped Paretsky's development of Warshawski's character. K. Edgington highlights this, noting, too, that with Warshawski, Paretsky "created a character whose personal struggle to establish a sense of a unified, autonomous self reflects the confusion and conflict prevalent in the 'consciousness-raising' phase of the feminist movement" (56). Paretsky herself stresses the connection between her feminist politics and rewriting of the crime genre (Beyer "Life" 214). She states in her autobiography, *Writing in an Age of Silence,* that "It was feminism that triggered my wish to write a private eye novel, and it shaped the character of my detective, V. I. Warshawski" (xvi).[9]

The novel's interrogation of the gender coding of violence also reflects an important aspect of second-wave feminist writing and underlines the close link between feminist critique and genre fiction that "seeks ambitiously to investigate the interrelation between a variety of different forms and manifestations" (Palmer 88).[10] A terrifying episode that sees Warshawski beaten up and warned off the case emphasizes that male criminals in *Indemnity Only* have no qualms about abusing their position and perpetrating violence against women (71). Their ruthlessness is shown to feed on a sense of entitlement and power. "He really could kill me and get away with it—he'd done it to others," Warshawski observes (73). *Indemnity Only* foregrounds male exploitations of power that permeate and negatively affect all strata of society—from organizations to educational establishments, to the family.

Paretsky constructs Warshawski's character with an acute sense of the complexity required to avoid stereotyping, thereby creating a female detective character who is tough, sharp-witted but sensitive, emotionally intelligent, and resilient in the face of difficulty. Commenting on how Warshawski was perceived when she first appeared, Gerrard calls her "a new style of feminist sleuth—modern, cool, witty, assertive" (129). This "new style" further reflects the era of second-wave feminism with which Warshawski coincided—a time when the complexities and contradictions of women's traditional roles became increasingly apparent. Warshawski comes across as having experienced life, not as girly and in need of rescue. Resisting the conventional restrictions on women presented by motherhood and marriage, she instead relishes her personal and financial space. This rejection of previous certainties is a specific dimension of feminist crime fiction. Heilbrun argues, "The refusal to dwindle into wife, seen as a pattern and not an anomaly, had to await the arrival of the female sleuth as protagonist" (427).

Thus, autonomy, integrity, and self-reliance are qualities central to Warshawski's character and how she defines herself in relation to her male counterparts (Beyer "Life" 215). LeRoy Panek, in his study of hardboiled detectives, explores these characteristics, observing, "part of independence in Paretsky also comes from pride in one's abilities and self-sufficiency" (78). He suggests later that Warshawski "fears entering into relationships because of their potential to erode her independence" (216). Warshawski herself says of her marriage, "My brief foray into marriage eight years ago had ended in an acrimonious divorce after fourteen months: some men can only admire independent women from a distance" (33). Her deadpan remark is carefully constructed to prevent her from appearing embittered or like a victim. On the contrary, as Natalie Kaufman and Susan Kaufman note, Warshawski "enjoys male company, but does not mind being single; she does not evaluate her life in terms of relationships with men" ("Food" 55).

In that independence is invested Paretsky's reimagining of the female detective within a feminist hard-boiled genre, along with her second-wave feminist aspirations and American models of self-reliance that further validate female independence (Beyer "Life" 215).[11] In this sense, Warshawski reflects the choices women have, in Paulina Palmer's words, of either "eluding or challenging phallocratic expectations of feminine behaviour" (37). In attempting both, she complicates one-dimensional representations of women in crime. Her independence is further emphasized in the novel's central focus on conflicts between fathers and daughters, and the daughters' struggle to liberate themselves from the "sins of the fathers" and the negative legacies of patriarchal oppression (*Indemnity Only* 277).

The first-person narrative dimension of *Indemnity Only* is crucial to establishing the connection between the woman reader and Warshawski and underpins its feminist perspective. Priscilla Walton argues that "When the female voice speaks the 'I' of the hard-boiled narrative, the agency of the mode shifts, for 'she' is not simply watching the detectives, but rather performing as a detective herself" ("Form" 134). The tactic of presenting a strong female figure telling her story represents a change in convention that promotes a sense of agency and a point of identification for women whereby narrative perspective becomes part of feminist consciousness-raising. Kinsman states, "Positioned at the center of the narrative, in the familiar first-person voice of the hard-boiled tradition embodied by Chandler's Philip Marlowe, characters such as Sharon McCone, Kinsey Millhone, and V. I. Warsawski were allowed agency, intelligence and action" ("Feminist" 148). Acknowledging the novelty of what Paretsky and her second-wave contemporaries have created, Kinsman explains that their female detective characters were "pioneering constructions" ("Feminist" 148). Thus the initiation of this narrative mode contributed to Paretsky's construction of a strong feminist voice with Warshawski.

The female detective character illustrates the fight against sexism in the public and private sphere, a concept central to both second-wave feminism and *Indemnity Only*. This ongoing conversation between feminism and fiction can be seen in the novel's portrayal of the gender politics of employment and the work environment, issues still pertinent in many ways in today's fourth wave of feminism, as noted by Cochrane. At the time of the novel's publication, a tough female private detective was still perceived as unconventional: "This really isn't a job for a girl to take on alone," Warshawski is told (6). Despite her hard demeanor, Warshawski has to defend herself against assumptions that her gender prevents her from being a successful detective, as when Bobby says, "Being a detective is not a job for a girl like you, Vicki" (33), and "for two cents I'd kick you in your cute little behind" (37). *Indemnity Only* portrays Warshawski having to fight sexism, including sexist language and assumptions, in both her professional and private life.[12]

In the novel, Warshawski's struggle against sexism is inspired by her mother, who taught her to aspire and to work for her goals rather than rely on her looks: "Any girl can be pretty—but to take care of yourself you must have brains. And you must have a job, a profession. You must work," she tells her (12).[13] This maternal advice establishes a powerful symbolic link of support and intellectual recognition between women (Panek 73). Warshawski mobilizes that maternal support to empower herself, stating, "I'm the only person I take orders from, not a hierarchy of officers, aldermen, and commissioners" (212). As Kaufman and Hevener argue, "The Paretsky oeuvre offers women an encouraging way to read the clues of socialization that can help them develop strategies to live and flourish in a patriarchal system" (27).

Through the novel's problematizing of gender and work, Paretsky demonstrates how genre fiction can promote feminist struggle. Warshawski's feminist consciousness is closely linked to her emotional intensity and engagement—and to her anger at injustice (Plain 155).[14] These responses and personal qualities are presented as manifestations of what Kinsman terms a feminist "resisting subjectivity" ("Feminist" 152), defined and shaped through its resistance to patriarchal domination on a number of levels—physical, emotional, intellectual, linguistic. The act of resisting dominant discourses of privilege and subservience is central to Warshawski's character and to her detective work, as it is to feminist consciousness-raising. Her readiness to admit to and express anger presents another break with conventional constructions of femininity. As Kaufman and Kaufman state, anger in women is taboo according to conventional constructions of femininity, but for the female detective, anger is "inevitable" ("Food" 51), and "V. I. is . . . effective in expressing it" (55). Edgington points out that Warshawski's "inner conflict keeps her in action physically, mentally, and emotionally, thereby providing her with a source of self-renewal and growth" (56). Nicole Décuré concurs in her assessment: "Sara Paretsky succeeds in being political, not by expounding feminist theory but by showing us women who LIVE as feminists, competent in their jobs, free, self-reliant, egalitarian" (237).

Thus, evaluating *Indemnity Only* and its relation to second-wave feminism more than thirty years after its publication, Warshawski's character emerges strongly, her anger and sense of women's solidarity contributing to the process of feminist consciousness-raising. Her "resisting subjectivity" is central to her appeal to women readers in particular, who identify with her righteous rage and take courage from it to translate it into their own lives. The novel achieves this not by presenting an idealized role model, but by exploring Warshawski's own personal issues and relationships, and by portraying her evolving feminist consciousness and politics through her various experiences as a detective.

Challenges: Feminist Themes and Debates

The topics and themes Paretsky treats in *Indemnity Only* reflect feminist revisionary efforts in the areas of genre and character, but also suggest unresolved tensions and issues within second-wave feminism as it evolved.[15] This political dimension of *Indemnity Only* reflects Paretsky's general preoccupation with the political (Rzepka 240). Feminist experimentation is evident in the novel, as we have seen, in the novel's re-visioning of genre and character, but also in the gender-political nature of the themes and ideas it explores. These topics reflect what Kinsman calls "explicitly feminist themes and feminist sensibilities" ("Feminist" 153), which had often been absent from mainstream crime fiction, despite their obvious relevance for women readers.[16] Paretsky and other second-wave women writers "appeal especially to the feminist reader because of their own feminist attitudes and assumptions and their sensitive depictions of women's lives and concerns" (DeMarr 32). This appeal is vital because it shows that women's writing, including feminist genre fiction, can have a consciousness-raising effect and can help build feminist community as well as strengthen the individual woman's sense of self and autonomy. Kinsman links this dimension to other women crime writers from the second-wave period: "Writers used their novels as spaces in which to explore the dilemmas germane to real women's lives. . . . Issues such as homelessness and poverty, homophobia, sexism and racism, domestic abuse, incest, pornography were taken up by many writers, bringing to the center what has often been marginalized or treated in stereotypical ways" ("Feminist" 154). *Indemnity Only*'s use of overtly gender-political themes is also an important aspect of feminist experimentation. Bringing to the center those topics and issues that have been silenced, and refocusing the crime fiction narrative and the characters that people it, is crucial to the impact feminist experimentation has had on genre. According to Kinsman, the function of feminist genre fiction is not to act "as a flag-waver for feminist identity, but as a vehicle for feminist debate" ("Feminist" 159). Paulina Palmer also highlights the capacity of feminist fiction to act as a vehicle to represent and "debate the controversial issues which perplex and divide feminists [and] experiment with a variety of different strategies" (61). Representing problems that demonstrate or create division among feminists can seem daunting, yet in Paretsky's novel these contradictions and disagreements are never treated superficially. *Indemnity Only*, along with other writing from the second wave, challenges readers and critics to interrogate and reconsider the meanings and parameters of both fiction and feminism.

Paretsky's portrayal of issues of body image is central to her feminist critique, foregrounding the significant second-wave feminist topic of the female body and food, an issue that remains relevant to twenty-first–century feminism.[17] Further examples of second-wave feminist critique of women's relationship to food and their bodies can be seen in 1970s–1980s texts such as Susie Orbach's *Fat Is a Feminist Issue* (1978) and Kim Chernin's *The Hungry Self: Women, Eating and Identity* (1985). These preoccupations were echoed in prominent texts by second-wave women writers during this period, thus illustrating how the female body was portrayed as a site of feminist struggle, a concern that reflects "the problematic relationship which, in a phallocratic culture, woman experiences with her body [and] the pressure put on her to conform to the images of feminine beauty promoted by the media and fashion industry. This motif also plays a key role in women's fiction" (Palmer 30).

Introducing such themes into a crime fiction setting draws attention to related concerns, such as anger, repression, anxiety, control, corporeality, and power. Paretsky's feminist stance is evident precisely in that she portrays her female protagonist struggling with these issues and working to resolve them like many other women, rather than presenting her as an ideal of feminist liberation; this is a very important aspect of Paretsky's critique. Critics, however, have had mixed responses to this focus on food and the female body. Kaufman and Kaufman note that Paretsky's Warshawski "reflects generally positive attitudes and behavior around food and anger" ("Food" 53), whereas Décuré argues that Paretsky's "concern with food and clothes clashes a little with a feminist approach" (237). I read Warshawski's character and Paretsky's problematizing of the female body as part of the politics of presenting a feminist detective, a central and ongoing aspect of second-wave feminist critique of patriarchy.

Warshawski's anxiety over aging and her awareness of the fragility and loss of agency it may bring is reflected in the attention she pays to a middle-aged female receptionist's upper arms and physical appearance (41). This passage is an indication of the way that patriarchy forces women, often unwittingly, to judge one another on physical appearance and to compete against one another, but it also reflects Warshawski's awareness of her own mortality and underlines the requirement for her to remain in physical top form to be able to meet the demands that her job and profession place upon her.[18] Kaufman and Kaufman's point supports this reading, as they observe that "V. I. runs on a regular basis, not to lose weight but to stay strong for the demanding physical part of her job" ("Food" 55).

Such references to food and body anxiety in *Indemnity Only* are incorporated into the fabric of the narrative for several reasons. First, they serve to problematize the construction of the female body in Western culture and its effect on women as part of a feminist debate. Second, they portray Warshawski as sharing commonalities with other women in terms of her insecurities and experience of corporeality; she is not idealistically portrayed as being somehow superior. Third, references to the female body and physical awareness for women emphasize the requirement for fitness and agility in the female detective. By introducing these issues and themes into her crime fiction, Paretsky contributes to important feminist debates. Central to Paretsky's portrayal of Warshawski in *Indemnity Only* is her awareness of her body and its gender-political dimensions as a work-in-progress, with ambiguities and contradictions, a realistic portrayal rather than one in which an idealized acceptance has been achieved. This complexity mirrors second-wave feminism's own increasing awareness of how the female body is politicized in patriarchal society, and also its recognition of the insidious ways that oppression may be internalized and form part of our lived experience.

Another feminist concern encountered in *Indemnity Only* is relations between women, including female friendship and women's community, but Paretsky also highlights differences between and among women.[19] Palmer argues that feminist literature is valuable as an intellectual engagement but that it also supports relations between women through thematic means, as it "provide[s] a valuable channel of communication, and create[s] a forum for both airing and debating ideas" (60). As part of its feminist engagement, *Indemnity Only* investigates what opportunities and spaces women have available to them (individually and as a group) to organize and be heard and foregrounds articulations of women's solidarity with other women. This emphasis is central to second-wave feminism, according to Palmer: "Sisterhood and women's community may be described, with some justification, as constituting the very heart and centre of contemporary feminism" (125). Rampton also highlights the importance to second-wave feminists of establishing "women-only" groups and organizations in order to resist marginalization. *Indemnity Only* uses a range of female characters to interrogate these ideas.

The shift from a male-centered plot, with females as minor characters, to a plot that features a female protagonist within an intergenerational context of women represents an important change of focus in crime fiction (Walton "Form" 136). Consequently, the counteremphasis in Paretsky's novel, according to Kinsman, is on female subject identity and female relations:[20] "The placement of these fictional female characters within solid yet dynamic communities of other female friends, relatives and associates . . . is one of the most important markers of the counter-tradition" ("Feminist" 155). What Palmer calls the "political significance of women's community" (125) and the portrayal of relationships between and among women in contemporary women's writing is emphasized in *Indemnity Only*. In its depiction of Warshawski's close friendship with her friend Lotty, the novel stresses the idea of female friendship based on unconditional acceptance, not competition for male attention. In this friendship, Warshawski encounters "no censure, no horror," and she concludes that this acceptance and reluctance to be shocked is "one of the things I liked in

Lotty" (125). The friendship is portrayed as constant since their student days, when both were involved in feminist reproductive politics (Décuré 233). The novel portrays Lotty's underground involvement as a vital service offered to women, assisting them in their plight and promoting a sense of choice. Thus, the two women share a political and emotional bond rooted in second-wave feminist struggles for women's reproductive rights and a sense of female solidarity. *Indemnity Only*'s treatment of the topic of abortion contributes to debates around women's reproductive rights and the attempts to control women's bodies and sexuality, debates, again, that still exist today.

The portrayal of relations between women and the rethinking of the mother-daughter relationship[21] has emerged as a central dimension of second-wave feminist writing (Palmer 112). The novel reflects this as well, by incorporating the theme centrally in the text—both in terms of problematizing the complexities and tensions in female relations, and in underscoring the positive aspects of solidarity and identification. Paretsky's portrayal of rich and complex relationships between women, albeit not sexual, suggests that her *Indemnity Only* and lesbian crime fiction are both nurtured by second-wave feminist commitment to representing female relations as central to women's lives, as friends, work colleagues, student activists, mother figures, daughters, lovers—and detectives.

Disagreements and divisions among women illustrate the complexity and internal contradictions of feminism that were becoming increasingly evident in the 1980s. The need for feminism to accept differences also remains important today, both in reappraising the second wave and in analyzing contemporary fourth-wave feminist issues. Paretsky's novel emphasizes this through its portrayal of feminist debate as a reflection of ongoing efforts to resolve internal feminist differences.[22] For example, in chapter 14, Warshawski attends a meeting with the University Women United student group at the University of Chicago to find further information about the missing woman, Anita McGraw, a student at the university, and what might have happened to her.[23] This provides a central opportunity to portray feminist debate and the voicing of different feminist positions; it enables *Indemnity Only* to use crime fiction to create representations of alternative, women-centered spaces, drawing attention to the significance of such groups, of woman-only spaces, and of female bonding more generally in the workplace, in education, and in detection.

In *Indemnity Only*, the meeting Warshawski attends does not merely present an opportunity to portray female fellowship and feminist debate, it also serves to explore intergenerational relations between women and the differences in opinion arising from these. On listening to the debates, Warshawski reflects,

"This was an old argument; it went back to the start of radical feminism in the late sixties: Do you concentrate on equal pay and equal legal rights, or do you go off and try to convert the whole society to a new set of sexual values?" (209). Although she recognizes the feminist positions rehearsed and the arguments used in the discussions as old, it becomes apparent during the course of the novel that each generation of women has to position itself in relation to these central questions, and that feminist struggle is urgent and ongoing.

In her discussion of the feminist debates that are rehearsed in *Indemnity Only*, Edgington argues that Warshawski perceives these feminist debates as "only a rehashing of 1960s Women's Liberation arguments" (60). However, my point is that the significance of the discovery of such ideas is relevant for women readers today, including readers of the younger generations, who may be in the process of discovering feminism for themselves as a lived experience, and for whom the consciousness-raising effect of connecting with such ideas and debates may be profound.[24] Twenty-first century manifestations of fourth-wave feminism, such as feminist student politics, "slut walks," and "pussy riots," demonstrate this point (MacDonald). Edgington echoes this. Commenting on Paretsky's representation of the female students, she notes, "the old issues don't prevent the young women from acting; the young feminists are impassioned and empowered in spite of or because of the complexities and debates of the feminist movement" (60).

This dimension is especially pertinent because, in an age some are calling "post-feminist" (Cochrane), the fact is that women are continuing to discover the relevance of feminist debate to their personal and professional lives.[25] The portrayal of these issues and topics draws attention to the ways in which crime fiction became explicitly politicized during the second-wave period, and it underlines the longer-term effects of this political and textual engagement. The inclusion of social and political themes in genre fiction adds depth and complexity, and it is one of the most significant ways in which second-wave feminism has contributed to literary innovation. Heilbrun comments on this facet of feminist crime fiction, arguing that female detectives "are incited by injustice" and do battle "against racism, or institutional bullying, or the illicit power of money. . . . They fight skullduggery in high places" (421).

Paretsky's treatment of such themes and ideas in *Indemnity Only* establishes her as among the first to represent an overtly feminist link between individual male crime and crime perpetrated by patriarchal power structures and social corruption and to suggest female solidarity as an alternative to that corruption and abuse of power—one of the most significant strategies identified by second-wave feminist criticism (Rampton).

Conclusion: "A Life-Changing Book"

Paretsky's 1982 *Indemnity Only* signaled a radical departure in its thematic concerns from those treated in the mainstream crime fiction tradition of its time. But, given that the novel is a part of feminism's second wave, does that make Warshawski a dated product of a particular feminist epoch? Or is her character (and her feminist struggle) still meaningful and relevant to younger generations of readers?

These questions are central to my inquiry in this chapter, as I consider the implications of feminist appropriations of popular genres. I have examined the extent to which this is an unproblematic and positive maneuver or a compromise to feminist political engagement. Mirroring this, Edgington says of Warshawski, that she "elects to locate herself within the mainstream, where she establishes a new space from which to operate and in which to grow" (63). I argue that although second-wave feminist engagements with genre fiction and mainstream culture are not unproblematic, *Indemnity Only* shows an acute awareness of nuance and a willingness to engage with the complexities of feminism in a way that continues to compel readers. In her discussion of feminist literature hitting "the mainstream," Nicci Gerrard examines the implications of interventions in popular culture for second-wave feminist political engagement. She specifically singles out Paretsky's work, referring to Warshawski as "a likeable and familiar figure: an engaging mixture of 1960s optimism and 1980s laid-back scepticism" (129). The ideas Gerrard highlights, optimism and pessimism, echo developments within second-wave feminism and trace the movement's journey from an early focus on possibilities for radical change, to the later acknowledgment of internal divisions and conflicts (Rampton). In that complex, evolving landscape, what has been the impact of Paretsky's crime novel *Indemnity Only*?

The long-term significance of *Indemnity Only* is the creation of the female detective character at the heart of the narrative (Heilbrun 428). Spearheaded by this "new female protagonist," the success story that is feminist crime writing is reflected in its appeal and diversity. The impact of this is evident not merely in the Warshawski series, but also in Paretsky's networking efforts on the crime fiction scene.[26] Those efforts have enabled other women writers and serve as an example of the practice of feminist sisterhood and solidarity. McDermid has credited Paretsky's *Indemnity Only* with changing her life and enabling her to become a successful crime writer by showing her a blueprint for a how a successful feminist crime novel, with a successful feminist sleuth, could look. "Thanks to *Indemnity Only*, I've had a career in writing that I could never have imagined. Now there's a life-changing book," she wrote recently (McDermid).

Through genre fiction, the second wave had an impact on popular culture that has had lasting significance. The increased appeal of popular culture to women writers brought new dimensions to the second wave, as Kaufman and Hevener state: "Popular culture can offer alternative strategies for reading the map of patriarchal society" (19). Similarly, Heilbrun posits, "We have now come to understand the importance and the influence of 'popular fiction' which can dare to embrace new ideas" (428). By appealing to women readers, something which Paretsky does very effectively through Warshawski, she reflects "the imaginative possibilities of feminism *as a process* involving both the writer and the reader" (Gerrard 171). Using popular culture to reread the "map of patriarchy" (to rephrase Kaufman and Hevener), second-wave feminism has shown the power of radical and challenging ideas to effect change when embodied within feminist practice.

Paretsky's *Indemnity Only* marks the emergence of a new type of hard-boiled feminist crime fiction, and her female private investigator character V. I. Warshawski is an embodiment of feminist consciousness-raising. Warshawski embraces feminism, "not as a theoretical treatise, but as a way of thinking, working, and living" (Décuré 228). With her doubts and struggles, and continual development as a character, she also typifies some of the tensions and problems that second-wave feminism and its ideas encountered in the 1980s. At the same time, Paretsky's insistence on the intersection of "the personal and the professional—the communities and the criminal" resonates profoundly with second-wave feminist ideals (Klein 146). As Heilbrun writes, noting the significance of the new second-wave female detective figures, "detective fiction featuring women sleuths are the readiest, the newest, the only stories waiting to alter society's expectations of women" (421).

Paretsky's reimagining of the crime fiction genre in *Indemnity Only* exemplifies how second-wave feminism embraced formal innovation as part of its impact on the mainstream. These formal innovations by feminist authors are as significant as the experimentations carried out by avant-garde and literary fiction authors. Feminist writing from the second wave challenges readers and critics to interrogate and reconsider the meanings and parameters of the term *experimental* beyond the avant-garde. This writing encourages readers and critics to expand those definitions to include the treatment of gender-political themes and motifs as part of an innovation strategy engaged in reformulating genre fiction. Through the consciousness-raising effects of those themes and motifs, and the sense of identification engendered in the reader, second-wave feminism has demonstrated its cultural importance and its political and aesthetic influence on the mainstream.

Re-visioning the crime fiction format in *Indemnity Only*, Paretsky's novel underlines the lasting impact and influence of second-wave feminist ideas, as new generations of women and girls realize the need to discover and live feminism for themselves and to engage in feminist struggle and resistance. Melissa Harrison writes in her article on the emergent fourth-wave feminism, "Each generation must reinvent feminism for itself, for while some things have improved for some women, new pressures and injustices have taken their place." *Indemnity Only* illustrates this through its portrayal of feminism as a work in progress. Paretsky affirms in *Writing in an Age of Silence* that, for her, feminism is as loud and urgent as ever: "I'm still doing feminism. And so is my detective, V I Warshawski" (77).

Notes

1. The quotation in the title of this chapter is taken from Paretsky *Indemnity Only* 6.

2. Broadly, second-wave feminism can be defined as "a social philosophy aimed at eradicating the pervasive sexism of our culture" (Dicker and Piepmeier 4) and promoting equal rights and reproductive control for women (Rampton). One of the most important aspects about second-wave feminism as a movement with long-term impact is its complexity and diversity (Rampton).

3. These include Décuré, Gerrard, Edgington, Kinsman, and Kaufman and Hevener.

4. I presented my developing reflections on related issues in a previous conference paper ("Still").

5. Writing as Amanda Cross (Kinsman "Feminist" 153).

6. See Gerrard for a discussion of feminist interventions in various genres, and the implications of mainstream appeal. See also Hawkins, Heilbrun, and Gerrard for more general reflections on these processes.

7. This promoted a radical shift in focus that affected several areas central to the crime fiction genre. The shift involved a changed perspective in several central areas: from featuring a male to a female detective, demonstrating a new and concerted effort to interrogate crime and criminality from a gender-political perspective, and incorporating portrayals of issues and problems specific to women's experience.

8. As Reddy points out, it was not until the 1990s that black women crime writers had their breakthrough (202), which shows the discrimination women face (as authors and fictional characters) through intersecting categories of oppression.

9. Also cited in Beyer "Life" 214.

10. A number of critics, including Panek, Walton, Walton and Jones, Palmer, Kinsman, Décuré, and myself ("Life") identify the themes of violence and violence against women as important preoccupations in Paretsky's work and feminist writing.

11. See also Beyer "Paretsky" 214.

12. Edgington further points out that, in *Indemnity Only*: "even her client, Andrew McGraw, balks when he realizes that V. I. is the detective, not the detective's receptionist or junior partner" (59).

13. For further discussion of the significance of the mother-daughter portrayal in Paretsky's oeuvre, see Kaufman and Hevener.

14. See my discussion of female anger in "Life" 216.

15. I am indebted to the analyses of Palmer and other critics cited here for their insights.

16. This can be found in her discussion of Amanda Cross (Carolyn Heilbrun) (Kinsman "Feminist" 153).

17. Critics such as Kaufman and Kaufman, Palmer, and Décuré have argued that the theme of food and the female body is significant to Paretsky and second-wave women's writing generally.

18. An issue also discussed in the context of second-wave women's writing by Palmer (38).

19. Critics such as Palmer, Kinsman, Décuré, Edgington, Kaufman and Hevener, and myself have identified the themes of female relations, the mother-daughter relationship, and feminist debate as central to Paretsky and second-wave women's writing, respectively.

20. See also my discussion of this topic in "Life" 219.

21. See also Kaufman and Hevener's examination of the mother-daughter relationship in Paretsky's fiction.

22. Palmer discusses the significance of feminist fiction of debate (60).

23. The missing student activist Anita McGraw, the daughter of the corrupt union leader Andrew McGraw at the center of the drama, is forced into hiding and assumes a fake identity as criminals seek to silence her. These criminals have already murdered her boyfriend, Peter Thayer, because he got involved (276). Anita courageously confronts her father with her knowledge about his criminal activity: "I know you've been using the union as a front for collecting money on illegal insurance claims" (276).

24. See also Miller's "I'm a Feminist—Loud and Proud."

25. The fourth-wave feminist revival is described by Cochrane, Harrison, Walby, Younis, and others.

26. Paretsky explains, "In 1986, when I started the organization Sisters in Crime, women published about a third of American crime novels. Today we make up almost fifty percent of active US crime writers" (*Writing* 69).

Works Cited

Beyer, Charlotte. "A Life of Crime: Feminist Crime/Life Writing in Sara Paretsky, *Writing in an Age of Silence*, P.D. James, *Time to Be in Earnest: A Fragment of Autobiography*, and Val McDermid, *A Suitable Job for a Woman: Inside the World of Women Private Eyes*." *Constructing Crime: Discourse and Cultural Representations of Crime and Deviance*. Ed. Christiana Gregoriou. Basingstoke: Palgrave Macmillan, 2012. 209–223. Print.

———. "Sara Paretsky, *Writing in an Age of Silence*." *American, British and Canadian Studies* 15 (2010): 214–216. Print.

———. "Still 'An Unsuitable Job for a Woman'? Some Reflections on Feminist Crime Fiction in the 1990s and post-2000, and Strategies for Teaching and Learning." Conference paper. The Mols Conference: Crime Fiction and Women, Experiences and Functions. 30 Nov.– Dec. 2009. Denmark.

Chernin, Kim. *The Hungry Self: Women, Eating and Identity*. New York: Times Books, 1985.

Cochrane, Kira. "The Fourth Wave of Feminism: Meet the Rebel Women." *The Guardian* 10 Dec. 2013. http://www.theguardian.com/world/2013/dec/10/fourth-wave-feminism-rebel-women?CMP=twt_gu. 1Accessed 8 Jan. 2014. Web.

Décuré. Nicole. "V. I. Warshawski, A 'Lady With Guts': Feminist Crime Fiction by Sara Paretsky." *Women's Studies International Forum* 12:2 (1989): 227–238. Print.

DeMarr, Mary Jean. "Joan Hess/Joan Hadley: Separating the Voices." *Women Times Three: Writers, Detectives, Readers*. Ed. Kathleen Gregory Klein. Bowling Green, OH: Bowling Green State U P, 1995. 29–42. Print.

Dicker, Rory Cooke, and Alison Piepmeier, eds. Introduction. *Catching a Wave: Reclaiming Feminism for the 21st Century*. Boston: Northeastern UP, 2003. 3–30. Print.

Edgington, K. "Defining the Enemy: Housewives and Detectives." *Clues: A Journal of Detection* 25:2 (Winter 2007): 55–63. Print.

Gerrard, Nicci. *Into the Mainstream*. London: Pandora, 1989. Print.

Harrison, Melissa. "Generation XX: Feminism Reinvented." *Financial Times* 4 July 2014. http://www.ft.com/cms/s/2/32497422–012f-11e4-a938–00144feab7de.html?ftcamp=published_links%2Frss%2Flife-arts%2Ffeed%2F%2Fproduct#slideo. Accessed 27 July 2014. Web.

Hawkins, Harriet. *Classics and Trash: Traditions and Taboos in High Literature and Popular Modern Genres*. New York: Harvester Wheatsheaf, 1990. Print.

Heilbrun, Carolyn G. "The New Female Detective." *Yale Journal of Law and Feminism* 14 (2002): 419–428. http://heinonline.org. Accessed 9 July 2013. Electronic.

Kaufman, Natalie Hevener, and Carrollee Kaufman Hevener. "Mythical Musical Connections: The Mother-Daughter Bond in the Work of Sara Paretsky." *Clues* 25:2 (Winter 2007): 19–28. Print.

Kaufman, Natalie Hevener, and Susan Kaufman. "Food, Anger, and the Female Detective." *Clues* 20:1 (1999): 49–62. Print.

Kinsman, Margaret. "Feminist Crime Fiction." *The Cambridge Companion to American Crime Fiction*. Ed. Catherine Ross Nickerson. Cambridge: Cambridge University Press, 2010. 148–162. Print.

———. "A Question of Visibility: Paretsky and Chicago." *Women Times Three: Writers, Detectives, Readers*. Ed. Kathleen Gregory Klein. Bowling Green, OH: Bowling Green State UP, 1995. 15–28. Print.

Klein, Kathleen Gregory. "Watching Warshawski." *It's a Print!: Detective Fiction from Page to Screen*. Ed. William D. Reynolds and Elizabeth Ann Trembley. Bowling Green, OH: Bowling Green State UP, 1994. 145–158. Print.

MacDonald, Fiona. "Pussy Riot, Femen and SlutWalk Are Working Hard To Give Feminism a Voice." *Metro*. 4 June 2013. http://metro.co.uk/2013/06/04/pussy-riot-femen-and-slutwalk-are-working-hard-to-give-feminism-a-voice-3826773/. Accessed 18 Jan. 2014. Web.

McDermid, Val. "Book of a Lifetime: *Indemnity Only*, by Sara Paretsky." *The Independent* 18 Sept. 2009. http://www.independent.co.uk/arts-entertainment/books/reviews/book-of-a-lifetime-indemnity-only-by-sara-paretsky-1789033.html. Accessed 9 July 2013. Web.

Miller, Danielle. "I'm a Feminist—Loud and Proud." *The Butterfly Effect* 10 Oct. 2013. http://enlighteneducation.edublogs.org/2013/10/10/im-a-feminist-loud-and-proud/. Accessed 19 Jan. 2014. Web.

Orbach, Susie. *Fat Is a Feminist Issue*. 1978. Reprint, London: Arrow Books, 2006.

Palmer, Paulina. *Contemporary Women's Fiction: Narrative Practice and Feminist Theory*. New York: Harvester Wheatsheaf, 1989. Print.

Panek, LeRoy. *New Hard-Boiled Writers: 1970s–1990s*. Bowling Green, OH: Bowling Green State UP, 2000. Print.

Paretsky, Sara. *Indemnity Only*. 1982. London: Hodder & Stoughton, 2007. Print.

———. *Writing in an Age of Silence*. 2007. London: Verso, 2009. Print.

Plain, Gill. *Twentieth-Century Crime Fiction: Gender, Sexuality and the Body*. Edinburgh: Edinburgh UP, 2001. Print.

Rampton, Martha. "The Three Waves of Feminism." *PACIFIC* (Fall 2008). http://www.pacificu.edu/magazine_archives/2008/fall/echoes/feminism.cfm. Accessed 9 July 2013. Web.

Reddy, Maureen. "Women Detectives." *The Cambridge Companion to Crime Fiction*. Ed. Martin Priestman. New York: Cambridge UP, 2003. 191–208. Print.

Rzepka, Charles J. *Detective Fiction*. Cambridge: Polity, 2005. Print.

Walby, Sylvia. *The Future of Feminism*. Cambridge: Polity, 2013. Kindle edition.

Walton, Priscilla L. "Form and Forum: The Agency of Detectives and the Venue of the Short Story." *Narrative* 6.2 (May 1998): 123–139. http://www.jstor.org/stable/20107143>. Accessed 9 July 2013. Web.

Walton, Priscilla L., and Manina Jones. *Detective Agency: Women Rewriting the Hard Boiled Tradition*. Berkeley: U of California P, 1999. Print.

Younis, Jinan. "What Happened When I Started a Feminist Society at School." *The Guardian* 20 June 2013. http://www.guardian.co.uk/education/mortarboard/2013/jun/20/why-i-started-a-feminist-society. Accessed 10 July 2013. Web.

Contributors

JILL E. ANDERSON is Assistant Professor of English and Women's Studies at Tennessee State University. Her work has appeared in *Ecozon@, The Journal of Ecocriticism, Margaret Atwood Studies,* and *The European Journal of Ecopsychology*. She is at work on a book project about queer eco-criticism and Cold War culture.

AGATHA BEINS is Assistant Professor of Women's Studies at Texas Woman's University. In addition to her work on feminism and print culture, her interests include art and activism, feminist geography and spatial politics, the institutionalization of women's studies, and theories and practices of the archive. She has published both scholarly and creative work, including poetry in *The Laurel Review, Blackbird, Newfound, Spiral Orb,* and *Fourteen Hills,* and articles in *Feminist Studies, Women: A Cultural Review, Sinister Wisdom,* and *Frontiers: A Journal of Women's Studies*. Beins is also co-editor of *Women's Studies for the Future: Foundations, Interrogations, Politics,* co-author of *Effective Writing in Psychology: Papers, Posters, and Presentations,* and editor of *Films for the Feminist Classroom,* an online journal that reviews primarily documentary films for their use and value to educators.

CHARLOTTE BEYER is Senior Lecturer in English Studies at the University of Gloucestershire, United Kingdom. She has published on contemporary literature, including a number of articles and book chapters on crime and spy fiction, and has also published on children's literature. She has a long-standing interest in women's writing and feminism. She is on the Steering Committee for the *Crime Studies Network* and on the editorial board for the journal *American, British and Canadian Studies.*

LISA BOTSHON is Professor of English and Women's and Gender Studies at the University of Maine at Augusta. Her publications have focused on women writers, popular culture, and the middlebrow. Her current project explores women's back-to-the-land memoirs from the interwar era.

JAIME CANTRELL is Visiting Assistant Professor of English at the University of Mississippi. Her research and teaching interests focus on how queer and feminist theories illuminate and complicate the intersections between canonical and obscure, queer and normative, and regional and national narratives. Jaime is co-editor of *Out of the Closet, Into the Archives: Researching Sexual Histories,* a collection of essays from SUNY Press's Queer Politics and Cultures Series (December 2015). Her current project, "Southern Sapphisms: Sexuality and Sociality in Literary Productions, 1969–1997," foregrounds the centrality of sexuality to the study of Southern literature as well as the region's defining role in the historiography of lesbian literature in the post-Stonewall-era.

JULIE R. ENSZER is Visiting Assistant Professor in the Department of Women's Studies at the University of Maryland. She is working on a book manuscript, "A Fine Bind: Lesbian-Feminist Publishing from 1969 through 1989," that examines the cultural and political significance of lesbian-feminist print culture. Her scholarly work has appeared or is forthcoming in *Frontiers, Journal of Lesbian Studies, Feminist Studies,* and *Southern Cultures.* Enszer is the editor and publisher of *Sinister Wisdom* and curator of the Lesbian Poetry Archive, www.LesbianPoetryArchive.org.

JENNIFER GILLEY is Associate Librarian in the Penn State University System and has been the Head Librarian at Penn State New Kensington since 2001. She has given presentations on feminist publishing at the National Women's Studies Association Conference, the International Conference on the Book, and the inaugural Publishing Feminisms symposium in Banff. She has also published articles in *NWSA Journal,* the *International Journal of the Book, American Libraries, Reference and User Services Quarterly,* and the *Journal of American Folklore.* A recipient of multiple archival research grants, she plans to continue unearthing publication histories of feminist texts to contribute to the emerging field of feminist print studies.

LAURA CHRISTINE GODFREY is a doctoral student in Medieval Studies at the University of Connecticut, where her research interests include medieval saints' lives, Middle English poetry, and late medieval lay devotion.

PHILLIP GORDON is Assistant Professor of English and Gay Studies Coordinator at the University of Wisconsin-Platteville. He has published on William Faulkner and gay Mississippi writer Hubert Creekmore. He is currently working on a book focused on gay representation in the works of William Faulkner.

JAIME HARKER is Professor of English and Interim Director of the Sarah Isom Center for Women and Gender Studies at The University of Mississippi. She is the author of *America the Middlebrow: Women's Novels, Progressivism, and Middlebrow Authorship between the Wars* and *Middlebrow Queer: Christopher Isherwood in America.*

JAY HOOD is a graduate of Mercer University, where he received his Bachelor of Arts in English and Southern Studies, and of the University of Mississippi, where he received his Master of Arts in English. His scholarship focuses on race, gender, the body, and formations of power between individuals and institutions. His most recent efforts have been in the investigation of the social and historical significance of popular and marginalized fiction in the middle Cold War. Jay Hood has presented papers at the South Central Modern Language Association conference and at the Southern Writers/Southern Writing conference at the University of Mississippi.

CECILIA KONCHAR FARR is Professor of English and Women's Studies, Chair of English, and a Carondelet Scholar at St. Catherine University's Women's College in St. Paul, Minnesota. A feminist critic, she writes about the novel and its passionate American readers, including a study of Oprah's Book Club, *Reading Oprah* (SUNY 2004), a collection of essays on Harry Potter coedited with her students, *A Wizard of Their Age* (SUNY 2014), and *The Ulysses Delusion* on how readers and critics judge novels and select the good ones (Palgrave 2016).

YUNG-HSING WU is Associate Professor of English at the University of Louisiana at Lafayette, where she teaches literary theory, the history of reading, and print culture studies. Her work on reading and reception has appeared in a variety of journals, including *Modern Fiction Studies, PMLA,* and *Profession.* Her current book project, "The Institution of Reading," argues that the remediation of reading embodied by the "late age of print" is as nostalgic and conservative as it is revolutionary. Writing this biography has helped her make the leap and decide on the title for the *next* project, *The Closeness of Reading,* which recounts a history of feminism through the movement's ongoing discomfort with reading.

Index

The University of Illinois Press
is a founding member of the
Association of American University Presses.

University of Illinois Press
1325 South Oak Street
Champaign, IL 61820-6903
www.press.uillinois.edu